Entangled Discourses

This book uniquely explores the shifting structures of power and unexpected points of intersection—entanglements—at the nexus of North and South as a lens through which to examine the impact of global and local circuits of people, practices, and ideas on linguistic, cultural, and knowledge systems. The volume considers the entanglement of North and South on multiple levels in the contemporary and continuing effects of capitalism, colonialism, and imperialism, in the form of silenced or marginalized populations, such as refugees, immigrants, and other minoritized groups, and in the different *orders of visibility* that make some types of practices and knowledge more legitimate and therefore more visible. It uses a range of methodological and analytical frames to shed light on less visible histories, practices, identities, repertoires, and literacies, and offers new understandings for research and for language, health care, education, and other policies and practices.

The book brings together an exciting mix of voices of both established and new scholars in multilingualism and diversity from a range of social, political, and historical contexts and provides coverage of areas previously under-represented in current research on multilingualism, globalization, and mobility, including Brazil, South Africa, Australia, East Timor, Wallis and Mayotte, Cape Verde, and Guinea-Bissau. This volume is key reading for scholars, researchers, and graduate students in multilingualism, globalization, sociolinguistics, mobility and development studies, applied linguistics, and language and education policy.

Caroline Kerfoot is Associate Professor at the Centre for Research on Bilingualism at Stockholm University, Sweden.

Kenneth Hyltenstam is Professor Emeritus at the Centre for Research on Bilingualism at Stockholm University, Sweden.

Routledge Critical Studies in Multilingualism

Edited by Marilyn Martin-Jones, MOSAIC Centre for Research on Multilingualism, University of Birmingham, UK and Joan Pujolar Cos, Universitat Oberta de Catalunya, Spain

For a full list of titles in this series, please visit www.routledge.com

Entangled Discourses

South-North Orders of Visibility

**Edited by Caroline Kerfoot
and Kenneth Hyltenstam**

Routledge
Taylor & Francis Group

LONDON AND NEW YORK

First published 2017 by Routledge

2 Park Square, Milton Park, Abingdon, Oxfordshire OX14 4RN

52 Vanderbilt Avenue, New York, NY 10017

Routledge is an imprint of the Taylor & Francis Group, an informa business

First issued in paperback 2019

Library of Congress Cataloging-in-Publication Data
A catalog record for this book has been requested.

ISBN: 978-1-138-19226-3 (hbk)
ISBN: 978-0-367-43031-3 (pbk)

Typeset in Sabon
by Apex CoVantage, LLC

To Christopher Stroud

Contents

Preface

This volume grew out of a symposium in honour of Christopher Stroud on his sixtieth birthday, celebrated in Stockholm in September 2013. The symposium was organized (in secret to the object of tribute) by his two home institutions: the Centre for Research on Bilingualism, Stockholm University, and the Department of Linguistics at the University of Western Cape. It focused on epistemological and methodological issues central to topics of Christopher's earlier and current sociolinguistic research such as new configurations of mobility and entanglements of identities, histories, languages, and literacies. Whereas the majority of the chapters of this book are elaborated versions of presentations at the symposium, other chapters have been added to achieve a more extensive and representative treatment of issues relative to the notions of entangled discourses, orders of visibility, and South-North dimensions of power and knowledge.

At a time when the world is experiencing unprecedented and deeply intertwined politico-economic, religious, martial, and climate-related turmoil, resulting in mass migration, demographic turbulence, and political instability, we are pleased to be able to contribute with this book to analyses and exploration of the sociolinguistic dimensions of the current commotion. We specifically hope that, in its focus on historical and contemporary South-North relations and social velocities, the book will add to the development of a sociolinguistics of the South and, more broadly, of the sociolinguistics of multilingualism and diversity for contemporary conditions.

We would like to thank the Centre for Research on Bilingualism, Stockholm University and, ultimately, Riksbankens Jubileumsfond for financial support for the symposium that was the impetus for this book. Our special thanks also go to Christopher Stroud, Tope Omoniyi, and the editors of this series, Marilyn Martin-Jones and Joan Pujolar, for their constant support and constructive help in the various stages of the making of the volume. We would also like to acknowledge that the quality of the book has been significantly improved by insightful comments and suggestions by 20 external, anonymous reviewers of the individual chapters. Our sincere thanks go to all of you.

Caroline Kerfoot and Kenneth Hyltenstam
Stockholm, August 2016

Introduction
Entanglement and Orders of Visibility

Caroline Kerfoot and Kenneth Hyltenstam

Rampant /ˈramp(ə)nt/ adj. **1** (placed after noun) *Heraldry* (of an animal standing on its left hind foot with its forepaws in the air (*lion rampant*) **2** Unchecked, flourishing excessively (*rampant violence*) **3** Violent or extravagant in action or opinion (*rampant theorists*).
—(Oxford English Dictionary 1995, 1135)

The unexpected but surprisingly appropriate pairing of 'rampant theorists'[1,2] in entry 3 above draws attention to the potential for violence inherent in any act of theorizing and indexes the fraught relationships between North and South which form the historical backdrop to this book. It points to the long reach of northern theories of cognitive, linguistic, social, economic, and political development constructed through interaction with colonized peoples, erasing in the process countless alternative ways of being, knowing, valuing, and languaging. Material destruction of libraries, archives, and artefacts marked a much deeper epistemicide (Santos 2014): the obliteration of social practices and other forms of knowledge by imposing a single perspective proclaimed to be universal, objective, and scientific and simultaneously making it appear that the histories of those colonized began with colonization (Fanon 1961). Acts of linguistic appropriation, description, invention, and invisibilization were a constitutive feature of this epistemicide (Makoni 2003; Makoni and Pennycook 2007; Mignolo 1992; Ngũgĩ 1986). The multiple acts of 'subaltern' resistance in response formed a largely invisible counterpoint.

In an effort to contribute to bridging the invisible 'abyssal line' that for Santos (2014, 118–24) separates 'modern' from other knowledges, this book seeks to bring into dialogue 'the south' and 'the north' not as separate or literal places of belonging but as a relation—a window onto a world of flows and connections and so 'transcendent of the very dualism of north and south' (Comaroff and Comaroff 2011, 47). Rather than fixed geographical locations or clearly delimited groups of states and societies, South and North are thus 'labile signifier[s] whose content is determined by everyday material and political processes' (Comaroff and Comaroff 2012, 127). Moreover, we follow, Santos (2012, 51) in understanding the South as:

> a metaphor of the human suffering caused by capitalism and colonialism at the global level, and a metaphor as well of the resistance to overcome or minimise such suffering. It is, therefore, an anticapitalist, anti-colonialist, and anti-imperialist South. It is a South that also exists in the global North, in the form of excluded, silenced and marginalised populations, such as undocumented immigrants, the unemployed, ethnic or religious minorities, and victims of sexism, homophobia and racism.

The South is thus 'a position and a politics' (Shepherd 2002, 81). Our volume aims to encompass both the North in the South in the form of entangled and evolving discourses and epistemologies and the South in the North, in the form of excluded, silenced and marginalized populations, such as refugees, immigrants, and ethnic minorities or minoritized groups. It has contributions from several 'southern' contexts less well represented in current research on multilingualism, globalization, and mobility: Australia (an economic North in the South), Brazil, Cape Verde, East Timor, Guinea-Bissau, South Africa, and Wallis (South Pacific).

The interaction of perspectives from the North and the South has at least two potential benefits: first, it creates the opportunity to revisit the limits of representation in mainstream social sciences, in epistemological terms, 'the missing links, the incomplete records, black holes, voids' along with absent knowledges and absent or silenced agents: an epistemology of absences (Santos 2014, 154). In this way dialogue across contexts opens up opportunities for reconstituting and expanding dominant theory so that it may become more productive in analyzing both northern and southern social realities.

A second potential benefit is that the interaction of perspectives can help expose limits to the capacity of the northern 'epistemological imagination' (Mbembe and Nuttall 2004) under current conditions. Driven by attempts to engage with rapid, unpredictable, and multidirectional shifts in social and cultural forms, research in Africa and the South more broadly has shown that the conceptual categories with which to account for rapid social change, the power of the unforeseen, and processes of unfolding need to be refined. So, too, does the language with which to describe people's ways of negotiating these conditions of turbulence (Mbembe and Nuttall 2004; Stroud 2013). Such turbulent conditions figure large in imaginings of Africa but also represent the experiences of those uprooted by economic or political instabilities in both North and South. It is often through the illumination of such instabilities and uncertainties that the most interesting insights and intuitions about realities and possibilities for change emerge (Bennett 2008). This point is also made by Santos (2014, 184) in calling for a sociology of emergences: 'a symbolic enlargement of knowledges, practices, and agents in order to identify therein the tendencies of the future (the Not Yet) upon which it is possible to intervene.' This dual focus on absences and emergences can help to reshape knowledge projects in socio- and applied linguistics, language policy and planning, education, anthropology, politics, and development studies.

This book will thus contribute to an understanding of the synergies between northern and southern perspectives and realities and also of the disciplinary and analytical challenges arising from dynamic and contentious configurations of identity, language, class, 'race', ethnicity, and gender in each context. While looking in this way at fields of discourse and exchange, at convergences, the book also considers the conditions under which social realities are rejected or disappear, becoming 'meaningless or unintelligible' (Hofmeyr 2004, 15) (see de Souza; Kerfoot and Tatah; Muni Toke, this volume).

With regard to language and linguistic practice, the volume focuses on linguistic diversity as it is constructed and managed in northern and southern education, health care, and other settings: while engaging at times with issues of hybridity, its purpose is to explore broader discursive formations and the limits or conditions of possibility they produce.

The Contributions to this Volume

The book is divided into four sections. The first part 'Southern perspectives' contains three chapters which explore entanglements of language, 'race', and ethnicity in southern contexts. The first by Valelia Muni Toke in the French Overseas territory of Wallis (South Pacific) and the second by Caroline Kerfoot and Gwendoline Tatah in South Africa analyze interactions in encounters across differences in health care and education, respectively. In both, the construction of orders of visibility is accompanied by a (re-)ethnicization of bodies and voices under a postcolonial gaze. In Muni Toke's study of 'silent patients' in a Wallisian hospital, the institutional gaze of the French Republic invisibilizes language practices viewed as 'culturally' different as well as their interpretative frames, erasing the historicity of social relations and continuing to impose a colonial racio-linguistic hierarchy. In Kerfoot and Tatah, a postcolonial gaze on a Cameroonian immigrant learner refracted through the everyday practices of young South African adolescents can be seen to refragment the black subject, undermining attempts at self-representation in new ways. Both chapters raise issues of epistemic justice. The third chapter by Zannie Bock, an analysis of South African university students' narratives on race, uses 'small stories' to counter dominant narratives, offering a view of complex configurations of identity, race, and class usually left unarticulated, and illustrating both the continuing hold of essentialist apartheid categories and glimpses of a re-imagined postracial future. Together these chapters make some of the 'ambiguous networks and trajectories of the postcolonial state legible' (Nuttall 2009, 13), underscoring the importance of southern voices in postcolonial contexts as objects for contemporary sociolinguistics and social science more broadly.

The second part, 'South-North Entanglements' contains two chapters. This section moves the level of analysis to 'trajectories', a neglected yet central concept in illuminating new circuits of people, resources, and practices in contemporary conditions of global South-North migration. The concept of trajectories enables a grounding of the universal deterritorialized narratives of mobility in specificities of dislocation and re-mooring (Estêvão Cabral and Marilyn Martin-Jones) as well as of involuntary immobility (Kasper Juffermans and Bernardino Tavares). The section explores South-North entanglements of language, migration, and social inequality in three contexts (East Timor-Northern Ireland, and Guinea-Bissau and Cape Verde-Luxembourg). It examines themes such as the mutual shaping of multilingual repertoires and mobilities and the ways in which these are bound up with desire, imagination, belonging, social status, and economic opportunities. It points to historical entanglements where colonially imposed geopolitical divisions along with contemporary political economies render some bodies and some languages more able to travel than others. It also emphasizes the importance of paying attention to less visible trajectories which disrupt conventional notions of South-North migration as unilinear, highlighting instead the temporal and spatial entanglements engendered by flows of people: lines of connectedness characterized by discontinuities, reversals, inertias, and especially absences: those trajectories that are desired, struggled for, yet ensnared by migration regimes, corruption, and a lack of material and/or linguistic resources.

The third part, 'Northern perspectives' moves analysis to the ideological tensions evident in policy and practice in educational contexts in the global north grappling with increased levels of diversity—a South moving North. It also addresses re-orderings of power, knowledge, and visibility in public health discourses through the emergence of online practices. The first two chapters (by Inger Lindberg and Karin Sandwall, and Lionel Wee) explore the complex effects of policy discourses on educational provision and equity for university students and for newly arrived migrants and refugees in adult education programs. Feeding into these discourses are debates over theoretical understandings of multilingualism as either a set of separate parallel systems or as a set of semiotically porous and dynamically interacting resources. In both settings, there is a visible ordering of fixed over flexible multilingualism. Here we see a universal logic of monolingualism bound up with essentializing ethnic and linguistic hierarchies within the nation-state and determining epistemic access, economic opportunity, and social belonging. A capitalist logic of productivity drives the adoption of quick-fix labour market tools at the expense of supporting long-term goals of active participation in society which, in turn, would require expanded understandings of the role of language and multilingualism in citizenship (cf. Stroud's 2001, 2009 notion of linguistic citizenship). In the third chapter, Hanell and Salö illuminate the ways in which knowledge practices travel not one way—from centre to periphery—but through many media, transforming in different sites and spaces, and convening different publics at different points. In this journey, at different times, some kinds of knowledge and some knowledge producers are rendered more visible and therefore more legitimate.

The final part, 'North-South dynamics in research and knowledge production', most explicitly addresses issues of the *coloniality* of power (Quijano 2000), the invisible and constitutive side of 'modernity' that inscribes a global racial/ethnic hierarchy itself entangled with other hierarchies: gendered, political, epistemic, economic, spiritual, and linguistic (Connell 2014; Grosfoguel 2007; Lugones 2008). The section contains three chapters, each grappling with research as a significant site of struggle between the interests and ways of knowing of the North and those of the Other and pointing to the complex ethical and political responses required to work towards mutual intelligibility and participatory parity.

The chapters by Tommaso Milani and Lynn Mario de Souza, written in very different contexts, show raced and gendered bodies refusing to respond to peremptory calls to inhabit certain subject positions. In his analysis of the disruption by black women of a Johannesburg Pride march, Milani, following Warner (2004), argues for a methodology of the margins that does not seek to make things intelligible in terms of dominant knowledge hierarchies but 'to find the words of the margins itself' (335). Here those in the margins speak through the public visibility of the body, suggesting the need for an expanded understanding of *linguistic citizenship* which takes account of the multi-semiotic and affective character of social activism. In his study of conflicting interpretations of indigenous educational policy in Brazil, de Souza argues that intercultural and bilingual education are not merely policy or linguistic issues, but epistemic issues. He draws attention to the operation of *lazy reason* (Santos 2002) in which policy makers, even benign ones, cannot escape from the confines of dominant forms of thinking and struggle to understand other, non-Eurocentric forms of reason, with the result that the rich diversity of knowledges that surrounds them remains invisible, at least to them. While the principle of incompleteness of all knowledges may be, as Santos (2014, 189) argues, the precondition for epistemological dialogue among different knowledges, the burden of intercultural translation tends to lie more heavily on southern scholars than on those in the North. The final chapter by Kathleen Heugh argues for the notion of *mestizo consciousness*, an *awareness of coloniality of being* (Kusch [1970] 2010; Mignolo 2011), as a lens through which to tease apart dissonances between universalizing theory and southern ways of knowing, being, and valuing.

An Afterword by Christopher Stroud re-examines the two core notions underpinning the volume, entanglement and orders of visibility, in relation to class, race, and gender in an upscale Cape Town market.

While the first and third sections group together southern and northern perspectives respectively, it should be emphasized that although this apparently geographical grouping is used for structural purposes, the North and South, as mentioned on page 1, are seen as a relation, as entangled, and mutually constitutive.

The remainder of this introduction elaborates the concepts 'entanglement' and 'orders of visibility', arguing for their potential to illuminate both absences in theory, knowledge, and representation and emergences in social and semiotic practices. We suggest that this dual focus on absences and emergences, following Santos (2014), is essential for the development of a sociolinguistics of the South.

Entanglement

In writing about the 'after apartheid' in South Africa, Nuttall (2009, 11) offers *entanglement* as a rubric by means of which we can 'draw into our analyses those sites in which what was once thought of as separate— identities, spaces, histories—come together or find points of intersection in unexpected ways.' These new points of intersection characterize not only South Africa and other postcolonial contexts but also, increasingly, contexts of the North. Indeed it has been argued that South Africa and other southern countries in many ways prefigured the conditions and forms of experience with which the North is increasingly challenged, namely, the spectacularly diverse linguistic and cultural make-up of the state, persistent high unemployment, growing informalization, the coexistence of mass poverty and mass democracy, massive inequalities within a single country, and ongoing battles between states and processes of spontaneous but illegal urbanization and migration (Comaroff and Comaroff 2011; Ferguson 2012).

It is a concern with these entangled and unpredictable social formations and their intersections with linguistic and other forms of diversity that form the basis of this book. 'Entanglement' indicates 'a relationship or set of social relationships that is complicated, ensnaring, in a tangle, but which also implies a human foldedness. [. . .] It works with difference and sameness but also with their limits, their predicaments, their moments of complication' (Nuttall 2009, 2). For Nuttall, the notion signals 'largely unexplored terrains of mutuality, wrought from a common, though often coercive and confrontational, experience' (2009, 11) (see also Bock, de Souza, Heugh, Milani this volume).

It is here that sociolinguistics and linguistic anthropology offer to social science a principled means of investigating the relationality of power, the mutual constitution of interactants, identities, and, over the longer term, social orders. It is notable that mainstream sociology has largely ignored this potential, only recently declaring that 'the problematic of agency is about attending to what even traditional sociology should attend to: *interactions*' (Go 2013, 14, orig. emphasis) (as opposed to universalizing and abstract categories such as agency vs structure).

Critical sociolinguists and linguistic anthropologists since Hymes (1974), Goffman (1981) and Gumperz (1982) in the 1960s have focused on the social tensions inherent in language, understanding it not as a 'neutral, abstract system of reference but a medium through which one participates in an historical flow of social relationships, struggles, and meanings' (Bailey 2011, 499–500). Several chapters in the book illuminate the ways in which language is used as a resource in constructing, naturalizing, or resisting inequality in everyday interactions and institutional sites (see chapters by Hanell and Salö, Lindberg and Sandwall, Kerfoot and Tatah, Muni Toke). The analysis of linguistic practices can thus provide a lens on the often invisibilized workings of power and the construction, reproduction, and contestation of inequalities in social processes.

Orders of Visibility

In engaging with the kinds of entanglements outlined above, the book will also aim to illuminate the ways in which different *orders of visibility* are constructed by conceptual, methodological, and analytical lenses. Here authors will explore the hierarchies of objects, social relations, ways of knowing, being, and saying concealed or embedded beneath the apparently common sense and taken for granted in policies and practices.

This concept has obvious resonances with Foucault's 'order of discourse' ([1970] 1981), 'a kind of gradation among discourses' (55) where some are ephemeral and disappear almost immediately and some over time become sedimented into religious, juridical, literary, and, to a certain extent, scientific texts. These processes of sedimentation are achieved through procedures for controlling, selecting, organizing and redistributing discourse which result in hierarchies of knowledge and semiosis and, hence, differential access. Discourse, following Foucault, refers to:

> ways of constituting knowledge, together with the social practices, forms of subjectivity and power relations which inhere in such knowledges and relations between them. Discourses are more than ways of thinking and producing meaning. They constitute the 'nature' of the body, unconscious and conscious mind and emotional life of the subjects they seek to govern.
>
> (Weedon 1987, 108)

Foucault's archaeological methodology was aimed at understanding the meaning-making practices of those who create discourses, to demonstrate the rules of discourse that allow such meaning-making to happen. It enables the understanding that 'what seems like the continuous development of meaning is crossed by discontinuous discursive formations' (Dreyfus and Rabinow 1983, 106). It also enables an analysis of the differential effects of meaning-making practices, of the ways in which these foreground certain modes of knowledge and semiosis and render others invisible. 'Systemic patterns of authority, of control and evaluation, and hence of inclusion and exclusion' (Blommaert 2010, 38) are continually challenged and reworked in new formations of order and disorder engendered by both local and global processes. The relations within and among these different orders of discourse are 'neither stable, nor constant, nor absolute' (Foucault 1981, 57). Such turbulent conditions create unpredictable surges and diminutions of the visibility of particular modes of being, saying, knowing, and valuing.

A goal of the book is therefore to illuminate the shifting structures of power and asymmetrical relations between North and South that render some types of knowledges, practices, repertoires, and bodies more legitimate, and therefore more visible, and thus construct different orders of visibility.

Absences and Emergences

To understand these discontinuities and asymmetries in visibility, we have to start with what brought them into existence: conquest, colonialism, and the world of neoliberal globalization which has generated new kinds of colonialism. Sociology, for example, was 'formed within the culture of imperialism, and embodied an intellectual response to the colonized world' (Connell 2007, 9). However, this context was concealed in early sociological work and then disappeared entirely in the perspectives that emerged in the post-war era' (Connell 2007), resulting in what Castro-Gómez (2007) terms the 'hubris of the zero point' of observation, apparently disembodied and unlocated but in fact masking a set of ethnocentric, geopolitical assumptions assumed to have universal validity (Mignolo 2007a, 2007b; Santos 2014; Santos et al. 2008).

This *grand erasure* (Connell 2007) of experiences of people of the Global South results in persistent forms of cognitive injustice (Santos 2014), silencing or consigning other epistemologies to the margins or a primitive past (Das 1997; Hountondji 1997; Medina 2013; Mignolo 2000, 2007a; Odora Hoppers 2002; Smith 1999). Most significantly, cognitive asymmetries were and still are perpetuated by an extractive economy of knowledge production in which knowledge is 'repatriated, capitalized and accumulated at the centre of the system' (Hountondji 1997, 11), invisibilizing scholarship of the global south and further entrenching what Mignolo (2009) terms epistemic silences. This epistemic hierarchy is carried through a linguistic hierarchy that privileges communication and knowledge production in European languages (Mignolo 2000) and serves to remove epistemic authority from speakers of other languages.

In his concern to retrieve and reconstitute absences in theory, knowledge, representation, and forms of sociability, Santos (2014) argues that non-existence is produced through five modes or logics, all of which have clear parallels in language and linguistic theory. The first and most powerful logic derives from the monoculture of knowledge identified above. One of its effects is to render those outside the charmed circle as ignorant or without culture (see chapters by Heugh, de Souza, Muni Toke, Hanell and Salö, this volume). This logic is connected to a second, that of the universal, global scale, creating an illusion of a homogenous 'totality' which in its invisibiliza-tion of the specificities of the local, renders social transformation impossible (Santos 2002; see de Souza, this volume).

Both logics are entangled with the logic of social classification which nat-uralizes raced, gendered, and linguistic hierarchies (see chapters by Bock, Kerfoot and Tatah, Milani). Under colonialism, linguistic descriptions cre-ated 'sociolinguistic hierarchies within and between languages which were projected onto categories such as class, gender, ethnicity, and which legiti-mized the exploitation of certain groups in labour' (Errington 2001; Stroud 2007, 26). This colonial project of 'ethno-linguistic essentialization' (Par-kin 2012, 76), an 'invention' of languages constructed as discrete bounded entities 'projected onto their putative speakers as indigenous languages' (Makoni and Pennycook 2007, 14; Mühlhäusler 1996) invisibilized the realities of everyday multilingual practices and complex social relations.

The same logics can be discerned underpinning linguistic stratification in the contemporary nation-state, tying the 'pure', standard varieties of lan-guages to certain bodies.

Silverstein (2015, 14) suggests that:

> At the imagined top-and-center are those with the 'voice from nowhere,' easily confused with Chomsky's [1965: 3–4] 'ideal speaker–hearer.' Those more and more 'down and out' show divergence from standard that becomes a negative index, an index of deficiency, speaking like one is demographically 'from somewhere'—Ethnic-and-Immigrant-land, Gender-land, Class-land—as opposed to communicating 'from nowhere at all'—a mere ethno-semiotic construct, to be sure—within the language community.

A fourth logic is the monoculture of linear time, the idea that history has a unique meaning and direction, constructed in different ways in the last 200 years as progress, revolution, modernization, development, and global-ization (Santos 2014, 172). In a discussion of temporality in constructions of language in colonial and postcolonial Mozambique, Stroud and Guissemo (2015) use Benjamin's (1991–99) distinction between 'empty homogenous time' and 'messianic time' to show how, in contrast to the 'flux and waning' of African languages according to shifting national narratives of modernity and progress, a *messianic* sense of Portuguese has throughout 'offered up organizing tropes of stability and national unity, stretching back into history and forward into new transnational spaces' (Stroud and Guissemo, 2015, 6). They follow Eisenlohr (2004, 81) in noting that '/languages/ contribute to the temporal structuring of social worlds by establishing relationships between linguistic forms, communicative practices and sociocultural valu-ations' (see chapters by Bock, Cabral and Martin-Jones, de Souza, Heugh, Juffermans and Tavares, Kerfoot and Tatah, Milani, Muni Toke, Wee).

A final logic, a capitalist logic of productivity, arguably underpins much of language policy today. It is particularly evident in countries of the South that feel the brunt of continued recycling and reworking of colonial lan-guage-in-education policies (Arthur Shoba and Chimbutane 2013; Chim-butane 2011; Heugh 2009, 2013; Kerfoot and Bello-Nonjengele 2016; Lin 2013; Makoe and McKinney 2014; Mohanty 2006; Pennycook 2007). It is used, too, to justify the postcolonial state's failure to resource diversity and multilingualism in any meaningful way (see chapters by Heugh, Kerfoot and Tatah, Muni Toke). This logic also figures in countries of the North as evi-dent in the increasing neoliberal focus in university education, adult educa-tion programs, and school language policies for immigrants (see chapters by Lindberg and Sandwall, Wee). It also shapes the trajectories of those driven by war and economic need to try and insert themselves in various ways into northern economies (see chapters by Cabral and Martin-Jones, Juffermans and Tavares).

This books thus seeks to build on socio- and applied linguistic work that grounds the view from nowhere (and the voice from nowhere) through his-torical, ethnographic, interactionist, and discourse analytic approaches to the analysis of language in the construction of social difference and inequal-ity (see, for example, Heller 1992, 1999, 2011, 2012; Heller and Martin-Jones 2001; Irvine and Gal 2000; Martin-Jones 2007; Woolard 1985, 1989).

Conclusion

In the ways outlined above, this book aims to contribute to the development of a sociolinguistics of the South and, thus, to the broader project of recasting the sociolinguistics of multilingualism to take account of contemporary con-ditions (see, for example, Heugh, Carino, and Stroud forthcoming; Martin-Jones, Blackledge, and Creese 2012; Martin-Jones and Martin forthcoming; also Borba 2015). It brings in the voices of the South as 'potential correc-tives and theoretical clarifications' (Connell 2007, 224) and, crucially, it draws attention to often invisibilized processes of cultural and knowledge production which can help lay the basis for conditions of mutual South-North intelligibility and engagement. Such examples of counter-hegemonic processes have the potential to provide ontological, epistemological, and axiological insights which could begin to shift the very terms of recogniz-ability (Butler 2010), illuminating the linguistic and epistemic authority of subaltern actors, and establishing their capacities both as subjects of knowl-edge and as givers of knowledge.

While fully aware of the complexity of the task of intercultural transla-tion (Santos 2014) and of de-colonial reconstruction (Smith 1999), we hope that the book as a whole could also be said to contribute to an 'ecology of knowledges' (Santos 2012) that encourages the destabilization of boundaries and the exploration of new relations, new ways of seeing and hearing, and an ethics of compassion and solidarity.

Acknowledgements

We would like to thank Marilyn Martin-Jones and Joan Pujolar for very helpful comments.

Notes

1 First drawn to our attention in Vladislavić (2005).
2 Given the lexicographers' location, this choice of example could be either unconscious irony or ironic reflexivity.

References

Arthur Shoba, J. and F. Chimbutane, eds. 2013. *Bilingual Education and Language Policy in the Global South*. New York: Routledge.
Bailey, B. 2011. 'Heteroglossia'. In *The Routledge Handbook of Multilingualism*, edited by M. Martin-Jones, A. Blackledge, and A. Creese, 499–507. New York: Routledge.
Bennett, J. 2008. 'Editorial: Researching for Life: Paradigms and Power'. *Feminist Africa* 11: 1–12.
Blommaert, J. 2010. *The Sociolinguistics of Globalization*. Cambridge, UK: Cambridge University Press.
Borba, R. 2015. 'A Sociolinguistics of the South? Discursive Colonisation, Epistemological Imbalances, and Rehearsed Narratives at a Brazilian Gender Identity Clinic'. *Working Papers in Urban Language and Literacies, No. 172*. Retrieved from http://www.kcl.ac.uk/sspp/departments/education/research/ldc/publications/workingpapers/abstracts/WP172-Rodrigo-Borba-2015.aspx.
Butler, J. 2010. *Frames of War: When Is Life Grievable?* Brooklyn, NY: Verso.
Castro-Gómez, S. 2007. *La Hybris Del Punto Cero: Ciencia, Raza E Ilustración En La Nueva Granada (1750–1816) [The Hubris of the Zero Point: Science, Race and Illustration in New Granada]*. Bogotá: Editorial Pontificia Universidad Javeriana.
Chimbutane, F. 2011. *Rethinking Bilingual Education in Postcolonial Contexts*. Bristol, UK: Multilingual Matters.
Chomsky, N. 1965. *Aspects of the Theory of Syntax*. Cambridge: MIT Press.
Comaroff, J., and J. L. Comaroff. 2011. *Theory from the South: Or, How Euro-America Is Evolving toward Africa*. New York: Routledge.
———. 2012. 'Theory from the South: A Rejoinder'. *Fieldsights: Theorizing the Contemporary, Cultural Anthropology Online*. Retrieved from https://dash.harvard.edu/handle/1/11204673.
Connell, R. 2007. *Southern Theory: Social Science and the Global Dynamics of Knowledge*. Cambridge, UK: Polity.
———. 2014. 'Margin Becoming Centre: For a World-Centered Rethinking of Masculinities'. *NORMA* 9 (4): 217–31.

Das, V. 1997. *Critical Events: An Anthropological Perspective on Contemporary India*. Delhi/New York: OUP India.

Dreyfus, H. L., and P. Rabinow. 1983. *Michel Foucault: Beyond Structuralism and Hermeneutics*. Chicago: University of Chicago Press.

Eisenlohr, P. 2004. 'Temporalities of Community: Ancestral Language, Pilgrimage, and Diasporic Belonging in Mauritius'. *Journal of Linguistic Anthropology* 14 (1): 81–98.

Errington, J. 2001. 'Colonial Linguistics'. *Annual Review of Anthropology* 30 (1): 19–39.

Fanon, F. 1961. *The Wretched of the Earth*. Translated by Richard Philcox. London: Grove.

Ferguson, J. 2012. 'Theory from the Comaroffs, or How to Know the World Up, Down, Backwards and Forwards'. *Cultural Anthropology*. Retrieved from https://culanth.org/fieldsights/271-theory-from-the-comaroffs-or-how-to-know-the-world-up-down-backwards-and-forwards.

Foucault, M. 1981. 'The Order of Discourse'. In *Untying the Text: A Poststructuralist Reader*, edited by R. Young, 51–78. Boston, London and Henley: Routledge and Kegan Paul.

Go, J. 2013. 'Introduction: Entangling Postcoloniality and Sociological Thought'. *Postcolonial Sociology* 24: 3–31.

Goffman, E. 1981. *Forms of Talk*. Philadelphia: University of Pennsylvania Press.

Grosfoguel, R. 2007. 'The Epistemic Decolonial Turn'. *Cultural Studies* 21 (2): 211–23.

Gumperz, J. J. 1982. *Discourse Strategies*. Cambridge: Cambridge University Press.

Heller, M. 1992. 'The Politics of Codeswitching and Language Choice'. *Journal of Multilingual and Multicultural Development* 13 (1–2): 123–42.

———. 1999. *Linguistic Minorities and Modernity: A Sociolinguistic Ethnography*. London: Longman.

———. 2011. *Paths to Post-Nationalism: A Critical Ethnography of Language and Identity*. New York: Oxford University Press.

———. 2012. 'Rethinking Sociolinguistic Ethnography: From Community and Identity to Process and Practice'. In *Multilingualism, Discourse, and Ethnography*, edited by S. Gardner and M. Martin-Jones, 24–33. New York: Routledge.

Heller, M., and M. Martin-Jones. 2001. *Voices of Authority: Education and Linguistic Difference: Contemporary Studies in Linguistics and Education, Volume 1*. Westport, CT: Ablex.

Heugh, K. 2009. 'Contesting the Monolingual Practices of a Bilingual to Multilingual Policy'. *English Teaching: Practice and Critique* 8 (2): 96–113.

———. 2013. 'Multilingual Education Policy in South Africa Constrained by Theoretical and Historical Disconnections'. *Annual Review of Applied Linguistics* 33: 215–37.

Heugh, K., A. Scarino, and C. Stroud, eds. (forthcoming 2017). *A Sociolinguistics of the South: Diversities, Affinities and Diasporas*. New York: Routledge.

Hofmeyr, I. 2004. 'Popular Literature in Africa: Post-Resistance Perspectives'. *Social Dynamics* 30 (2): 128–40.

Hountondji, P. J. 1997. *Endogenous Knowledge: Research Trails*. Oxford, UK: African Books Collective.

Hymes, D. 1974. *Foundations in Sociolinguistics: An Ethnographic Approach*. Philadelphia, PA: University of Pennsylvania Press.

Irvine, J. T., and S. Gal. 2000. 'Language Ideology and Linguistic Differentiation'. In *Regimes of Language: Ideologies, Polities, and Identities*, edited by P. V. Kroskrity, 35–79. Santa Fe, NM: School for Advanced Research.

Kerfoot, C., and B. O. Bello-Nonjengele. 2016. 'Game Changers? Multilingual Learners in a Cape Town Primary School'. *Applied Linguistics* 37 (4): 451–73, first published online September 20, 2014.

Kusch, R. [1970] 2010. *Indigenous and Popular Thinking in América*. Durham, NC: Duke University Press.

Lin, A. M. Y. 2013. 'Breaking the Hegemonic Knowledge Claims in Language Policy and Education: "The Global South as Method"'. In *Bilingual Education and Language Policy in the Global South*, edited by J. Arthur Shoba and F. Chimbutane, 223–31. London: Routledge.

Lugones, M. 2008. 'The Coloniality of Gender'. *Worlds & Knowledges Otherwise* Spring: 1–17.

Makoe, P., and C. McKinney. 2014. 'Linguistic Ideologies in Multilingual South African Suburban Schools'. *Journal of Multilingual and Multicultural Development* 35 (7): 658–73.

Makoni, S. 2003. 'From Misinvention to Disinvention of Language: Multilingualism and the South African Constitution'. In *Black Linguistics: Language, Society, and Politics in Africa and the Americas*, edited by S. Makoni, G. Smitherman, A. Ball, and A. K. Spears, 132–51. London: Routledge.

Makoni, S., and A. Pennycook. 2007. *Disinventing and Reconstituting Languages*. Bristol, UK: Multilingual Matters.

Martin-Jones, M. 2007. 'Bilingualism, Education and the Regulation of Access to Language Resources'. In *Bilingualism: A Social Approach*, edited by M. Heller, 161–82. New York: Palgrave Macmillan.

Martin-Jones, M., A. Blackledge, and A. Creese. 2012. 'Introduction: A Sociolinguistics of Multilingualism for Our Times'. In *Routledge Handbook of Multilingualism*, edited by M. Martin-Jones, A. Blackledge, and A. Creese, 1–26. Abingdon, OX: Routledge.

Martin-Jones, M., and D. Martin. (forthcoming 2017). 'Introduction'. In *Researching Multilingualism: Critical and Ethnographic Perspectives*, edited by M. Martin-Jones and D. Martin, 1–27. Abingdon, OX: Routledge.

Mbembe, A., and S. Nuttall. 2004. 'Writing the World from an African Metropolis'. *Public Culture* 16 (3): 347–72.

Medina, L. R. 2013. *Centers and Peripheries in Knowledge Production*. New York/London: Routledge.

Mignolo, W. D. 1992. 'On the Colonization of Amerindian Languages and Memories: Renaissance Theories of Writing and the Discontinuity of the Classical Tradition'. *Comparative Studies in Society and History* 34 (2): 301–30.

———. 2000. *Local Histories/Global Designs: Coloniality, Subaltern Knowledges, and Border Thinking*. Princeton: Princeton University Press.

———. 2007a. 'Introduction: Coloniality of Power and De-Colonial Thinking'. *Cultural Studies* 21 (2–3): 155–67.

———. 2007b. 'Delinking: The Rhetoric of Modernity, the Logic of Coloniality and the Grammar of De-Coloniality'. *Cultural Studies* 21 (2–3): 449–514.

———. 2009. 'Epistemic Disobedience, Independent Thought and Decolonial Freedom'. *Theory, Culture & Society* 26 (7–8): 159–81.

———. 2011. 'Geopolitics of Sensing and Knowing: On (De)coloniality, Border Thinking and Epistemic Disobedience'. *Postcolonial Studies* 14 (3): 273–83.

Mohanty, A. K. 2006. 'Multilingualism of the Unequals and Predicaments of Education in India: Mother Tongue or Other Tongue?' In *Imagining Multilingual Schools: Language in Education and Globalization*, edited by O. Garcia, T. Skutnabb-Kangas, and M. E. Torres-Guzman, 262–83. Bristol, UK: Multilingual Matters.

Mühlhäusler, P. 1996. *Linguistic Ecology: Language Change and Linguistic Imperialism in the Pacific Region*. New York: Routledge.

Ngũgĩ, T. 1986. *Decolonising the Mind: The Politics of Language in African Literature*. Rochester, NY: J. Currey.

Nuttall, S. 2009. *Entanglement: Literary and Cultural Reflections on Post Apartheid*. Johannesburg: Wits University Press.

Odora Hoppers, C,. ed. 2002. *Indigenous Knowledge and the Integration of Knowledge Systems: Towards A Philosophy of Articulation*. Claremont: New Africa Books.

Parkin, D. 2012. 'From Multilingual Classification to Translingual Ontology: Concluding Commentary'. *Diversities* 14 (2): 73–85.

Pennycook, A. 2007. 'ELT and Colonialism'. In *International Handbook of English Language Teaching*, edited by J. Cummins and C. Davison, 15: 13–24. New York: Springer US.

Quijano, A. 2000. 'Coloniality of Power and Eurocentrism in Latin America'. *International Sociology* 15 (2): 215–32.

Santos, B. de S. 2002. *A Crítica Da Razão Indolente: Contra O Desperdício Da experiência [A Critique of Lazy Reason: Against the Waste of Experience]*. São Paulo: Cortês.

———. 2012. 'Public Sphere and Epistemologies of the South'. *Africa Development* XXXVII (1): 43–67.

———. 2014. *Epistemologies of the South: Justice against Epistemicide*. Boulder, CO: Paradigm.

Santos, B. de S., T. B. G. Egziabher, M. F. Alonso, L. C. Arenas, and J. P. B Coelho. 2008. *Another Knowledge Is Possible: Beyond Northern Epistemologies*. New York: Verso.

Shepherd, N. 2002. 'Heading South, Looking North'. *Archaeological Dialogues* 9 (2): 74–82.

Silverstein, M. 2015. 'How Language Communities Intersect: Is "Superdiversity" an Incremental or Transformative Condition?' *Language & Communication* 14: 7–18.

Smith, L. T. 1999. *Decolonizing Methodologies: Research and Indigenous Peoples*. London: Zed Books.

Stroud, C. 2001. 'African Mother-Tongue Programmes and the Politics of Language: Linguistic Citizenship versus Linguistic Human Rights'. *Journal of Multilingual and Multicultural Development* 22 (4): 339–55.

———. 2007. 'Bilingualism: Colonialism and Postcolonialism'. In *Bilingualism: A Social Approach*, edited by M. Heller, 25–49. Basingstoke: Palgrave Macmillan.

———. 2009. 'A Postliberal Critique of Language Rights: Toward a Politics of Language for a Linguistics of Contact'. In *International Perspectives on Bilingual Education: Policy, Practice, and Controversy*, edited by J. E. Petrovic, 191–218. Charlotte, NC: Information Age.

———. 2013. 'Turbulent Mobility and Superdiversity'. Keynote presentation. First International Conference on Language and Super-diversity: Explorations and Interrogations, June 5–7, Jyväskylä, Finland. Unpublished.

Stroud, C., and M. Guissemo. 2015. Linguistic Messianism. *Multilingual Margins* 2 (2): 6–19.

Vladislavić, I. 2005. 'Meeting Halfway'. *Art South Africa*. Retrieved from http:// artsouthafrica.com/archives/archived-featured-articles/212-main-archive/archi ved-featured-articles/1358-meeting-halfway.html.

Warner, D. 2004. 'Towards a Queer Research Methodology'. *Qualitative Research in Psychology* 1 (4): 321–37.

Weedon, C. 1987. *Feminist Practice and Poststructuralist Theory*. Cambridge, MA: Wiley-Blackwell.

Woolard, K. 1985. 'Language Variation and Cultural Hegemony: Toward an Integration of Sociolinguistic and Social Theory'. *American Ethnologist* 12 (4): 738–48.

———. 1989. *Double Talk: Bilingualism and the Politics of Ethnicity in Catalonia*. Stanford, CA: Stanford University Press.

Part I
Southern Perspectives

1   On the Margins of the Republic

Medical Encounters in a Postcolonial Setting and the Construction of Sociolinguistic Orders of Visibility

Valelia Muni Toke

Introduction

'French Overseas territories' is a political and administrative category that encompasses a wide range of heterogeneous postcolonial cases—from places which have held penal colonies (French Guiana, New Caledonia)[1] to places that have been dominated by slavery (Martinique, Guadeloupe, La Réunion) and to ancient protectorates which have not been colonies of settlement (French Polynesia, Wallis-and-Futuna, Mayotte). These territories are now divided between *départements* on the one hand—an administrative status that matches the one of mainland France—and *collectivités* on the other hand, which have a hybrid administrative status: they keep local and traditional forms of governance alongside the French administration. This is the case of Wallis (South Pacific), on which this chapter focuses. The island[2] became been a French protectorate in 1842, and served as a military base for the American army during World War II. Its population is now ca. 8900 inhabitants. After a referendum in 1959, in which French citizenship was offered to inhabitants while preserving both the royalty and the influence of the Catholic Church—[3]an option that received 100 percent of favourable votes from the population (Henningham 1992, 1995)—Wallis became a *territoire d'Outre-mer (TOM)* in 1961 and is now labelled as a *collectivité d'Outre-mer (COM)*. In practice, an aristocratic regime that includes kings, ministers, and village chiefs[4] decides land ownership issues (a conflictual question in postcolonial settings), while the French State keeps all executive power on all other domains (notably justice). Administration and public service such as schools and hospitals are run in French exclusively, although almost 25 percent of the population in Wallis declares itself non-French speaking according to the 2011 census. The vast majority of Wallisian children speak a Polynesian language, *Faka'uvea*,[5] at home and start learning French when they go to school, from the age of three (Muni Toke 2012). The island thus stands as a case of State's monolingual management that relies on the French Constitution, of which article number 2 says: 'The language of the Republic is French'.

This chapter postulates that the contemporary political situation of the French Overseas territories provides a unique observatory to the sociolinguistic inquiry that concerns the politics of multilingualism and diversity in a globalizing world. Language and citizenship issues are often addressed from the perspective of migration (Moyer and Rojo 2007), which is definitely a valid one when it comes to French Overseas territories as well, especially because some of them receive significant incoming migration fluxes (French Guiana and Mayotte, for instance). But the particular question that these southern territories raise is the one of autochthony and indigeneity in a post-colonial era (Gausset, Kenrick, and Gibb 2011). Being politically dependent on a European metropole, yet displaying socio-economic characteristics of the so-called Southern countries, French Overseas territories allow the investigation of the fact that 'there is much South in the North, much North in the South' (Comaroff and Comaroff 2012, 127). In this sense, they stand on the margins of the Republic, geographically, politically, and socially: in all of them, indicators are alarming when compared to mainland France. Infant mortality is much higher than in metropolitan France (Cour des Comptes 2014),[6] cost of living is significantly higher although unemployment is a major issue, which leads to social protests and feelings of despair (Gordien 2014), and school dropout is also worrisome (Doligé 2009). The ethnographic work that I present here takes health care settings in Wallis as privileged sites for observation and analysis of multilingual practices within the public service.

As Wallis has never been a colony of settlement, almost the totality of the population was born and raised on the island, or on the island of Futuna that is 250 kms away, or within Wallisian and Futunian families who migrated to metropolitan France or to New Caledonia (another French territory which is only a three-hours flight away). A minority of French expats lives on the island as well, mostly in order to run the administration and public service in general. In the 2011 census, approximately 90 percent of the population declared that Wallisian is the language that they use primarily at home. In this sense, it is irrelevant here to talk about minority (in the quantitative sense) languages or migrant languages (or even of urban settings, as these islands are small and entirely rural) as in many contexts where contemporary multilingualism is studied. What we deal with is rather a case of political minoritization of autochthonous languages through State's actions—notably through the provision of public service (education, health care) in French only. The objective of this chapter is precisely to shed light on the way metropolitan State governance in postcolonial settings and institutional monolingualism creates locally an interpretative lens through which social positionalities get assessed within local economies of communication (Bourdieu 1977a; Bourdieu and Bensa 1985; Stroud 2007). I here understand economies of communication as situated and embodied interactions, discourses, and metapragmatics—they are sites that produce, reproduce, and impact socially significant discourses and practices; sites where indexicalities attached to social positionalities get reshuffled and renegotiated. This renegotiation praxis is not confined to the here and now of linguistic events but can rather be understood as organized in a scalar way (Blommaert 2007a; Collins and Slembrouck 2007; Herod and Wright 2002), articulating the level of individual interaction to the postcoloniality of the political regime in place. In the case of Wallis, the fact that care is provided by a hospital run by the French State (there is no private medical practice on the island) sets a particular frame for communication: health care is provided in a top-down movement, from the French State (all doctors are from metropolitan France) to the autochthonous, sometimes non-French speaking population, and competes directly with the local, traditional non-biomedical approaches to care.[7] One thus needs to understand what is at stake in medical encounters in these particular settings, the hypothesis being that the State hospitals achieve a social task that goes beyond health care provision, as this task is embedded within politicized issues of racialization, legitimacy of (bio-)medical knowledge, and colonial history.

This chapter relies on fieldwork that I have undertaken since 2010 in Wallis,[8] living mostly among families—and mostly with my own relatives, as my father is Wallisian and migrated as an adult to metropolitan France where I was born and raised. When in the field, I am therefore ethnically perceived by my interlocutors in various ways. I am a metropolitan researcher as I work for a French public research institute, but people who define themselves as Wallisians on the island alternatively refer to me as a '*métisse*' ('mixed-race') and as a Wallisian, depending on how these categorizations and terms appear relevant in a particular conversational context. When categorized only from a phenotypical perspective, I am often seen as 'White' as well.[9] My position in the field is therefore privileged, as I am granted access to many local private settings and conversations, and comforted into some sense of legitimacy regarding my presence on the island—but it is also sometimes uncomfortable in case of conflicts between local inhabitants and metropolitan State representatives, for instance, as both parts would claim my loyalty and expect me to understand and support them. In the data that follows, one should keep in mind that most of the patients see me as a Pacific Islander whom they explicitly want to help in her work by sharing their experience,[10] when doctors would take various stances towards me, alternatively speaking to the metropolitan researcher (seeking closeness in the exchange) and to the Wallisian woman (usually praising quite artificially in my view, seemingly to please me, the 'local culture').

In what follows, after pointing out how the construction of 'orders of visibility' is related to the process of 'seeing like a state' (section 2), I take the case of the voices of patients who are perceived as indigenous in public health care settings in Wallis (section 3). They seem to remain largely inaudible, possibly because these patients are not expected to speak in the first place: they are often viewed by the French doctors as preferring to communicate through the gravity of silence—which would be a Polynesian cultural practice—or, in other cases, as being untrustworthy anyway. In a context where the French State representatives work along with the local aristocratic regime, I argue that this ethnicization of the bodies and voices might mirror the somehow hybrid political management—the local population being expected to preserve its Otherness while being French. This chapter thus contributes to a linguistic anthropology of visibility by exploring how gazes get positioned and how they get to construe indexicalities in resonance with social orders in which they take part.

Orders of Visibility and the Historicity of Economies of Communication

Drawing on Foucault's notion of 'order of discourse' (1971), the sociolinguistic notion of 'order' refers to the hierarchical organization of social practices as well as to the preservation of established situations; to the metapragmatic regimentation of meaningful semiosis; to the legitimization of certain discourses while other voices are silenced (Blommaert 2007b, 2009). The term 'orders of visibility' invites us more precisely to displace the focus of the analysis from the *logos* to the *nomos*, in the sense of Bourdieu (1993, 58, 2012, 611); that is, from the discourse to the 'principle of vision and of division' through which we see and interpret the organization of the social world, inasmuch as it is mostly provided to us by the State:

> we are never done with getting rid of the self-evidence of the social; and, among the instruments of production of self-evidence, of feeling of self-evidence, the State is probably the most powerful.[11]
>
> (Bourdieu 2012, 578) [My translation]

This relates to what Bourdieu (1993, 2012) calls 'State's thinking', and to what Scott (1999) calls 'seeing like a State'. Classifications that are elaborated by and for governance are first circulated in a top-down process, erasing the permeability and the hybridity of actual social practices, and transforming territories as well as languages in homogeneous, discrete entities (Silverstein 2015). In this sense, these State categories of languages, speakers, and territories are the situated product of, as well as (re-)producing, language ideologies (Schieffelin, Woolard, and Kroskrity 1998) which, in practice, suffuse processes of social differentiation:

> *Erasure* is the process in which ideology, in simplifying the field of linguistic practices, renders some persons or activities or sociolinguistic phenomena invisible. Facts that are inconsistent with the ideological scheme may go unnoticed or get explained away.
>
> (Gal and Irvine 1995, 974)

According to Bourdieu, the social order as constructed by the State has the property to appear as self-evident; sociology is about making visible again the historicity of social order so it can be questioned:

> Making this detour via the genesis [of the State; Bourdieu is here commenting on the overall structure of his course on the State at Collège de France] is to give ourselves some chance to escape from the State's thinking, which is one of the empirical ways to practice the radical doubt. It is in my opinion the major function of history: giving tools to unravel the commonplace and to denaturalize.[12]
>
> (Bourdieu 2012, 578) [My translation]

Historicizing the economies of communication in the contemporary French Overseas territories remains a thorny task. The mere existence of such places challenges *de facto* any idea of a clear-cut distinction between a North and a South, as well as the idea that decolonization would be a linear and teleological process. Sometimes called an 'unorthodox decolonization' (Deville and Georges 1996), the way these territories have been integrated into the present French Republic proves itself quite complex to analyze—and ethnographic studies question the idea of a contemporary non-colonial situation (Blanchard 2007; Dimier 2005; Lemercier, Muni Toke, and Palomares 2014; Trépied 2012). To avoid entering a sterile discussion on the objective historical value of the prefix post- in 'postcolonial' when applied to Wallis, I rather choose to follow Clifford's claim that:

> three narratives [have been] active in the last half-century: decolonization, globalization, and indigenous becoming. They represent distinct historical energies, scales of action, and politics of the possible.
>
> (Clifford 2013, 8)

These three narratives delineate differentiated images of the world, from an ancient bipolar opposition between the colonized and the decolonized, the South and the North; to the interconnectedness that would characterize current globalizing processes; and to the re-emergence of indigenous claims.[13] Rather than clear-cut periods organized in a sequential order, these narratives of decolonization, globalization and indigenous becoming point to 'unfinished, excessive historical processes' (Clifford 2013). It is as such fuzzy and heteroglossic entities that they get entangled in contemporary economies of communication. The ways they construct and shape social orders of visibility are therefore often contradictory—sometimes locking speakers in essentialized identities and/or racialized bodies; sometimes giving them a unique opportunity to gain agency in an otherwise inequitable or uncertain situation.

Focusing on the role of the State, I hereby address social processes of visibilization and erasure that remain themselves almost invisible—precisely because they reinforce apparently self-evident, mostly unquestioned, and State-related categories in economies of communication. Social visibility is indeed ambiguous—as suggested above, largely because it is historically constructed along lines of power disputes. A lack of social visibility indexes the belonging to the discriminated, unrecognized, and often racialized margins (Brighenti 2007)—which could paradoxically open sometimes onto a fruitful perspective on the hidden backstage of social order (Rollock 2012). In this sense, a linguistic anthropology of visibility cannot be limited to the top-down and explicit manifestations of erasure that the State can perform about speakers and language practices. It also has to take into account (1) what is discursively made visible instead of what is being invisibilized, and how indexicalities of citizenship, in particular, shift accordingly; and (2) how social visibility or invisibility might be rationalized metapragmatically in ways that would invisibilize the actual State influence. It is such contradictions pertaining to social visibility that I intend to analyze here—its shifting indexical values, and its complex relation to the power of the State.

Wallis: Indigenous Bodies and Inaudible Voices

The Contradictions of Apparent Sociolinguistic Freedom

This section is meant to provide an illustration of the way the State constructs sociolinguistic orders of visibility. Wallis, as presented in section 1, is a peculiar example of hybrid governmentality. The French State kept in place a system in which families of *'Aliki* (nobles) get to elect, among their members, kings or queens who are assisted by ministers and chiefs in districts and villages. It is therefore common to see customary ceremonies that are attended by the representative of the French State, the *préfet*—whose local name is *Kovana*, an adaptation of the ancient title 'Governor'—and in which only customary chiefs give speeches, all in *Faka'uvea*. This visibility and constant displaying of the aristocratic custom is a key component of the public life on the island. In this sense, Wallis stands as a remarkable political exception within the Republic (Chave-Dartoen 2002). East Uvean is a language that is seemingly spoken everywhere, from the numerous churches where frequent Catholic masses are held, to the households and conversations between co-workers on construction sites. French language comes into play when the French State authority or responsibility is involved, whether in the educational system, the administration, or the health care system. French public school—which was installed in 1961 only, in replacement of the missionaries' boarding schools that recruited only a limited number of children—has not yet allowed the vast majority of the population to access certain employment sectors, such as medicine.

The French monolingualism that prevails at school has therefore progressively become a subject of questioning—although in Wallis, as in any other part of France, the possibility of a bilingual teaching that would include local languages cannot be performed within the public frame. When this particular issue is raised during conversations, the cheerful image of a local language that would be proudly spoken—and powerful as it is associated both with the religion and the kingdom—crackles. For instance, during an interview, a social worker from mainland France deplores: 'When you ask youngsters and students why they keep speaking the language [and not French], their reply is often: *we are afraid that people make fun of us, because we speak in a bad way*' [My translation]. In other words, they prefer keeping their French unheard instead of taking any risk of ridicule: erasure is, in the end, self-performed to avoid an uncomfortable visibility that is predicted as socially endangering. There is, of course, no direct relation between any kind of 'linguistic competence' as it would be measured in an educational setting, for instance, and behaviours of avoidance such as this one. In this sense, what speakers perform here by ruling themselves out of French language practices has very much to do with the fact that their own language is stigmatized as useless on the economic market—a very common discourse as in many, if not all, minoritization contexts—whereas French would be the gate to success. Dropping out of this unfair and seemingly already settled competition might be a drawback economically, as these young people would sometimes avoid applying for jobs, but it would definitely serve face-preserving purposes. In this particular case, self-invisibilization comes as a resource when reversing the stigma by claiming 'Wallisianness' does not seem to stand as one: the way young adults see their practice of East Uvean can in fact also be rather negative (Muni Toke 2011). They sometimes praise the language of the 'Ancients' and make theirs the common critiques of a contemporary decadence of the local language that would be too often mixed with French and would in the end lose its authenticity.[14]

The multilingual practices that take place on the island seem therefore to be marked with forms of linguistic insecurity, whatever language is in use. The most crucial point in this diagnosis is that actual multilingualism at the individual level does not mean that speakers feel like using any language in any context. For instance, an interpreter works in court: my observation of audiences shows that people might choose to rely on the interpreter's service even if they were supposed to be able to 'speak French' otherwise. So, when given room for their own sense of agency, so-called bilingual speakers would be able to determine for themselves the language in which they were the most comfortable in court. The mere presence of a permanent, State-funded interpreter in court shows that the French State acknowledges the need for a language mediator in this particular place. In fact, the State is bounded by law to provide an interpreter to any defendant, understanding one's trial being a fundamental individual right within the French justice system. This perspective of individual rights is not the most interesting for analysis, however: why would it be a legal right to understand one's trial, and not one's education or one's medical consultation? The provision of language services within the health care system is indeed not regulated in France, being left to the discretion of institutions: ad hoc interpreters such as nurses, medical secretaries, and family members are therefore the most common case.[15] One could consequently say that when the State must be understood and must understand, communicational issues are addressed in a pragmatic frame that could at first sight appear as contradicting the doctrine of State's monolingualism. I here argue that there is no contradiction is such a situation. In fact, the institution does not primarily provide a language service to the user, but rather settles for itself the conditions of felicity of interactions that bear a legal value.[16] Language practices that differ from the official language of the institution acquire a temporary visibility in the eyes of the State—but only to confirm that they are, as a common metaphor puts it, 'a language barrier'.

Talking about Silent Patients

In Wallis, the health care system is entirely free of charge, being provided directly by the French State. The public hospital is therefore an institution that is worth observing when it comes to the State's regimentation of language practices. In the following, I quote excerpts of interviews I had with several doctors over the years—the turn-over is important as they usually sign short-term contracts that go from one month to two years, and then fly back to France or to another French Overseas territory. These interviews were for me the opportunity to shed light on a conversational phenomenon that I find throughout all the consultations that I have recorded so far: silence is a core component of the interaction. The excerpt of a medical consultation below gives an example of a completely silent patient, to whom the doctor (DOC) tries to talk, while getting replies from the accompanying person (a family member) only (ACC):

DOC je vais te faire un papier pour [nom d'une infirmière] tu reviendras te faire contrôler ta tension la semaine prochaine/ et tu lui expliques qu'on va l'allonger qu'on va lui faire ça d'accord [mais je te donne] ACC [non/ c'est bon elle en]tend DOC elle a compris\ d'accord// mais si c'est élevé si ça reste élevé on verra si je te donne un traitement ou pas mais pour l'instant non hein on va vérifier d'abord et pour les yeux c'est pas vous avez déjà pris rendez-vous là-haut ACC non ils ont dit de venir par ici	DOC *I'm going to give you a paper for [name of a nurse] you'll come back to get your blood pressure checked next week and you explain to her that we'll have her lying down and we'll do that to her ok [but I give you]* ACC *no but it's ok she hears this* DOC *she understood ok but if it's high if it stays high we'll see whether I give you a treatment or not but for the moment no ok we'll check first and for the eyes you already have made an appointment upstairs?* ACC *no they said to come here*

The referent of the second person pronoun 'you' is permanently shifting—as is the participation frame. The doctor talks primarily to the family member who seems to be in charge of the patient ('I'm going to give you a paper',

'Have you made an appointment'), but he also addresses the patient directly ('your blood pressure', 'whether I give you a treatment'). His attempts to make sure that he is understood ('you explain to her') get quite bluntly rebutted by the family member ('no but it's ok she hears this', *overlap*). And the patient gives no verbal or bodily sign of understanding. In this case, the doctor shared, after the consultation, his concerns for the patient, deploring in his own words the 'lack of trust' that, in his view, suffused most of the interactions he had with patients. I did attend many consultations where mutual misunderstanding was salient, and the results of the communicational issues potentially dramatic—some patients understand neither the diagnosis nor the treatment, and end up, for instance, conscientiously taking paracetamol every day to treat high blood pressure.

Spending time with aged and diabetic patients at their homes, I learned that they disliked medical consultations, and that they were happy to keep them as short as possible—which was another take on silence, and gave their own explanation for it. Away from doctors and the hospital, they were voicing profound discontent with the health system, saying that medical consultations were a place where they mainly got reproaches about their dietary habits and their non-observance of the treatment. They felt like they were infantilized. Sometimes giving a fatalistic explanation for their condition, such as a divine punishment, they saw the whole biomedical frame as hostile and displayed more trust towards Holy Water bottles and local healers whom they knew personally, and with whom they would speak in *Faka'uvea*. Even if these two last options would probably fall under the label 'superstition' from a biomedical perspective, the rationality of these patients' discourse—which contrasted with the irrational behaviour that numerous doctors would describe to me when talking about the non-observance of treatments or the avoidance of care—is moreover supported by the fact that, as the health care facilities located in Wallis are basic, any serious diagnosis can lead to a medical evacuation towards New Caledonia, Australia, or even mainland France. If some patients actually wished to leave the territory and get closer to their families who had emigrated there, some also feared the possible isolation that would ensue. They consequently avoided the public health care institution as much as possible and cut short when dialoguing with doctors. In these cases, diseases had to be kept unknown from and invisible to the medical institution in order to avoid changes in their daily lives that they perceived as more frightening than the disease itself.

This rationale, that is very much embedded in the materiality and economic poverty of a postcolonial, Southern context,[17] often appears to be quite opaque to the doctors. One says, dismissing the overall validity of verbal interaction in favour of physical observation:

> I don't really take it [the patients' discourse] into account although it is said that it is so important but here I don't really take it into account. We have learned to be clinical, we care about the clinical observation

more than about the questioning, even if we have an interpreter I don't trust the questioning.

[My translation]

The blame is put during this interview on the 'language barrier', as well on the fact that patients tend to give distorted accounts of their actions and symptoms—especially when it comes to the daily management of diabetes. The economy of communication is ruled by mutual defiance: the patients' declarations stand as untrustworthy, while, in the patients' eyes, the doctors' opinion and public health concerns are mainly reprimands. The medical act is therefore preferably reduced by the doctor to an examination of the body—which is seen as not being able to conceal what the discourse would otherwise try to keep hidden. As Foucault (1963) puts it, the clinical gaze relies on the belief that all that is 'visible' is 'sayable', and vice versa: the bodily symptom becomes language through the practitioner's sense of medical analysis. In the example provided above, it is clear what relation the clinical gaze has with discursive practices: it is entirely a doctor's activity, independent from the patient, whose language and words are carefully put aside and ignored, in the fear that they would interfere with the quality of the medical diagnosis.

If doctors sometimes denounce silence as an intentional dissimulation of the truth, many also share their puzzlement about the silence of the patients when it comes to the expression of pain. A recurring statement in the interviews is: 'They never complain'. Some doctors even claim that they now dislike having 'White' patients, because they, on the contrary, 'complain all the time and for nothing'. Racialization is here invoked to distinguish between two groups of patients, Wallisians being this time on the right side of the axiological evaluation. In my view, this seems to result from a culturalist view that sees Pacific Islanders as inheriting the courage of their ancestors, and as being natural born 'warriors'. A doctor affirms:

I get angry [with the patients], and I'm not afraid of getting angry, yeah I get angry. 'You smoke, you walk barefoot and your foot is damaged, you come barefoot? I don't want to see you. You go and get shoes for yourself.' And it works. Because these Wallisians they develop better, like their ancestors, in conflict, in brutal relation, in big voice. You see?

[My translation]

In this account, the doctor is proud 'not to be afraid' to provoke warlike patients. He is even prouder to have found what he thinks is the most adapted way of talking to them: 'conflict' and 'brutal relation' are the modes of communication that they are supposed to understand better, in virtue of their 'culture'. Old modes of colonial regimentation re-emerge in this somehow picturesque narrative in which an indigenous person walks barefoot, seemingly unaware of the lack of respect and possibly poor hygiene that it indexes in the eyes of the Western health care institution—so the doctor has to play the role of the educator. In this process, both the colonial aspects of the past and present social inequalities get erased. A patient says, talking about the non-availability of good quality food, which in her ironic view is a continuation of colonization in the form of controlled markets:

> [only bad quality food is imported] because Wallisians only eat *tini* [corned beef] and chicken everybody knows that (laughs). Anyway, we don't need to eat vegetables, everybody knows that, we are *warriors* [in English] we are invincible. So [the doctors say] 'oh, don't drink alcohol!'—well, yeah, in the meantime their biggest benefits they make on alcohol tobacco, *tini* and chicken.
>
> [My translation]

It is unclear who 'they' refers to—she seems to denounce a conspiracy that would bring together a colonizing state, doctors, and economic networks at the expense of the local population. She also includes the customary authorities—being born in a family without political legitimacy, her voice has only a small chance of being heard on that side either. What is particularly interesting here is the contestation that she makes of public health discourses regarding diets, on a political and economic basis—contradicting the doctors' view, which is often that Wallisians have happily rejected 'their traditional ways of eating', and are therefore guilty victims of modernity. On the same subject, taking a political stance and expressing empathy for the patients who feel mistreated by doctors who reproach them about their weight and dietary habits, a member of the medical staff says:

> for them [certain doctors] it's [the patients] almost, excuse me for the term—it's cattle. You should see what terms they use, it's unacceptable. A doctor talked [about a patient] in an extremely offensive way, and I mean extremely offensive. Those who were here were in shock, but they didn't react. Why don't they react?
>
> [My translation]

Silence is once again evoked—this time, as an inapprehensible acceptance of derogatory discourses that are performed in a language that is nevertheless understood by the patient, even if she doesn't speak it. In the same interview, usual economies of communication are explicitly analyzed as indexing an asymmetrical state-citizen relationship (Stroud 2007) that is marked by implicit racialization:

> [the people from mainland France] they are not aware of this, that people [Wallisians] can understand [French]. They always start by saying *tu* [instead of *vous*]. It profoundly bothers me. Because he is old, because

he's Wallisian, they say *tu*? According to me, this is colonialism, this is racism.

[My translation]

This politicized view (which is almost unique in my corpus so far) is countered by another kind of discourse, as shown below by an interview with another doctor—on the basis of which domination is performed by the patients to the detriment of the medical staff from mainland France. In this case, conflicts would not result from a colonial history, but rather from the inner flaws of the 'customary system' that would stand against modernity and the French State, and would end up producing White racism:

> I know that it is not nice to say this but I hate this customary system, I see it as a total perversion ; I don't know how it was a hundred years ago, I wasn't there fifty years ago, same thing, but I can't stand it [. . .] I got sick of this ambient xenophobia [. . .] you should see anyhow that we attend conversations between customary chiefs [. . .] and that the medical secretary, who is there translating with the doctor [. . .] soon realizes that those customary chiefs who claim to be monolingual in fact master French, and they know how to use it when the moment comes, and they display a certain contempt towards the medical staff, with sometimes tones, things that are said in a somehow threatening way— and there you see immediately that language is a weapon.
>
> [My translation]

The image of the warrior comes back, under the guise of a verbal war ('language is a weapon') in which dishonesty rules the whole economy of communication. Dissimulating their actual competence in French, customary chiefs would not hesitate to 'threaten' the medical staff, using both silence and the local language to avoid dialoguing with the doctor—a behaviour that is here interpreted as 'xenophobia'. Although history is evoked ('I don't know how it was a hundred years ago'), nothing is said about the political dependence that the island and its traditional leadership have constructed with mainland France. The 'Natives' are here confined in a mode of thought (Appadurai 1988) that is irremediably attached to the 'local'—a scalar view that ends up denying them access to global modernity (Briggs 2004). The medical staff's metapragmatic discourses therefore tend to rationalize their actions and those of the patients by falling back on cultural explanations— in which culture is viewed as an immemorial and homogeneous entity that any member of a given 'community' would receive equally and display in any of her actions. This culturalism performs the erasure of other explanations, among which are the historicity of social relations as well as the inner rationality of behaviours—such as silence—that can on the contrary be in some cases interpreted as forms of resistance, as attempts to deal with unequal social orders.[18]

The fact that 'local customs' are officially made visible on the island probably put the doctors, as well as all residents from mainland France, in the position of spectators of a 'culture' that preserves—notably because of the language it mainly draws on—a part of 'exoticism'.[19] Letting the local culture be visible is anyhow rather innocuous for the French State's authority, as the territory is, at the end of the day, under French governance.[20] In this sense, the current, hybrid political situation can be interpreted as a continuation of the gaze that the Europeans had on the Pacific islanders three centuries ago. In a paradoxical Othering process, they first admired them as 'almost White' (Tcherkézoff 2009) and were impressed by their 'aristocratic' organization. In this romantic view, Polynesia appeared as 'a lost civilization which could be equated to that of the Ancient Scots or the Hebrews of the time of King David' (Guiart 1982, 139). In other words, Polynesians appeared as 'relatively civilized and could easily be improved' (Guiart 1982).[21] So, presently, visible manifestations of Polynesian traditions, which have always been officially acknowledged and tolerated by the French State, seem to be easily instrumentalized by culturalist interpretations of the economies of communication. They stand, as it were, as an opaque veil that conceals the complex historical construction of social relations—and their fundamentally political dimension.

Conclusion

I have here illustrated the ways in which sociolinguistic orders of visibility get constructed by the State in a postcolonial situation. Counter-intuitively, the official visibility of 'local culture' and 'local languages' in Wallis does not seem to lead to any accuracy of the French State's evaluation of the sociolinguistic situation.[22] It rather seems to lead to the erasure of the historical construction of economies of communication, and of the political asymmetry they rely on, promoting culturalist explanations when interactional issues emerge. The State's hospital in Wallis does provide care, although it goes beyond this point by being embedded within a postcolonial context that sets uncertain parameters for interaction: are the patients 'cultural Others'? Are they 'rational' at all? Are doctors benevolent? Are they trustworthy? Strategies elicited on both sides, from avoiding consultation on the side of the patients to ignoring patients' discourse on the side of the doctors, stand as the symptom of deregulated, chaotic even, economies of communication. As it seems to be so common, mutual mistrust can hardly be blamed on psychological, individual factors, but should rather be understood in the political context in which takes place. By reducing the patients' voices either to silence or to an irrational discourse that challenges the rationality of biomedicine, doctors paid by the State sometimes continue forms of colonial education that show that the health institution achieves far more than just providing care. It stands in fact as a crucial element in the French

State's postcolonial management of the territory, giving patients little chance of expressing their own voice and sense of agency.

What the Wallisian case thus shows is that the gaze of the State, achieved here by the public hospital and the metropolitan doctors, does not only perform the invisibilization of language practices that are viewed as 'culturally' different. More importantly, it tends to make invisible the relevant interpretative frames for these actual language practices. States' modes of classification present themselves as self-evident, as Bourdieu notes, but also as ahistorical—erasing the historicity of the construction of social relations, as well as the social inequalities that result from this history.

As I suggested it, a crucial question when it comes to seeing language practices 'like a State' regards the legal frame that the State imposes for itself. More work should be done on how economies of communication are conditioned by the State's legal concerns. In which cases does the State judge it important that things that are said should be understood by all interlocutors? This question seems to provide an efficient explanatory frame for resolving apparent contradictions in the acknowledgement of linguistic diversity by the State—imposing monolingual teaching while praising 'cultural' preservation, or providing interpreters in courts but not in medical consultations. Far from being unfortunate exceptions or marginal cases, Southern voices in postcolonial contexts therefore stand as a crucial object for contemporary sociolinguistics—because their analysis requires the sharpening and development of a general theory of the State within the discipline.

Notes

1 New Caledonia is the only one for which the French State currently acknowledges the colonization process. A referendum will be held in 2018 regarding independence or permanent attachment to the French State.
2 The administrative and hyphenated name 'Wallis-et-Futuna' refers to the whole *collectivité*. In fact, Wallis and Futuna (the latter comprising two islands) are 230 kms far from each other. They have different languages, social histories, and contemporary challenges. My fieldwork so far is based in Wallis only, so I avoid adding the name of 'Futuna' systematically—although a large number of my observations here would probably be applicable to its situation.
3 Primary schools are up to now under the responsibility of the Catholic Church, being nevertheless ruled by the Ministry of National Education when it comes to the content and overall goals of the programs.
4 This local authority network is referred to as *la chefferie* ('leadership') or *les coutumiers* ('customary chiefs').
5 Also called *East Uvean* in English, and *wallisien* in French. See (Moyse-Faurie 2016).
6 In Wallis, more than 80 percent of the adult population is considered overweight or obese, and over 18 percent has diabetes (Girin et al. 2014). Infant mortality is 5.5 percent, as compared to 3.3 percent in mainland France (2011).
7 I won't address these issues of competing care approaches in this chapter, but it is worth mentioning that many metropolitan practitioners mostly tolerate, within the hospital rooms even, traditional healing practices as long as they

don't interfere too much with biomedical treatments. For instance, patients can call on a traditional massage practitioner to relieve their pain, but won't be allowed to drink therapeutic plants infusions.

8 The data presented in this chapter has been collected through an ethnographic work that is still ongoing, and that started in 2010 in educational and health care settings in Wallis. It has been funded by IRD (Institut de recherche pour le Développement) and by the research unit SeDyL (CNRS—INALCO—IRD) in 2013 and 2015–16, and consists of two to three months of field-work per year.

9 This variability of ethnic categorization sometimes creates awkward situations on first encounters with people on the island. What we deal with here is the social perception of bodies (Bourdieu 1977b), my interlocutors judging my phenotype and overall appearance as congruent or dissonant with the identity they would spontaneously assign to me. One day when I was wearing a traditional outfit at the hospital, a metropolitan person (whom I had only emailed so far and was supposed to interview on that day) started our conversation by laughing out loud: 'Oh, so you're all ready for the costume ball!'. Apologies followed when this person understood where I was coming from—as well as a comment on the 'ridicule' of 'Whites going Natives' when being expats, which was supposed to be a justification for the preceding laughter. On the contrary, I also got annoyed comments by Wallisian persons working at the hospital on days that I came with outfits that they judged as improper for a Wallisian: they would say to me that I was dressed as a '*Papalagi*' (the local term in use to refer to 'Whites' and metropolitan French) with too short a skirt or too tight a T-Shirt, for instance—as one local mainstream discourse is very much about the *Papalagi* having no sense of modesty. The way the latter deal with the tropical climate is indeed often by wearing as little clothing as possible, which is sometimes interpreted as a provocative disrespect for the local customs.

10 I often get comments such as 'We want to tell you anything that can help with your work, it is important that a Wallisian person succeeds in what you do'.

11 '[. . .] on n'en finit jamais de se libérer de l'évidence du social et, parmi les instruments de production d'évidence, de sentiment d'évidence, l'État est sans doute le plus puissant.'

12 'Faire ce long détour par la genèse, c'est se donner quelques chances d'échapper à la pensée d'État, ce qui est une des manières empiriques de pratiquer le doute radical. C'est à mon avis la fonction majeure de l'histoire: fournir des instruments pour débanaliser et pour dénaturaliser.' (ibid.)

13 See also (Gausset, Kenrick, and Gibb 2011). In this chapter, I am interested in how people express various senses of belonging, sometimes seeking attachment to a 'nation' ruled by a 'State'; sometimes getting estranged from it and, whether it is their own choice or not, finding themselves attached to another political and social organization which I call here 'indigenous' or 'autochthonous'. Often pertaining to ethnicization and racialization processes, this idea of a 'group' within the 'national group', whose existence would historically precede the one of the latter, is particularly fruitful when it comes to the study of the contemporary French Overseas territories.

14 In places where a so-called 'heritage language' is confronted to another one that comes to index 'modernity', responsibility for the feeling of loss can create complex intergenerational issues (Kroskrity 2009), that get entangled with academic discourses on the necessity of 'preserving the local culture'.

15 As I have seen during fieldwork in public hospitals in metropolitan France (2012), some places choose to devote a specific budget to professional interpreters working over the phone, in consultations primarily dedicated to asylum seekers. But this is clearly not the general situation within the French public

health system, nor a model that is followed in the French Overseas territories for autochthonous people who would not speak French.

16 I here take inspiration from Fassin (2008, 124), who studies the emergence of boards of ethics in anthropology. The author suggests that their primary function could be seen as one of legal self-protection for the institutions. In my case, I argue that the provision of 'language service' in courts appears as user-driven when in fact it probably mainly serves the legal interests of the institution itself. Otherwise, such language services would be found in any other kind of public setting where language needs would emerge—which is not the case, as there are notably no official interpreters in the hospital, for instance.

17 From an economic perspective, the part of the informal sector is prevalent, and only 30 percent of the population is employed. Within this percentage, the public sector counts for 65 percent. So it is fair to say that a large part of the population relies on the salaries of the few family members who are actually employed. Money games such as the 'bingo' are very popular as well, especially among the elderly who have no retirement pensions, when it comes to try to earn money. Being evacuated as a patient to New Caledonia or to France usually means that a family member will be accompanying, dropping his or her job for a while, or at least paying for a plane ticket, and then for food and gifts to thank the emigrated Wallisian family that would usually provide accommodation on site. This is a heavy economic cost that all patients have in mind when they are confronted to medical evacuations, even if the health institution primarily sees that it is 'free of charge'.

18 As such, culturalism is 'a poor social theory' (Fassin 2001).

19 See Bensa (2006) for a critique of 'exoticist' and ahistorical positionalities in anthropology.

20 In the absence of local economic resources, funding relies on the French State, which confers a solid basis for its political power and legitimacy.

21 As the populations of the South Pacific got divided between Polynesians and Melanesians, the latter came to be considered inferior, and mistreated accordingly: they endured massacres, their lands were grabbed, and they were put to forced labour. This is notably the history of the Kanak people in New Caledonia. The fallacy of a racial divide between Polynesians and Melanesians has had a long life, and still has contemporary ethnicizing effects.

22 And nor does the census that I quoted in the beginning of this chapter, which is public statistics but does translate into State's language policies.

References

Appadurai, A. 1988. 'Putting Hierarchy in Its Place'. *Cultural Anthropology* 3 (1): 36–49.

Bensa, A. 2006. *La Fin de L'exotisme: Essais D'anthropologie Critique*. Toulouse: Anacharsis.

Blanchard, E. 2007. 'Fractures (post)coloniales à Mayotte'. *Vacarme* 38 (1): 62.

Blommaert, J. 2007a. 'Sociolinguistic Scales'. *Intercultural Pragmatics* 4 (1): 1–19.

———. 2007b. 'Sociolinguistics and Discourse Analysis: Orders of Indexicality and Polycentricity'. *Journal of Multicultural Discourses* 2 (2): 115–30.

———. 2009. 'Language, Asylum, and the National Order'. *Current Anthropology* 50 (4): 415–41.

Bourdieu, P. 1977a. 'L'économie Des échanges Linguistiques'. *Langue Française* 34 (1): 17–34.

―――. 1977b. 'Remarques Provisoires Sur La Perception Sociale Du Corps'. *Actes de La Recherche En Sciences Sociales* 14 (1): 51–54.

―――. 1993. 'Esprits d'Etat [Genèse et Structure Du Champ Bureaucratique]'. *Actes de La Recherche En Sciences Sociales* 96 (1): 49–62.

―――. 2012. *Sur l'Etat : Cours au Collège de France*. Edited by Patrick Champagne, Remi Lenoir, Franck Poupeau, and Marie-Christine Rivière. Paris: Seuil.

Bourdieu, P., and A. Bensa. 1985. 'Quand Les Canaques Prennent La Parole'. *Actes de la Recherche en Sciences Sociales* 56 (1): 69–85.

Briggs, C. L. 2004. 'Theorizing Modernity Conspiratorially: Science, Scale, and the Political Economy of Public Discourse in Explanations of a Cholera Epidemic'. *American Ethnologist* 31 (2): 164–87.

Brighenti, A. 2007. 'Visibility: A Category for the Social Sciences'. *Current Sociology* 55 (3): 323–42.

Chave-Dartoen, S. 2002. 'Le paradoxe wallisien : une royauté dans la République'. *Ethnologie française* 32 (4): 637–45.

Clifford, J. 2013. *Returns: Becoming Indigenous in the Twenty-First Century*. Cambridge, MA: Harvard University Press.

Collins, J., and S. Slembrouck. 2007. 'Goffman & Globalisation: Participation Frames and the Spatial & Temporal Scaling of Migration-Connected Multilingualism'. *Working Papers in Urban Language & Literacies, No. 46*. Retrieved from http://www.kcl.ac.uk/sspp/departments/education/research/ldc/publications/workingpapers/46.pdf.

Comaroff, J., and J. L. Comaroff. 2012. 'Theory from the South: Or, How Euro-America Is Evolving toward Africa'. *Anthropological Forum* 22 (2): 113–31.

Cour des Comptes. 2014. 'La Santé Dans Les Outre-Mer, Une Responsabilité de La République'. Retrieved from http://www.ccomptes.fr/Publications/Publications/La-sante-dans-les-outre-mer-une-responsabilite-de-la-Republique.

Deville, R., and N. Georges. 1996. *Les départements d'outre-mer : L'autre décolonisation*. Paris: Gallimard.

Dimier, Véronique. 2005. 'De la France coloniale à l'outre-mer'. *Pouvoirs* 113 (2): 37–57.

Doligé, E. 2009. 'Les DOM, Défi Pour La République, Chance Pour La France, 100 Propositions Pour Fonder L'avenir', 519. Paris: Sénat. Retrieved from http://www.senat.fr/rap/r08–519–1/r08–519–1121.html.

Fassin, D. 2001. 'Culturalism as Ideology'. In *Cultural Perspectives on Reproductive Health*, edited by Carla Makhlouf Obermeyer, 300–17. Oxford: Oxford University Press.

―――. 2008. 'Extension du domaine de l'éthique'. *Mouvements* 55–56 (3): 124.

Foucault, M. 1963. *Naissance de la clinique*. Paris: Presses Universitaires de France—PUF.

―――. 1971. *L'Ordre du Discours*. Paris: Gallimard.

Gal, S., and J. T. Irvine. 1995. 'The Boundaries of Languages and Disciplines: How Ideologies Construct Difference'. *Social Research* 62 (4): 967–1001.

Gausset, Q., J. Kenrick, and R. Gibb. 2011. 'Indigeneity and Autochthony: A Couple of False Twins?' *Social Anthropology* 19 (2): 135–42.

Girin, N., R. Brostrom, S. Ram, J. McKenzie, A. M. V. Kumar, and C. Roseveare. 2014. 'Describing the Burden of Non-Communicable Disease Risk Factors among Adults with Diabetes in Wallis and Futuna'. *Public Health Action* 4 (1): 39–43.

Gordien, A. 2014. 'Guadeloupe, l'après LKP : Anticolonialisme, identité et vie quotidienne'. *Revue Asylon(s)* 11. Retrieved from http://www.reseau-terra.eu/article1275.html.

Guiart, J. 1982. 'A Polynesian Myth and the Invention of Melanesia'. *The Journal of the Polynesian Society* 91 (1): 139–44.

Henningham, S. 1992. *France and the South Pacific: A Contemporary History.* Honolulu, HI: University of Hawaii Press.

———. 1995. *The Pacific Island States.* Basingstoke: Palgrave Macmillan.

Herod, A., and M. W. Wright. 2002. 'Introduction: Scales of Praxis'. In *Geographies of Power*, edited by A. Herod and M. W. Wright, 215–23. Malden, MA: Blackwell.

Kroskrity, P. V. 2009. 'Language Renewal as Sites of Language Ideological Struggle: The Need for "Ideological Clarification"'. In *Indigenous Language Revitalization: Encouragement, Guidance and Lessons Learned*, edited by J. Reyhner and L. Lockard, 71–83. Flagstaff: Northern Arizona University.

Lemercier, É., V. Muni Toke, and É. Palomares. 2014. 'Les Outre-Mer Français: Regards Ethnographiques Sur Une Catégorie Politique'. *Terrains et Travaux* 24: 5–38.

Moyer, M., and L. Martin Rojo. 2007. 'Language, Migration and Citizenship: New Challenges in the Regulation of Bilingualism'. In *Bilingualism: A Social Approach*, edited by M. Heller, 137–60. Basingstoke: Palgrave Macmillan.

Moyse-Faurie, C. 2016. *Te lea faka'uvea / Le wallisien.* Leuven: Peeters.

Muni Toke, V. 2011. 'Deontological Issues, Language Ideologies and Reflexivity in Linguistics: "Native" Competence vs Scientific Knowledge?' *Pragmatics and Society* 2 (2): 205–33.

———. 2012. 'Les Présupposés Ethnodidactiques de La Coupure Disciplinaire FLE/FLS/FLM'. *Le Français Aujourd'hui* 176: 11–24.

Rollock, N. 2012. 'The Invisibility of Race: Intersectional Reflections on the Liminal Space of Alterity'. *Race Ethnicity and Education* 15 (1): 65–84.

Schieffelin, B. B., K. A. Woolard, and Paul V. Kroskrity. 1998. *Language Ideologies: Practice and Theory.* New York: Oxford University Press.

Scott, J. C. 1999. *Seeing like a State: How Certain Schemes to Improve the Human Condition Have Failed.* New Haven, CT: Yale University Press.

Silverstein, M. 2015. 'How Language Communities Intersect: Is "Superdiversity" an Incremental or Transformative Condition?' *Language & Communication* 44: 7–18.

Stroud, C. 2007. 'Bilingualism: Colonialism, Postcolonialism and High Modernity'. In *Bilingualism: A Social Approach*, edited by Monica Heller, 25–49. New York: Palgrave Macmillan.

Tcherkézoff, S. 2009. *Polynésie/Mélanésie—L'Invention française des 'races' et des régions de l'Océanie.* Pirae (Polynésie française): Au vent des iles.

Trépied, B. 2012. 'Une Nouvelle Question Indigène Outre-Mer ?' *La Vie Des Idées* 15 mai. Retrieved from http://www.laviedesidees.fr/Une-nouvelle-question-indigene.html.

2 Constructing Invisibility

The Discursive Erasure of a Black Immigrant Learner in South Africa

Caroline Kerfoot and Gwendoline Tatah

Introduction

The end of apartheid changed South Africa from a refugee-producing to a refugee-hosting country. Since 1994 increasing numbers of refugees and economic migrants from across Africa have made their way to South Africa, an economic 'north' in the south. Such South-South flows fall largely outside the purview of sociolinguistic research yet have distinct discursive and material effects in that a black 'other' is inserted into a postcolonial order which itself, as Fabricio (2014) points out, consists of reworked and recycled entextualizations of colonial hierarchies and indexicalities. The majority of migrants, with a few exceptions, tend to circulate on the peripheries across local, national, or transnational spaces, disrupting local economies of meaning and becoming entangled with historical and contemporary discourses of race and difference in ways that are little understood.

Migrant families bring with them children who are generally invisible in educational research or official statistics yet often bear the brunt of integration pressures as they enter the turbulent environments of post-apartheid schools. This chapter analyzes some of the discursive interactions through which a 13-year-old francophone Cameroonian student attempts to construct new social and academic identities. In so doing, it illustrates a process of erasure in which her affective and epistemic stances are consistently disbarred and through which linguistic features of her repertoire and other material markers become enregistered as ethnically and linguistically 'other'. Through these processes, while she becomes marked and highly visible as 'other', her identities as competent linguistic, social and academic performer are erased. Here Kulick's (2003, 2005) concept of *dual indexicality* is used to point to 'absent presences' that render certain subject positions impossible.

The chapter builds on research on the situated co-construction of microinteractional identities and macro-social categories such as ethnicity and race (Bailey 2007; Bucholtz 1999; Goodwin 2003; Ibrahim 2009). Through this analysis we draw attention to the ways in which discursive processes construct *orders of visibility*, both momentary and of longer duration. As with Foucault's *regimes of truth* (1971), the concept of orders of visibility draws attention to the shared frames of reference and meaning-making practices that construct, legitimate, and obscure relations of power, foregrounding certain modes of knowing, being, and saying, and rendering others invisible. Through these meaning-making processes, certain features of identity such as ethnicity or accent are made salient and inserted into hierarchies of power located within racialized structures of meaning, obscuring other attributes and possible categories.

Visibility in this sense relates to *erasure* (Gal and Irvine 1995), an ideological process which 'renders some persons or activities or sociolinguistic phenomena invisible' (974). Erasure is achieved through making particular linguistic forms or features iconic of the social identities of speakers, positioning these differences so as to produce 'normal' and 'other' identities, then ignoring facts that contradict this ideological framing in order to maintain such distinctions. However, these ideological frames and the hierarchies constructed though them are continually reworked; they are unstable and open to challenge, particularly amidst postcolonial realities which hold in tension inherited colonial orders and emergent formations characterized by ruptures and upheavals. Such turbulent conditions create unpredictable surges and diminutions of the visibility of particular modes of being, saying, and/or identity attributes of speakers.

This chapter illustrates the disjunctive interplays of visibility and invisibility that characterize the trajectory of a Cameroonian immigrant student, Aline, as she moves through new diasporic and educational spaces in Cape Town. Crucially, in tracing complex processes of visibilization and invisibilization, we argue that what is often missing from accounts of identity construction and identification in school and other settings is attention to *absences:* to what should be visible but is not, what is deliberately obscured, what slips quietly out of view, or is painted over with ideological veneers.

Background

Despite attempts to build a more equitable postracial order in South Africa, race is still a key marker of privilege. However, the forms of social division, disparity, and marginalization are becoming increasingly complex (Mbembe 2014) and African immigrants are increasingly positioned as the new 'other', often occupying the lowest rungs of the new order and subject to widespread but not universal prejudice and exclusion. Foreign Africans are frequently and contemptuously referred to as 'amakwerekwere' from the isiXhosa *ama*, a plural prefix, + *kwerekwere* imitative of unintelligible sound or babble (Collinsdictionary.com. 2015). Here the overt labelling, imbued with power, indexes foreign, incomprehensible, and, more insidiously, something to be despised, a nuisance, widely perceived as a threat to economic and physical security, and subject to harassment and stigmatization by political parties, the media, and the communities in which they settle (Meda 2014; Nyamnjoh 2006). Pervasive xenophobic discourses exacerbated by high levels of poverty and unemployment accompanied by a long history of racial politics have led to frequent outbursts of violence with alarming surges in 2008 and 2015.

There has thus been a shift in racism from notions of biological superiority to exclusion based on cultural or ethnic difference. There is no pan-ethnic formula but a restratification of 'race' where otherness is read through ethnicity, where degrees of blackness, dress, accent, or other cultural markers determine who one is seen to be as well as access to material and other forms of capital. While the colonial gaze fragmented the black subject and reconstituted that subject on its own terms (Fanon [1967] 2008), so now a postcolonial gaze refragments the black subject, undermining attempts at self-representation in new ways. Here we see a new field of visibility being constituted.

Immigrant children are caught in these entanglements of contemporary and historical discourses. Official educational policies (as manifested in schools via textbooks and school-level policies) are inclusive (Bentley and Habib 2008), but this does not prevent widespread experience of prejudice by young immigrants. While there is a small body of work focusing on processes of school integration for groups previously separated under apartheid (Kerfoot and Bello-Nonjengele 2016; Makoe 2014; McKinney 2010; Ndlangamandla 2010), this study is one of very few to focus on immigrant children in South African schools.

Theoretical Framework: Constructing Orders of Visibility

Our focus on linguistic practices in settings characterized by multilingualism and diversity locates the study theoretically within Linguistic Ethnography (LE) (Creese 2008; Rampton 2007). Through its combination of Interactional Sociolinguistics and ethnography, LE enables an examination of the ways in which power asymmetries are constructed through interaction and individuals may thereby be rendered unable to construct or negotiate desired identities and identifications. It is thus appropriate for exploring the fluid, entangled multiplicity of identities and identifications in contemporary South Africa and the processes by which they are constructed or constrained. This context of rapid social change calls for a focus on how individuals' performances constitute or reconstitute identity across social sites, how speakers invoke, challenge, or redefine social norms and roles through sociolinguistically inflected choices (Jaffe 2009) and how categories such as race and ethnicity are 'enacted, produced and negotiated in specific social contexts' (De Fina 2007, 373; Ochs 1992).

Our focus on how young adolescents use interactional resources to build, sustain, and regulate local hierarchies also resonates with work done within the language socialization (LS) paradigm. Here a central finding in recent work has been the key role of peers in determining inclusion or exclusion of minoritized 'others' (e.g., García-Sánchez 2014; Ochs et al. 2001). Both

LE and LS accord centrality to the interactional practices through which affective and epistemic stances are constructed, negotiated, or disallowed. Studies in schools characterized by increasing diversity have shown how young adolescents use multilingual repertoires to negotiate identities, shape new interaction orders, and restructure linguistic and other hierarchies of value including 'race' and ethnicity (e.g., Banda 2010; Bucholtz 2004; Kerfoot forthcoming 2017; Kerfoot and Bello-Nonjengele 2016; Rampton 1995, 2006). Others have shown, however, how complex entanglements of ideology, class, 'race', ethnicity, and language often promote the hegemony of the dominant language and perpetuate inequitable relations of power (e.g., Evaldsson 2005; Evaldsson and Cekaite 2010; Makoe 2007; Makoe and McKinney 2014).

In order to understand these processes, Wortham (2005) has stressed the importance of examining both typical and atypical trajectories of socialization in order to learn about both 'the individual's particularity and the collective resources used to accomplish that particularity' (97). In this chapter we analyze Aline's gradual invisibilization as an indexical process achieved through a set of inter-related semiotic phenomena such as those identified by Bucholtz and Hall (2005): explicit use of identity labels, implicatures and presuppositions regarding identity positions, and evaluative and epistemic stances in relation to ongoing talk. These semiotic processes are tied into local, national, and transnational discourses of belonging and constrained by, but not necessarily ordered by, institutional frameworks. They are thus partly produced by the differential valuation in different social and educational fields of key elements of embodied social and cultural capital such as race, ethnicity, gender, class, and linguistic repertoire (cf. Luke 2009). Such evaluative distinctions help to define lines of social stratification, belonging, or exclusion, and, by extension, the degrees of visibility of speakers.

However, we go further than other research in this area by analyzing the operation of *dual indexicality*[1] (Kulick 2003, 2005) in processes of identification whereby a refusal to acknowledge a particular interpellative call is at the same time a form of acknowledgement. Here Kulick (2005) argues that the 'more or less conscious claim-staking' by which *identity* is generally represented within sociolinguistic and linguistic anthropological work should not be conflated with *identification* which is concerned with 'the operations through which the subject is constituted' (615). Identifications are not entirely conscious nor do they constitute a coherent set of relations. Within a performative framework, examining interactions 'not by asking: who says it? But, rather: what does saying it—*or not saying it*—produce?' (Kulick 2003, 149, emphasis added) enables an exploration of the processes whereby some kinds of identifications are authorized and others are delegitimized. So behind the visible construction of identities and identifications through interaction lie other desired but invisible, unauthorized identifications.

Acts of identity and identification can be seen as constructed through affective and epistemic stance-taking in which speakers seek to shape subject positions, both their own and others (Du Bois 2007; Jaffe 2009; Ochs 1996). This chapter thus analyzes, first, how stances are interdiscursively achieved or disbarred and, second, how the accretion and/or absence of stances over time have longer lasting consequences, helping to construct (or erase) more durable social categories (Jaffe 2009; Wortham 2005).

Method

In order to explore these processes, we collected observational, interview, and audio-recorded interactional data in Cape Town among a group of Cameroonian[2] immigrant youngsters in classrooms, playgrounds, and home settings over five years. Twelve youngsters aged 10–14 (of which two were girls) were participants in the project, the full contingent of Cameroonian learners in one school. Nine were from the Anglophone sector of Cameroon and three from the Francophone, with a wide range of Cameroonian indigenous languages spoken at home. Participant observation was carried out in classrooms, playgrounds, and a variety of home and social settings. Over the years the focus gradually narrowed to two key participants as representative of broader patterns of inclusion and exclusion: one Francophone, the focus of this chapter, and one Anglophone. Learners carried pocket recorders: the data consists of 80 hours of audio recordings complemented by interviews in French and/or English following learners' leads. Video was found to be too intrusive; as a result, only field notes could be used to capture the embodied resources such as gesture, gaze, which co-produce stance. Wherever possible, findings and interpretations were checked with participants in follow-up meetings.

All families of participants and their interactants were given bilingual permission forms. It was initially difficult to get full participation given the precariousness of immigrant positions politically, economically, and legally. For this reason, some learners chose not to be recorded but agreed that their responses could be written down. Great care has been taken to ensure anonymity; all names are fictional. The caregivers of other learners with whom the participants interacted in recordings also signed informed consent forms.

Setting

The parallel medium school[3] was located in a low income suburb of Cape Town where the language of instruction was either English or Afrikaans. Of the 1455 learners in 2013, 50 percent were white, 35 percent Black/African, 11 percent 'coloured'[4] and 6 percent Indian or Asian (School, 2013). No information on the number of immigrant children in these statistics was available. Of the seven classes for each grade, five were for English-speaking learners and two for Afrikaans learners. In the English-medium classes, where Aline was placed, the majority of children were local isiXhosa speakers who travelled in from the townships, children from other provinces in South Africa with different home languages, and foreign learners from all over the world: most learners did not have English as a home language. The Afrikaans-medium classes by contrast contained only white and coloured learners speaking Afrikaans as a home language. Teachers in all classrooms were white Afrikaans first language speakers, many of whom had been in the school for more than 20 years. In this school, field conditions were fairly stable and a linguistic regime (Kroskrity 2000) firmly in place, ranking repertoires and linguistic practices.

The participant in this chapter comes from the French-speaking part of Cameroon. Her trajectory differs markedly from those of Anglophone Cameroonian youngsters in the same schools who despite similar ages, educational backgrounds, and home conditions, eventually became ratified members of local social groups.

Aline

When this research began in 2008, Aline was 13 years old and was repeating Grade 2 in her second South African school. She had been in South Africa since late 2006. She left Cameroon in the equivalent of Grade 6 in South Africa. Her family's first stop was in Brazzaville, Republic of Congo. Here she progressed again to what would be Grade 7 in South Africa. Once in South Africa, she attended three different primary schools as her parents moved around the peripheries of Cape Town in search of work. On arrival in South Africa, she had been assessed on English and Mathematics and placed in Grade 1 along with six-year-old learners. She then failed Grade 2 in 2007, partly as a result of changing schools within the same area. In 2010 she stayed out of school for a year, citing unhappiness at repeated failure and disagreements with her parents as the reasons, then moved into a new school in 2011. In an interaction with author B and her peers, she labelled herself 'nearly 14, old in primary school' (Table 2.3, turn 43) and, after five years when she was 18 in Grade 3, felt that the best solution for her would be a return to the Cameroons, pointing out that 'if I were in the Cameroons or Congo now, I would be at university' (interview, 8 May 2013). The dramatic drop in status which resulted from her initial placement and later grade repetition had a profound effect on her, making her linguistic and academic competence invisible, as will become apparent below.

Her linguistic repertoire included Duala—her language of inheritance, French—her language of schooling or expertise, and a set of translingual practices popularly known as Camfranglais or Francanglais[5] which included features of French, English, Cameroonian Pidgin English (CPE) and various indigenous languages. Her family members spoke CPE as a lingua franca with other Cameroonians.[6]

Here we present three extracts of data: two in a diasporic social setting 18 months after Aline's arrival in South Africa and one on the playground of her second school six months later. We also draw on classroom observations from both schools as well as interviews throughout the research period. These extracts illustrate representative moments in her trajectory across social and educational spaces and highlight the ways in which a series of communicative events, interdiscursively and indexically linked, shaped possibilities for stance and the emergence of particular social and academic identities.

Negotiating Linguistic and Moral Orders

The extracts below in Tables 2.1 and 2.2 are part of a longer interaction among a group of Cameroonian youngsters at a social gathering chatting in one room of an apartment. The adults were in the other room and in the kitchen frantically preparing for the occasion. Those present were 11 Cameroonian and two South African/Cameroonian children ranging in age from seven to 13. Some were long-standing friends who had known each other in Cameroon; others became acquainted on arrival in South Africa while some had only just met. James and Jim were brothers. Awah and Bih had come from Cameroon to spend their vacation with their parents. Tasneema considered herself South African: her father was Cameroonian and her mother a coloured South African. With the exception of Tasneema and Aline, all came from the Anglophone part of Cameroon so, while they spoke eight different Cameroonian languages, English was an everyday medium of communication. The Anglophone youngsters had varying levels of competence in French, taught as a subject in Cameroonian schools but not in South Africa. It is clear that Aline, the only one without much English in her repertoire, nevertheless follows the gist of the interaction.

As the extract opens, a heated argument had been interrupted by the ringing of Aline's mother's phone. After ending the call, Aline's mother threatened the youngsters with a cane (*molongo* in Duala) if they did not reduce the noise level, before leaving the room. This threat provoked a flurry of questions and exclamations, most notably Simon's judgment of Aline's mother as "scary". The focus in this analysis is on Aline's vigorous defence of her mother's image in the extended sequence which follows.

In analysing this data, we focused both on mood structures of conversational clauses and the *moves* made by participants and the languages in which they are made. A *move* is defined here by two criteria: as 'a clause which selects independently for mood' (Martin 1992, 40) and prosodic factors such as rhythm and intonation which 'interact with grammatical structure to signal points of possible turn transfer' (Eggins and Slade 2004, 188). One speaker turn can realize several discourse *moves* (or speech functions) through one or more clauses and through nonverbal means.

Identifying what interactants are doing as they speak to one another, for example, 'challenging' or 'supporting', and relating these *move* types to the grammatical and semantic resources used to realize them, offers sophisticated

Table 2.1 Extract of Community Gathering, March 2008, 18 Months After Arrival (See Appendix A on page 243 for transcription key)

Move	Turn	Participant	Utterance
	25	Aline's Mother	[Rushes to answer call. Speaks in CPE to caller for 30 seconds then turns and shout to the children] "SHUT UP! **TAISEZ-VOUS!** *(BE QUIET)* I AM TALKING ON THE PHONE! **AU TELEPHONE!** Ok *naw so (2) bye noh*. ^[Turns around and confronts the group of children] Next time MOLONGO will talk to you, not me (3) *wona hear*? [Leaves the room in anger].
O:R:	26	Simon	i) ↑Whaow! (.) Your mom's scary (.)
R:track: clarify	27	John	i). Mo what?
R:	28	Edi	Mmm ^[Inaudible whispering]
R: track: clarify	30	Aline	i) Scary **veut dire quoi**? (*'Scary', what does that mean?*)
R: track: clarify	31	John	i) What is MOLONGO?
Res: resolve	32	James	i) Scary means (.) the undertaker; ii) you know (.) [Raising his arms and shaking them][[fear (.) frighten.
R	33	All except Aline	[[laugh]
R: track: clarify	34	John	i) ↑What is MOLONGO ?
Res: resolve: elaborate	35	James	i) Cane (.)Sticks. Our teacher used to beat us with MOLONGO
Rej: confront:	36	Aline	**Un bâton pour frapper les mal élevés comme toi!** (*A cane for beating badly brought up people like you.*)
R: track: clarify	37	Simon	i) ↑What was that? ii) ↑ What did she say?
Res: resolve	38	James	i) I think she was insulting you.
R: clarify	39	John	ii) ↑How do you know?
Res: extend	40	James	i) I don't speak French (.) ii) but I think: :
Res: resolve: elaborate	41	Mark	: : i).I know (.) ii) she says you have no manners
Rej: confront: challenge	42	Aline	i) ↑YOU RUDE TO **MA MERE!** (.) ii) **n'insulte plus ma mère** (.) (*Don't insult my mother again*)
Rej: confront: elaborate	43	Simon	i) That was being honest not rude (.) ii) she scared the hell (.) (Laughing) out of me.
Rej: rebound: rechallenge	44	Aline	i)↑**TA** (.) **mère aussi** (.) **elle est costaude** (.) [Pauses as if searching for words] ii) FAT! (*Your mother also, she is very fat*)
Rej: challenge	45	John	i) ↑Ok, that's enough (.) ii) you can't do that : :
Rej: rechallenge	46	Simon	: : i) Foolish girl (.) let her speak (.) And in English.

Move	Turn	Participant	Utterance
Rej: elaborate: challenge	47	James	i) ↓↑She can't really speak English (.) ii) only tries (2) don't you dare try to
R: track	48	John's M	[Shouting attracts attention of hostess] i) *Egainha* John? (*What is happening here John?*)

tools for illuminating processes of stance-taking, positioning, and (dis)alignment. Moves have been categorized following Eggins and Slade (2004) with a focus on a subset of 'sustaining' moves necessary to keep a conversation going: reacting speech functions. Reacting moves are generally either 'responses', which move the exchange towards completion, or 'rejoinders', moves representing dispreferred options which 'in some way prolong the exchange',[. . .] set underway sequences of talk that interrupt, postpone, abort, or suspend the initial speech function sequence' (Eggins and Slade 2004, 200, 207). Move analysis is complemented by other analytical resources from Interactional Sociolinguistics such as turn-taking, interactional frames (Goffman 1974), participation frameworks, and footing (Goffman 1981).

Our aim is to establish the ways in which social relations are constructed through discursive moves within and across turns and in different languages.

In turn 30, Aline, having perceived from Simon's tone that his comment about her mother was unflattering, asked for the meaning of the word 'scary' before launching a counter-attack which then developed through the subsequent turns, with John and James acting as translators and mediators.

James did his best to explain the meaning of scary with accompanying gestures indicating something huge and alarming. Her response perhaps aggravated by this explanation as well as the others' laughter, Aline elaborated James' subsequent definition of molongo in English to make a point of moral sanction against Simon but in French, intensified by a nonverbal act of pointing (*A cane for beating badly brought up people like you*) (turn 36). Here, while she ostensibly addressed Simon, she knew he would not understand, and her actual addressees were those in the group who understood French and would grasp her intention. A feature of all Aline's recorded interactions was her ability to laminate (Goffman 1981) participation frameworks through the skilful use of different languages, simultaneously engaging different participants for different communicative purposes.

A few turns later when Mark had translated this confronting move for Simon, she elaborated (42) her reasons for this sanction. Here she started off in English to be sure of being understood by Simon but then continued in French, perhaps reverting to a more familiar language under the pressure of strong emotion but also once again making explicit to others in the group the reasons for her strong affective stance. This stance is augmented in turn 44 where, responding again to Simon's countering move in 43 and in particular to his laughter, she started in French, emphasizing the 'TA mère' (your mother) to return the perceived insult and translating 'costaude' into English at the end of the move to be sure she was understood by Simon. However, only French speakers would have appreciated the full indexical force of 'costaude': heavyset, powerful, and perhaps menacing.

When John tried to resolve the conflict, Simon escalated it instead by inscribing a judgment of 'Foolish girl' and trying to impose his own set of linguistic norms. James leapt to her defence in 47, aligning with her right to use French, before being interrupted by John's mother who arrived to deal with the noise level. Here the interaction and linguistic orders were under negotiation.

In order to illustrate the semiotic means through which Aline and her interactants enacted and constructed their relationships during the interaction, we will briefly analyze the interaction from two perspectives: grammar (the constituent mood structures of conversational clauses) and discourse (the types of moves made).

Asserting a Moral Order

In this interaction, Aline had fewer turns than others but is nevertheless a participant on equal terms. Her interactional competence was unquestioned, she was able to construct desired positions and respond assertively to challenges. Her ability to construct an assertive stance is evident in her choice of declaratives and imperatives for her counter-challenges to Simon (turns 42, 44). The use of an elliptical declarative in 36 extends James' definition in 35 and encodes a judgment of Simon's upbringing. Together with the unmodalized declaratives in turns 42, 44 these moves can be seen as asserting her status as able to set the moral ground rules for the interaction (cf. Eggins and Slade 2004, 53–4). She also used an imperative in turn 41 to make it clear to Simon that the interaction order (Goffman 1983) should not include insults. These stances of righteous indignation were implicitly aligned with by others as no-one contradicted her except Simon. Pushed to more forceful retaliation by Simon's laughing justification of his comments, she herself, however, resorted to an insult in 44, a move which was swiftly censured by John. In terms of discursive moves, apart from one clarifying move at the beginning, all Aline's moves were rejoinders, either counter-challenges or elaborations of previous challenges in which she justified her outrage, often intensifying the affect through rising pitch and volume. Such confronting moves play the most significant role in the negotiation of interpersonal relationships (Eggins and Slade 2004).

Through her mood choice, discursive moves, and encoding of evaluation, she constructed affective stances which by indexing shared, cultural values such as respect for elders (turn 36, 42) enabled her to claim an identity as moral arbiter. This stance is also evident in Extract 3 discussed below where she asserted the right to correct others' behaviour towards adults. In neither extract were her claims to a social or moral identity disaligned with, partly because earlier in this interaction other participants had also found Simon to be rude.

Simon's patterns of mood choice and discursive moves were similar, ending with his dismissive 'Foolish girl' in 46 and his lofty, barbed 'let her speak and in English', assuming authority for assigning speaking rights and defining the linguistic order, perhaps also animating an institutional voice (Goffman 1981) which seeps through the porous boundaries between spaces.

Shifting Indexicalities

Throughout this excerpt, Aline used French unhesitatingly as a stance resource, amplifying negative appraisal and constructing complex interwoven participation frameworks, indexing 'the ease that comes from being in one's place' (Bourdieu 2000, 184). Her translingual utterances indicate that she perceived the use of Francanglais as 'unmarked', an accepted part of the interaction order in this diasporic space. However, the ground was shifting under her: while only Simon explicitly disaligned with her use of French, the others implicitly evaluated her practices as inappropriate, a judgment evoked by the fact that even those who spoke sufficient French did not reply to her in this language (dispreferred responses in this sense only). Even James who acted as mediator and supported Aline against Simon (turn 46) responded to her in English. Only once in the full extended interaction did anyone address her in French and as a greeting only.

So here we see the 'interactive emergence of the indexical ground' (Hanks 1992, 66): the shifts in what it means to be Cameroonian in South Africa. The policing of the emerging linguistic regime, resignifying the links between nation, ethnicity, and language, was reinforced in another sequence later in the interaction on the subject of ovens:

Table 2.2 Community Gathering, March 2008, Continued

103	Aline	i) Ma mère aussi (2) elle fait toujours dans le microwave (2) ii) it's good . . . (*My mother also always makes it in the microwave*)
104	Bih	i) HEY! Leave people with that your French
105	Aline	i) But we are Camerounais, n'est-ce pas? (*not so?*)
106	Bih	i) SO? Must you remind me? (.) I KNOW!

Here Aline implicitly laid out her understanding of Cameroonian identity (turn 105), that it allows the use of either language unproblematically in this diasporic space. The tag '*n'est-ce pas?*', however, while inviting a compliant response, indicates some uncertainty. Indeed, this metalinguistic stance was not taken up by the others; it is explicitly and forcefully countered by Bih (turn 104) who, by identifying French as Aline's possession rather than a common resource, undermined her appeal to a common Cameroonian identity, thus continuing the gradual delegitimization and invisibilization of French and Francanglais.

Disbarred Affective and Epistemic Stances

The next extract in Table 2.3 was recorded a few months later in the same year. The interaction took place during lunch break on the playground at Aline's school. Aline was with two coloured South African friends who were also in grade 2; they had been friends for close to a year.

Table 2.3 Playground Interaction, November 2008

Move	Turn	Speaker	Data
Res:D: P:extend P:extend P: probe	19	Author B	i).Talking of your mum (.) ii) I saw her here the other day (.) iii) your papa too (.) ↑iv) problems?
Res: disagree: P: enhance	20	Aline	i)**Non** (.) ii) **Le professeur voulait parler avec eux.** (*No, the teacher wanted to speak to them*).
Rej: challenge P: elaborate P: elaborate P: enhance D: query	21	Michelle	i).There she goes again (.) ii) packler packler (.) iii) she is always packlaying (.) (Laughter) iv) Says she speaks French (2) v) Do you speak French also?
Res: reply Continue: monitor	22	Author B	i) **Mais oui bien sur** (*But yes of course*) [. . .] v) How is everything?
Res:affirm	23	Chorus	↑Fine!
Rej: track: probe P: extend	24	Michelle	i)↑Are you sure? ii)You were just complaining a moment ago (2)
Res: track: probe x 2	25	Author B	About what? Schoolwork?
Res: D: elaborate P: extend	26	Michelle	i).She was saying it was boring here and ii) she hates the fact that=
Rej: confront P: extend P: rechallenge	27	Aline	i) = **N'écoute pas!** (2) ii) **Je n'ai rien dit** (3) iii) SHE LIE TOO MUCH ! (*Don't listen to her. I didn't say anything*)
Rej: refute P: extend P: rechallenge	28	Michelle	i)↑Oh no! ii) You know I am not LYING (2) iii) tell her the truth.
Rej: rechallenge x 2	29	Aline	i)↑**Quoi?** (.)ii) ↑WHAT?
Res: monitor	30	Author B	i).I am listening (.)
Res: append	31	Aline	(2) ↑Yes? [to Michelle]
Res: develop P: extend x3 P: enhance	32	Michelle	i) ↑Ok (.) let me help her (.) ii) she hates Afrikaans and Math (.) iii) she is trying in English now (.) iv) she never spoke when she first came (.) v) I also don't like Afrikaans.
- -			
Res: track: check	42	Author B	i) How old are you?
Res: answer P: enhance	43	Aline	i) **Presque quatorze ans** (.) ii) Old **en primaire school.** (*Nearly 14 years. Old in primary school.*)

Move	Turn	Speaker	Data
Res: query	44	Michelle	i) ↑And you? ii) How old are you? [to researcher]
Rej: challenge: P: enhance x2	45	Aline	i) [to Michelle] **Tu ne dois pas** (2) she is big (2) ↑**Adulte** (*You must not*)
Rej:s: track: clarify	46	Michelle	i) So you have been here for ten years?
Rej::refute P:extend x3 P: enhance	47	Author B	i) No ii) She said two years (2) iii) she was born in Cameroon iv) and she just came here (.) v) so can't be ten (.)
Res: repair Res: check	48	Michelle	i) I was joking (.) ii) where is Cameroon?
Rej: disengage	49	Author B	i)Ask your friend.
Rej: counter	50	Michelle	i) She will never succeed in that her broken English.
Rej: rebound	51	Aline	i) You foolish [[hhh.
Rej: rebound P:extend	52	Michelle	i) [[See who is calling names (.) ii) you were two years in grade 2
Rej: rebound x 2	53	Aline	i) **Et puis?** (*And so?*) (1.5) ii) ↑So?
Res: resolve O:probe	54	Author B	i) It's alright (.) how are you coping?
Res: answer	55	Aline	i) ↑Fine.
Rej: contra-dict P:extend	56	Michelle	i) She is a bit slow in math (.) ii) very slow I mean (.) in her work
Rej: refute: P:elaborate	57	Aline and Kelly	i)NO! OH NO (.)ii) NO YOU DONT (2x)
Rej: counter: enhance	58	Aline	i)>\<I hate [[Afrikaans
Rej: contradict: Rej: rechallenge	59	Michelle	i) [[Oh no (.)ii) tell her the truth.
Rej: confront	60	Kelly	i) Don't you dare mmm (.)
Rej: challenge P:extend	61	Michelle	i)Not only Afrikaans (.) you make mistakes . . .
Rej: rebound: P: extend: clarify x2	62	Aline	i) **Je suis** (.) I am **un peu** (2) I mean (.) ha (.) problems in some place. (*I am*. I am *a bit*)
Rej:s:track: check	63	Author B	i) On what?
Res:answer	64	Kelly	i) Mostly Afrikaans
Rej :refute: P:extend	65	Michelle	i) ↑NO! ii) She is also slow in maths (.) and in doing her homework (laughs)
Rej: rechallenge	66	Aline	↑Shut up!
Rej: counter:extend	67	Michelle	i)I am concerned (.) really concerned for her (2) ii) doesn't ask for help (receives a punch)
Rej:rebound P: elaborate	68	Aline	i) You lie! (2) ii) I ask teacher
Res:resolve: P:elaborate	69	Author B	i) Okay don't worry. ii) We will sort you out.

Note. English and French phonetic symbols are used to indicate French accented pronunciation of English by Aline

The interaction began when Aline along with her friends approached author B who is also Cameroonian. Her use of French in turn 20 in response to an inquiry from author B triggered the first of a sequence of attacks by Michelle which occurred in two waves (reflected in the text in turns 21–32 and turns 50–67) separated by a patch of quiet water where participants compared origins, trajectories, and ages. It is important to note that these attacks were delivered and received in a light-hearted, joking manner so that much of the sting appeared to be removed. The cumulative effect is, however, a devastating assault on Aline's ability to speak for herself, to articulate her own experiences and emotions, as well as a damaging appraisal of her linguistic and academic abilities.

In this interaction we see Aline constantly on the defensive against a barrage of criticism from Michelle so intense that even Kelly, a ratified but silent participant, is moved to defend Aline at key points (turns 57, 60). Michelle's denigration of Aline's linguistic repertoire was carried out as follows: in turn 21 she laughingly parodied Aline's French. Moreover, the clause 'says she speaks French' presented the proposition as arguable, thereby hinting at a possible lack of veracity which would incur social sanction. In turn 46 she suggested that Aline had been in Cape Town for ten years, later metapragmatically labelled as a joke in turn 48. However, the implicature seemed to be that Aline should therefore be doing much better in English as this is followed in turn 50 by her labelling of Aline's English as 'broken' and her statement that Aline would therefore not succeed in explaining where Cameroon is. This implies a double lack of capacity: linguistic and epistemic. The modal 'will never succeed' is categorical, closing down all possibility.

This negative valuation of Aline's epistemic ability is applied also to her capacity to do mathematics and Afrikaans in turns 32, 56, 61, 65. In 32 Michelle animated Aline's voice again, taking up the stance of a helpful friend 'let me help her'. She was animator and author, the selector of the sentiments expressed and the order in which they are presented, but simultaneously suggested that Aline was the principal responsible for the words in the first place and committing her to this position. Halfway through this turn, she changed footing and presented her own account of Aline's actions when she arrived and added, perhaps in an attempt to mitigate, that she herself did not like Afrikaans (32 iv and v). Despite Kelly's attempt in turn 64 to limit Aline's difficulties to Afrikaans where many learners struggled and so to reduce her isolation, Michelle insisted that Aline was slow in mathematics as well and expanded this judgment to include doing homework in general. Aline's entire academic identity is thus disparaged and made worthless, constituting very serious acts of identity ascription albeit carried out in a joking manner.

A second feature of Michelle's positioning of Aline is a constant questioning of her ability to speak for herself and a frequent usurping of Aline's turns in order to speak for her. In turn 24 she questioned Aline's assertion that she was fine and thereby her ability to articulate her own state of being, and in turn 26 she seized Aline's turn, animating her voice and denying her the chance to speak for herself. 'Speaking for another' (Schiffrin 1993) who is present in a judgemental rather than supportive manner is traditionally associated with male stances (Hoyle and Adger 1998). This has been shown not to hold true for girl talk in research by Goodwin (1998) and similarly here was used by Michelle in order to position herself as more knowledgeable than Aline about Aline's own feelings. In turn 28 she did align with Aline's obvious discomfort but took an even more serious step by implying that Aline was lying about her own feelings, exhorting her here and in turn 59 to 'tell her the truth', thus positioning her as untruthful. In 52 she responded to Aline's calling her foolish by counterchallenging 'see who is calling names' and providing evidence for her position in that Aline had spent two years in grade 2. In turn 56 she once again usurped Aline's turn, asserting the right to speak for her and offering a negative appraisal of her ability to do mathematics and in turns 59 and 61 again positioning her as untruthful, amplifying the element of social sanction: not only does Aline lack academic capacity but also moral standing.

Michelle's various 'footings' as joke teller, concerned friend, engaged listener, mask a devastating assault achieved through indexical layering: the meaningless babble of 'packler packler' (21), lack of truthfulness (28, 59), 'broken' (50), 'slow' (56), mistakes (61). Aline's reactions were to contradict Michelle and challenge her veracity, telling author B not to listen to her (27), to call her foolish (51), to question the relevance of her proposition (53), to mitigate (58) by claiming an affective reason for her lack of success in Afrikaans, to claim repeatedly to be fine (23, 55) admitting only 'problems in some places' (62), to tell her to shut up (66) and finally to accuse Michelle again of lying (68). The punch Aline gave Michelle in turn 67 when Michelle claimed she didn't ask for help is perhaps the only indication we get of frustration, a violation of the speaking subject which finds its response in a multidimensional physical embodiment of internal distress. However, Aline's attempts to save face were not honoured.

Thus, Aline was forced into a positioning on Michelle's terms. While all her signifying acts (Urciuoli 1995, 193) were referable to a shared frame, it is what they are NOT able to achieve that is significant: 'what is not or cannot be performed' (Kulick 2005, 615) are her desired stances as competent learner and interactant. Her use of French indexes these briefly visible traces of aspects of her identity. In an interview two years later, Aline expressed her extreme frustration at not being able to have a 'real' conversation and her sense of social isolation:

The others make fun of you when you try to manage in English and they don't take the time to explain anything to me so when I want to speak, really speak, I give them only French even if they don't understand. That's their problem.

(trans.)

It is important to note that unlike other school-based research on language socialization (Evaldsson and Cekaite 2010; Karrebæk 2013), there was no transforming of faulty talk, no attempt to assist Aline by her peers. Thus, faced with constant disparagement of her abilities and her feeling that she can never 'really speak', she adopted a solitary stance of resistance, persisting in her use of French in the full knowledge that no-one would understand.

Despite her increasing isolation, Aline continued to engage in social encounters on the playground on her own terms. However, in the classroom she hardly ever spoke: there is no data on her classroom interactions in either of the two schools she attended during this research. Generally, she sat at the back in a corner. In the first school she stopped talking because of continual mockery:

> In class, I don't waste my time talking because the learners will laugh. One day, they laughed when I was reading and I know that every time they talk in their patois, they say my name and laugh. But they are foolish. I don't care.

In the second school her silence became more acute: she and the girl she sat next to hardly ever spoke to each other and she wandered about on her own in the playground. In this school, classroom conditions were so noisy that the teacher paid no attention at all to those like Aline who tried to learn, his energies taken up with controlling the class. Here her silence embodies a logic of invisibility,[7] a response to symbolic violence and institutional erasure. Once again she was unable to construct a successful academic identity.

Discussion

In Aline's trajectory across social and educational spaces, we have traced disjunctive interplays of visibility and invisibility constructed through interactional, institutional, and pedagogical practices that legitimated certain ways of being and speaking and rendered others invisible. Interactionally, invisibility was constructed over time through a number of inter-related indexical processes. These included the repeated usurpation of her voice and ability to speak for herself along with other evaluative and epistemic orientations to her stance projections which undermined or disbarred them completely, implicatures regarding her veracity and academic abilities, and indexical layering through which both her French and English language practices became identified with a particular social identity and a metalinguistic label 'broken English'. Simon began to use this label as a name for Aline (interview, 8 May 2013) and it subsequently surfaced in many other interactions as seen above in Table 2.3. The iterations of this interdiscursive link were tied into circulating discourses of otherness and belonging as well as institutional and pedagogical practices. Thus, this index moved across discursive fields, among classroom, playground and diasporic spaces, enregistering an indexical relationship between a set of speech practices and a particular persona (cf. Silverstein 2003; Urciuoli 2010). The effect of these iterations was to invisibilize her linguistic and epistemic resources. Here the operation of dual indexicality can be seen in Aline's response to the interpellative call of 'broken English' that even in refusing it, affirms it (cf. Kulick 2003, 149). Examining what 'not saying it' (Kulick 2003) *in English* produced enables an exploration of the processes by which Aline's desired identifications are delegitimized. Forced into attempts to save face, her subject positions were constituted by denials and disavowals rather than affirmations ('I didn't say anything', 'Oh no, you don't', 'You lie'). These were the only options available: her rejection of other options was ideologically constrained by the lack of legitimate language resources with which to construct desired stances. In the dual indexicality of 'broken English' against the erased, invisible, 'excellent French' lies the 'not-there, or, rather, the unsaid traces, the absent presence, that structure the said and the done' (Kulick 2005, 615): this absent presence made certain subject positions impossible.

What was 'not there' was absent because it was not 'sayable' in English but also because of the cumulative effects of strategies of condescension or disparagement and metalinguistic stance-taking (Evaldsson and Sahlström 2014; Jaffe 2009), both inscribed and evoked, all refracted through institutional discourses and pedagogical practices as well as broader ideologies of language and belonging. 'Strands of interdiscursivity' (Agha and Wortham 2005) carrying negative evaluations of her linguistic practices circulated among spaces, with indexical entailments for who she could be in each interactional moment but also more durably as subsequent interactions increasingly came to 'presuppose identities signaled in earlier ones' (Wortham 2005, 98). Unable to transform others' 'schemes of perception and appreciation' (Bourdieu 1989, 20), Aline resorted to silence in the classroom, invisibilizing herself, and to resistance on the playground, continuing to use French in defiance of the linguistic regime and thus rendering herself permanently visible as 'other'. In this inverse play of visibility and invisibility, she was constructed as doubly inarticulate, in both French and English: 'what then is articulateness but the right to speak in ways that others can hear?' (McDermott 1988, 62), a position she acknowledged in that when she wanted to 'really speak' she did this in French, addressing an audience that would not hear. What became invisible were her identities as a confident social participant, moral arbiter, articulate French speaker, and strong student, the losses in social and linguistic capital entwined with those in cultural capital, pointing to the ways in which social identification and learning partly constitute each other (Wortham 2004).

It appears then that Aline's linguistic repertoire was decisive in determining patterns of social and academic success. As Busch (2015, 17) argues 'the linguistic repertoire reflects the synchronic coexistence of different social spaces in which we participate as speakers, and it points diachronically to different levels of time.' Aline's repertoire largely pointed backwards to a lost world of competence, 'ease', and belonging, the scars of the present visible in her defiant linguistic practices, her silence, and solitude. Because Aline was unable to expand her linguistic repertoire sufficiently quickly, to build up the 'stance accretion' (Rauniomaa 2003) necessary for the production of social identity over time, her ethnicity became reinforced, she remained 'other', fixedly Cameroonian. Language here was a constant in defining her 'otherness', 'French' remained a clearly bounded entity tied to a nationality. This re-essentialization of ethnicity was at odds with the dynamic and fluid processes of incorporation of Anglophone immigrants in the schools where the broader racialized category of 'black' expanded locally to include them (Kerfoot ftc 2017). Here we see the crucial role of linguistic repertoires in the resignification or sedimentation of local racial and ethnic categories. In Aline's case, this ethnicization was entangled with her age, loss of social and academic status and of social networks, and her embodied unhappiness,[8] all of which fed into how her linguistic resources were valued.

Conclusion

In southern contexts complex histories of engagement across differences lie behind each interactional moment: each moment carries the potential to either shift or reproduce racialized indexicalities and thereby either transform or reinforce the local social order.

This chapter has traced complex and contradictory processes of visibilization and invisibilization in the trajectory of an immigrant youngster, illustrating the identities that came to be 'indexically entailed in-and-by the use of certain language forms' (Silverstein 2014, 153; cf. 2003). In the emerging social orders of these schools, some like Aline remained excluded: the local racial hierarchy was restratified and re-ethnicized, creating a new order of visibility.

Those like Aline who circulate on the peripheries across local, national, and transnational spaces in Africa become entangled in circuits of legitimacy cycling through social and educational spaces. Detailed analyses of interactions and the processes through which inarticulateness and invisibility were constructed point to the importance of absences: those practices which could or should be there but are barred from performance and disappear soundlessly beneath the weight of the prevailing order. This chapter thus aims to contribute to an epistemology of the global South (Santos 2012) by pointing to invisibilized processes of cultural and educational production, a necessary starting point for conditions of greater ethical engagement and mutual intelligibility.

Acknowledgements

We would like to thank Chris Stroud, Kenneth Hyltenstam, Natalia Ganuza, Manuel Guissemo, Patric Lebenswerd, Ben Rampton, Linus Salö, and especially David Karlander and anonymous reviewers for illuminating comments on this paper. This research was supported in part by the National Research Foundation (NRF) of South Africa under grant 62314.

Notes

1 Kulick distinguishes his definition of the term from that of Hill (1995) who uses it to characterize the way in which 'humorous' utterances of Mock Spanish by Anglo speakers assign desirable qualities to Anglos and undesirable qualities to members of historically Spanish-speaking populations.
2 Cameroon is among the five top African countries for economic migrants to South Africa (Statistics South Africa 2014, 35). Like other African nationals, Cameroonians migrate to escape the economic hardships plaguing the country. Many also flee for political reasons: a dictatorial order, political instability, press and speech censorship, and exclusion of certain regions of the country from power, as well as political murders (Pineteh 2007).
3 Parallel medium schools are defined as those where speakers from two different groups each receive instruction through the medium of his or her home language. They have been used in South Africa since at least 1943 (Malherbe 1943) with regard to the only two languages with symbolic power under apartheid, English and Afrikaans, and continue in some cases today.
4 Under apartheid, the designation 'coloured' was a category constructed for all those of 'mixed' heritage, including descendants of Indonesian and Malay slaves as well as the Khoe-San. Because it incorporates a number of culturally distinct groups, the word is generally written today with a lower case 'c'. In post-apartheid South Africa, the terms Black, African, and coloured are used variously and never without contestation. For statistical purposes, the present government retains the former apartheid "race" categories in order to implement policies designed to ensure redress and equity.
5 Camfranglais emerged in the mid-1970s among high school and college students after the reunification of Francophone and Anglophone Cameroons (Kouega 2003) and often indexes rebellion against authority (Ewané 1989).
6 As observed by Author B, who is Cameroonian.
7 We thank David Karlander for this point.
8 While gender may well have played a role, a different research design would have been necessary to investigate this.

References

Agha, A., and S. Wortham, eds. 2005. 'Discourse across Speech-Events: Intertextuality and Interdiscursivity in Social Life'. *Special Issue: Journal of Linguistic Anthropology* 15 (1): 1–150.
Bailey, B. 2007. 'Language Alternation as a Resource for Identity Negotiations among Dominican American Bilinguals'. In *Style and Social Identities: Alternative Approaches to Linguistic Heterogeneity*, edited by P. Auer, 29–56. New York: Mouton de Gruyter.
Banda, F. 2010. 'Defying Monolingual Education: Alternative Bilingual Discourse Practices in Selected Coloured Schools in Cape Town'. *Journal of Multilingual and Multicultural Development* 31 (3): 221–35.
Bentley, K., and A. Habib, eds. 2008. *Racial Redress & Citizenship in South Africa.* Cape Town, SA: Human Sciences Research Council.
Bourdieu, P. 1989. 'Social Space and Symbolic Power'. *Sociological Theory* 7 (1): 14–25.
———. 2000. *Pascalian Meditations.* Translated by R. Nice. Stanford: Stanford University Press.
Bucholtz, M. 1999. 'You Da Man: Narrating the Racial Other in the Production of White Masculinity'. *Journal of Sociolinguistics* 3 (4): 443–60.

————. 2004. 'Styles and Stereotypes: The Linguistic Negotiation of Identity among Laotian American Youth'. *Pragmatics* 14 (2-3): 127–47.

Bucholtz, M., and K. Hall. 2005. 'Identity and Interaction: A Sociocultural Linguistic Approach'. *Discourse Studies* 7 (4–5): 585–614.

Busch, B. 2015. 'Expanding the Notion of the Linguistic Repertoire: On the Concept of Spracherleben: The Lived Experience of Language'. *Applied Linguistic*. First published July 23, 2015. doi: 10.1093/applin/amv030.

Collinsdictionary.com. 2015. 'Amakwerekwere'. *Collinsdictionary.com*. Retrieved from http://www.collinsdictionary.com.

Creese, A. 2008. 'Linguistic Ethnography'. In *Encyclopedia of Language and Education*, edited by K. King and N. Hornberger, 229–41. New York: Springer.

De Fina, A. 2007. 'Code-Switching and the Construction of Ethnic Identity in a Community of Practice'. *Language in Society* 36 (3): 371–92.

Du Bois, J. W. 2007. 'The Stance Triangle'. In *Stancetaking in Discourse: Subjectivity, Evaluation, Interaction*, edited by R. Englebretson, 139–82. Philadelphia: John Benjamins.

Eggins, S., and D. Slade. 2004. *Analysing Casual Conversation*. London: Equinox.

Evaldsson, A.-C. 2005. 'Staging Insults and Mobilizing Categorizations in a Multiethnic Peer Group'. *Discourse & Society* 16 (6): 763–86.

Evaldsson, A.-C., and A. Cekaite. 2010. ' " 'Schwedis' He Can't Even Say Swedish": Subverting and Reproducing Institutionalized Norms for Language Use in Multilingual Peer Groups'. *Pragmatics* 20 (4): 587–604.

Evaldsson, A.-C., and F. Sahlström. 2014. 'Metasociolinguistic Stance-Taking and the Appropriation of Bilingual Identities in Everyday Peer Language Practices'. In *Children's Peer Talk: Learning from Each Other*, edited by A. Cekaite, S. Blum-Kulka, V. Grøver, and E. Aldea, 149–68. Cambridge: Cambridge University Press.

Ewané, L. M. 1989. 'Le Camfranglais, Un Cousin Du Verlan?' *Afrique Elite* 36: 18–19.

Fabrício, B. F. 2014. 'Policing the Borderland in a Digital Lusophone Territory: The Pragmatics of Entextualisation'. In *Global Portuguese: Linguistic Ideologies in Late Modernity*, edited by L. P. Moita-Lopes, 66–86. London: Routledge.

Fanon, F. [1967] 2008. *Black Skin, White Masks*. Translated by R. Philcox. London: Grove.

Foucault, M. 1971. *L'Ordre du Discours*. Paris: Gallimard.

Gal, S., and J. Irvine. 1995. 'The Boundaries of Languages and Disciplines: How Ideologies Construct Difference'. *Social Research* 62 (4): 967–1001.

García-Sánchez, I. M. 2014. 'Language Socialisation and Exclusion'. In *The Handbook of Language Socialization*, edited by A. Duranti, E. Ochs, and B. B. Schieffelin, 391–419. Chichester, UK: Wiley-Blackwell.

Goffman, E. 1974. *Frame Analysis: An Essay on the Organization of Experience*. Cambridge, MA: Harvard University Press.

————. 1981. *Forms of Talk*. Philadelphia: University of Pennsylvania Press.

————. 1983. 'The Interaction Order: American Sociological Association, 1982 Presidential Address'. *American Sociological Review* 48 (1): 1–17.

Goodwin, M. H. 1998. 'Games of Stance: Conflict and Footing in Hopscotch'. In *Kids Talk: Strategic Language Use in Later Childhood*, edited by S. M. Hoyle and C. T. Adger, 23–46. New York and Oxford: Oxford University Press.

————. 2003. 'The Relevance of Ethnicity, Class, and Gender in Children's Peer Negotiations'. In *The Handbook of Language and Gender*, edited by J. Holmes and M. Meyerhoff, 229–51. Chichester, UK: Blackwell.

Hanks, William F. 1992. 'The Indexical Ground of Deictic Reference'. In *Rethinking Context: Language as an Interactive Phenomenon*, edited by A. Duranti and C. Goodwin, 46–76. Cambridge: Cambridge University Press.

Hoyle, S. M., and C. T. Adger, eds. 1998. *Kids Talk: Strategic Language Use in Later Childhood*. New York and Oxford: Oxford University Press.

Ibrahim, A. 2009. 'Operating under Erasure: Race/ Language/ Identity'. In *Race, Culture, and Identities in Second Language Education: Exploring Critically Engaged Practice*, edited by R. Kubota and A. M. Y. Lin, 176–94. New York: Routledge.

Jaffe, A. 2009. *Stance: Sociolinguistic Perspectives*. New York: Oxford University Press.

Karrebæk, M. S. 2013. ' "Don't Speak like That to Her!": Linguistic Minority Children's Socialization into an Ideology of Monolingualism'. *Journal of Sociolinguistics* 17 (3): 355–75.

Kerfoot, C. forthcoming. 'Linguistic Shifters: Multilingual Learners and the Construction of Postracial Orders in Two South African Primary Schools'. In *Diversities, Affinities and Diasporas*, edited by K. Heugh, A. Scarino, and C. Stroud. New York: Routledge.

Kerfoot, C., and B. O. Bello-Nonjengele. 2016. 'Game Changers? Multilingual Learners in a Cape Town Primary School'. *Applied Linguistics* 37 (4): 451–73, first published online September 20, 2014.

Kouega, J.-P. 2003. 'Camfranglais: A Novel Slang in Cameroon Schools'. *English Today* 19 (2): 23–9.

Kroskrity, P. V. 2000. *Regimes of Language: Ideologies, Polities, and Identities*. Santa Fe, NM: School of American Research Press.

Kulick, D. 2003. 'No'. *Language & Communication* 23 (2): 139–51.

———. 2005. 'The Importance of What Gets Left out'. *Discourse Studies* 7 (4–5): 615–24.

Luke, A. 2009. 'Race and Language as Capital in School: A Sociological Template for Language-Education Reform'. In *Race, Culture, and Identities in Second Language Education: Exploring Critically Engaged Practice*, edited by R. Kubota and A. M. Y. Lin, 286–308. New York: Routledge.

Makoe, P. 2007. 'Language Discourses and Identity Construction in a Multilingual South African Primary School.' *English Academy Review* 24 (2): 55–70.

———. 2014. 'Constructing Identities in a Linguistically Diverse Learning Context'. *International Journal of Bilingual Education and Bilingualism* 17 (6): 654–67.

Makoe, P., and C. McKinney. 2014. 'Linguistic Ideologies in Multilingual South African Suburban Schools'. *Journal of Multilingual and Multicultural Development* 35 (7): 658–73. doi:10.1080/01434632.2014.908889.

Malherbe, E.G. 1943. *The Bilingual School*. Johannesburg: Central News Agency.

Martin, J. R. 1992. *English Text: System and Structure*. Philadelphia: John Benjamins.

Mbembe, A. 2014. 'Class, Race and the New Native'. *Mail and Guardian*, September 26.

McDermott, R. P. 1988. 'Inarticulateness'. In *Linguistics in Context: Connecting Observation and Understanding: Lectures from the 1985 LSA/TESOL and NEH Institutes*, edited by D. Tannen, 37–68. Norwood, NJ: Praeger.

McKinney, C. 2010. 'Schooling in Black and White: Assimilationist Discourses and Subversive Identity Performances in a Desegregated South African Girls' School'. *Race, Ethnicity & Education* 13 (2): 191–207.

Meda, L. 2014. 'The Mist That They Declared to Be Over Is Still around: Xenophobic Experiences of Refugee Children Living at a Community Centre in South Africa'. *Child Abuse Research in South Africa* 15 (2): 72–82.

Ndlangamandla, S. C. 2010. '(Unofficial) Multilingualism in Desegregated Schools: Learners' Use of and Views towards African Languages'. *Southern African Linguistics and Applied Language Studies* 28 (1): 61–73.

Nyamnjoh, F. 2006. *Insiders and Outsiders: Citizenship and Xenophobia in Contemporary Southern Africa*. Dakar, Senegal: Zed Books.

Ochs, E. 1992. 'Indexing Gender'. In *Rethinking Context: Language as an Interactive Phenomenon*, edited by A. Duranti and C. Goodwin, 335–58. Cambridge: Cambridge University Press.

Ochs, E. 1996. 'Linguistic Resources for Socialising Humanity'. In *Rethinking Linguistic Relativity*, edited by John J. Gumperz and Stephen C. Levinson, 407–37. Cambridge: Cambridge University Press.

Ochs, E., T. Kremer-Sadlik, O. Solomon, and K. Sirota. 2001. 'Inclusion as Social Practice: Views of Children with Autism'. *Social Development* 10 (3): 399–419.

Pineteh, E. A. 2007. 'Narratives of Homelessness and Displacement: Life Testimonies of Cameroon Asylum Seekers in Johannesburg'. Ph.D. dissertation, University of the Witwatersrand.

Rampton, B. 1995. *Crossing: Language and Ethnicity among Adolescents*. London and New York: Longman.

———. 2006. *Language in Late Modernity: Interaction in an Urban School*. Cambridge: Cambridge University Press.

———. 2007. 'Neo-Hymesian Linguistic Ethnography in the United Kingdom'. *Journal of Sociolinguistics* 11 (5): 584–607.

Rauniomaa, M. 2003. 'Stance Accretion'. Paper presented at the Language, Interaction, and Social Organization Research Focus Group, University of California, Santa Barbara, February.

Santos, B. de S. 2012. 'Public Sphere and Epistemologies of the South'. *Africa Development* XXXVII (1): 43–67.

Schiffrin, D. 1993. 'Research Talk on, for, and with Social Subjects'. *Language & Communication* 13 (2): 133–6.

Silverstein, M. 2003. 'Indexical Order and the Dialectics of Sociolinguistic Life'. *Language & Communication* 23 (3–4): 193–229.

———. 2014. 'Denotation and the Pragmatics of Language'. In *The Cambridge Handbook of Linguistic Anthropology*, edited by N. J. Enfield, P. Kockelman, and J. Sidnell, 128–57. Cambridge: Cambridge University Press.

Statistics South Africa. 2014. 'Documented Immigrants in South Africa, 2013'. *Statistical Release P0351.4*. Pretoria: Statistics SA.

Urciuoli, B. 1995. 'The Indexical Structure of Invisibility'. In *Human Action Signs in Cultural Context: The Visible and the Invisible in Movement and Dance*, edited by B. Farnell, 189–215. Metuchen, NJ and London: Scarecrow.

———. 2010. 'Entextualizing Diversity: Semiotic Incoherence in Institutional Discourse'. *Language & Communication* 30 (1): 48–57.

Wortham, S. 2004. 'The Interdependence of Social Identification and Learning'. *American Educational Research Journal* 41 (3): 715–50.

———. 2005. 'Socialization beyond the Speech Event'. *Journal of Linguistic Anthropology* 15 (1): 95–112.

3 'Why Can't Race Just Be a Normal Thing?'

Entangled Discourses in the Narratives of Young South Africans

Zannie Bock

Introduction

South Africa is a country with a fraught history of inequality and racial oppression. Racism has been a pervasive feature, first as part of the colonial project, and then entrenched as a legalized system during the apartheid years (1948–94). With the first democratic elections in 1994, the official discourse changed radically from one which promoted racial difference, to one in which the need for social, political, and economic transformation is legitimated. Despite the demise of apartheid, race has continued to permeate many aspects of public and private life (Bundy 2014). Whereas social integration in public spaces has seen some progress, less has been achieved in private, with research showing that South Africans still prefer to associate in social groups based on race, ethnicity, and language (Lefko-Everett 2012; Seekings 2008).

For young people growing up in the 'new' South Africa, the terrain of racial positioning is difficult and uneven. Referred to as the 'born free' generation, they aspire to be liberated of the past, yet are themselves shaped by and positioned within its legacy (Bundy 2014). This chapter explores how the discourses of 'born frees' at a tertiary institution in South Africa both reproduce and transform inherited racial identities and positions. It forms part of a larger research project which analyses focus group interviews held between 2009 and 2014 on two campuses, one 'historically black' and the other 'historically white' (Bock and Hunt 2015).

This chapter takes up the metaphor of entanglement which frames this book by focussing on the points in the data when 'identities, spaces, histories—come together or find points of intersection in unexpected ways' (Nuttall 2009, 11). It asks: to what extent do these participants reproduce or transform inherited racializing discourses? What kinds of (dis)entanglements do they express and how do these help us understand South Africa post-apartheid? It uses a focus on narrative, in particular 'small stories', to provide insight into the complex and dialogic ways in which participants discursively enact their racialized identities and (seek to) imagine the future.

The data are complex, full of ambiguities and contradictions, a web of tangled threads. Many different interpretations and lines of argument could be made, several of which are covered in other papers (Bock 2014; Bock and Hunt 2015). These point to the underlying racism in much of the corpus and argue that despite the stated desire to move on, and in the absence of an alternative non-racial discourse, participants reinvoke the apartheid racial hierarchy as an explanatory framework for their everyday experiences. In this chapter, however, the analysis picks up a different thread and explores those points where different discourses intersect and commonalities emerge. It argues that despite the racial anxiety suffusing the data, the participants seek to disentangle from the apartheid past and position themselves in a postracial future. Although they are uncertain on how this can be achieved, they primarily identify interracial social interaction as key.

Racial Classification

Although scholars generally agree that there is no biological basis to race, it is, as demonstrated in this chapter, still experienced by South Africans as very real (Soudien 2013). During the apartheid years, a raft of discriminatory legislation determined people's life prospects based on their racial classification. In terms of the Population Registration Act of 1950, people were divided into three racial categories: *black*, *coloured*, and *white*. *Asian*, or *Indian*, as a fourth category, was added later. This, Posel (2001) shows, was often a relatively arbitrary decision based more on social standing and acceptance into the broader community than on genetic inheritance, yet it served to fix one's position within a racial hierarchy, firmly associating 'whiteness' with power, privilege, and opportunity and 'blackness' with dispossession, poverty, and lack of advancement. Being 'coloured' or 'Indian' meant occupying a rank somewhere in between.[1]

Despite the dismantling of apartheid in 1994, race has continued to have a profound effect on people's lives. As many scholars have argued, institutionalized racism entrenches structures of privilege and disadvantage which shape families for decades even after the legal system has been abolished (Bundy 2014). One of the ways in which the post-apartheid government sought to transform this legacy was through a policy of affirmative action which requires public and private sector institutions to ensure demographic representivity in the workplace by giving preferential employment to people from previously disenfranchised groups. To this end, many institutions use racial quotas to regulate admissions or employment. A consequence of this is that all South Africans are required to identify themselves in terms of the old apartheid categories on all official application forms. Thus, another reason why race is still so pervasive in contemporary South Africa is that it has been reinvigorated in the name of redress and used to favour applicants who were disadvantaged by apartheid, in particular, black applicants. In a context of high unemployment (currently 25.5 percent, Statistics SA 2014), different racial groups are thus set in competition for scarce job and study opportunities.

This chapter uses these racial labels conscious of their history and contested meanings. Erwin (2012) cautions that their use inevitably runs the risk of further entrenching those same categories, and that researchers should work to critique and destabilize these naturalized classifications. This chapter aims to draw attention to the ways in which race is reproduced in discourse and so to raise awareness about how this may shape or constrain progress towards postracial ways of thinking, speaking, and being.[2]

Race in Higher Education

Under apartheid, all educational institutions, including universities, were segregated according to race. The better resourced universities were reserved for those classified white (and included separate English and Afrikaans medium campuses), whereas the rest of the population attended institutions organized along racial and ethnic lines (Walker 2005a). (In contemporary discourse, the former are referred to as 'historically white' institutions, whereas the latter are *collectively* referred to as 'historically black'). However, in the early 1980s, in defiance of the apartheid laws, several more progressive campuses began admitting black students, with the University of the Western Cape (UWC), University of Cape Town (UCT) and the University of the Witwatersrand leading the way.

Although, since 1994, schools and universities have become increasingly racially diverse, research continues to point to the ongoing salience of race in these settings. Scholars have investigated how young South Africans negotiate their racial identities in ways which either perpetuate or destabilize the essentialized apartheid categories (e.g., Dolby 1999; Kerfoot and Bello-Nonjengele 2016; McKinney 2007). What is common to all these accounts is recognition of the difficulties young people face when navigating this terrain and the strategic ways in which they deploy their repertoire of identity options to enact shifting (dis)alignments as demanded by a given context.

Research by Pattman (2007), Wale (2010) and Walker (2005a, b) in higher education contexts explores how racialized discourses are reproduced or transformed on campuses which, in the past two decades, have undergone considerable transformation including mergers between formerly white and black universities. Walker's study takes place at a formerly white Afrikaans university code-named 'Northern University'. Pattman's participants are students on a historically white English campus, now part of the merged University of KwaZulu Natal (UKZN). Wale's research takes place on two sites: the former white English campus of UCT, and the University of Johannesburg (UJ), the latter a product of a merger between a black campus and a former white Afrikaans one. All researchers conclude that despite much greater racial integration and diversity since 1994, these campuses remain socially divided by race. Further, their studies also show how new identities have emerged based on class or perceived educational advantage. For example, those black, coloured, and Indian students who have attended former white schools in the wealthier suburbs, are often derogatively labelled 'coconuts' (i.e., black on the outside, white on the inside) or 'Model C's' (a reference to former white schools) by their peers who attended the poorly resourced township schools (Pattman 2007). Where racial integration does occur, argue both Wale and Pattman, it tends to be assimilationist in nature and serves to subtly reinforce and reproduce the greater social and cultural power of middle-class whiteness.

Walker's (2005a, b) study shows how in an historically white Afrikaans institution, students engage in complex webs of acknowledgement and denial, alignment and rejection in relation to their racial identities, creating, she argues, a context in which 'race is nowhere and race is everywhere' (2005b, 41). Here racial relations are more strongly polarized into black and white extremes, a legacy of the university's history as a site for the reproduction of racist Afrikaner nationalism. According to Walker, many of her young white participants adopt a range of discursive positions to remain securely within their racial and social positions (white, Afrikaans, Christian). Where they do admit to some reflexivity about race, they do not interrogate their positions too closely, preferring to 'otherise softly' (Bonilla-Silva 2003, in Walker 2005a, 134) by using discursive strategies which include denying or minimizing the impact of racism and emphasizing the importance of individual effort (not race) as a predictor of success. In this context, she argues, 'racist discourse mutates but does not disappear' (2005a, 140).

Whereas the findings referred to above reflect issues in historically white institutions (or partly white in the case of the merged institutions), little research has been conducted on racial discourses in institutions which can be described as historically black. This chapter, then, seeks to address this gap by reporting on the salience of race in the discourses of students at the University of the Western Cape (UWC) in the period 2009–14. One of the major differences between this corpus and those referred to above is that the UWC participants talk uninhibitedly about race in ways which sometimes include racial labelling and stereotyping. By contrast, Pattman, Wale, and Walker note that their participants avoid racial references. Pattman argues that silence is in fact a way of policizing these boundaries: by refusing to confront them, they remain unaddressed and untransformed.

It is important to note that subsequent to the above studies, and very recently, the issue of race has exploded on many South African campuses. It began with the action of a UCT student, who, on 9 March 2015, flung human excrement over a statue of Cecil Rhodes, a British colonialist and imperialist from the late nineteenth century, and declared: 'There is no black collective history here—where are our heroes and ancestors?' (Robins 2015). This action sparked the growth of a student movement known as Rhodes Must Fall, which spread to other (formerly white) campuses nationally and initiated debates on race, normative whiteness, and the need for transformation in higher education. Since October 2015, these debates have heightened as additional campuses, including historically black ones, began protesting the high cost of higher education under the umbrella of Fees Must Fall. Whereas this movement garnered widespread support across a range of groups and institutions and succeeded in securing a number of concessions, including a national moratorium on tuition fee increases for 2016, the protest turned violent on several campuses, including UWC, further polarizing the student body. Thus, the research reported on here needs to be read as occurring prior to these events, but as a precursor to the new (dis)entanglements that will emerge through 2016 and beyond.

Research Site and Data Description

UWC was established as a tertiary institution for coloured students in 1960, but, as noted above, it opened its doors to black students in defiance of the apartheid laws in the early 1980s. It has historically served students from more marginal educational and social backgrounds. Whereas the current enrolment of over 20,000 includes students from all over South Africa and, increasingly, African countries to the north, it still predominantly draws on students from two provinces in South Africa: the Western Cape (in which the university is situated) and the Eastern Cape. As such, the student population reflects the social demographics of these regions (predominantly coloured and black) and students generally speak English, Afrikaans, and/ or isiXhosa as well as local mixed varieties of these languages. English, as medium of instruction, is the language of prestige, both regionally and nationally. Whereas UWC shares some of the same racial problems as those of former white institutions, the 'shape' of these problems is somewhat different given that only 5 percent of the student population is white. However, as will be seen below, racial distrust between different student groups, and in relation to the predominantly coloured university administration, persists.

The data for this chapter are based on six focus group interviews conducted between 2009 and 2014 at UWC. All interviewers are students who selected their own interviewees, generally third year or post-graduate students. The interviewees were generally known to each other, either loosely as fellow students (in the case of the multiracial focus groups—Lebo, Chad, Janette), or more intimately as close knit friendship groups (for the monoracial groups—Dineo, Bianca, Charlene). This differential composition affected the data in that the talk in the racially mixed interviews generally promoted more non-racial values, whereas in the racially homogenous groups, the discussions were more 'frank' and stigmatizing (see Lefko-Everett 2012, 133, for a similar observation).

Data were elicited using a number of open-ended questions which asked students what they knew about apartheid, how they felt about it, and how it

Table 3.1 Overview of Focus Groups

Group	Interviewer	Participants	Date	Duration
Dineo*	black female	2 black females 1 black male	2009	2:10
Bianca*	black female	6 coloured females	2009	0:55
Lebo	black female	3 coloured females 1 black female 1 white male	2009	0:28
Chad	coloured male	2 black males 1 coloured male	2010	0:32
Charlene	coloured female	2 coloured males 3 coloured females	2013	0:57
Janette	coloured female	1 black female 2 coloured males 1 white male	2014	0:45

* Note: 'Bianca' and 'Dineo' were conducted by the same interviewer, but are given different pseudonyms to distinguish them

had affected them. Asking students about apartheid proved to be very generative and stimulated rich discussion about the students' own experiences of racism. The dominant language of the interviews was English, although interviewees in Charlene's interview code-switched between Afrikaans and English. The interviews were transcribed and analyzed using narrative analysis, as outlined below.

Narrative Analysis

Narrative analysis encompasses 'a minefield of multiple and at times competing perspectives' in a wide range of disciplines (De Fina and Georgakopoulou 2012, 1). The concept of 'small stories' (Georgakopoulou 2007, 2015) was chosen as an analytical lens as it helps to retain a sense of the complexities and ambivalences of the different voices in the data. Bamberg and Georgakopoulou (2008, 379) argue that people use small stories to 'create (and perpetuate) a sense of who they are' both in the interactional moment as well as in relation to the dominant discourses which constitute their context. Small stories may refer to events in the distant or recent past, or to incidents which are imagined or hypothetical. They may serve as 'reworked slices of life' arising as participants recount experiences (Georgakopoulou 2007, 150) or they may be offered as a way of elaborating or backing up an argument in conversation. They provide a sense of how people interact with the social discourses in their everyday contexts and provide counter positions and ambivalences often lost in the homogenizing master narratives. In this way, they are an important epistemology for capturing silenced, under-represented voices and subjectivities which are not yet fully articulated (Georgakopoulou 2015).

As the oral historian, Portelli (1991), reminds us, narratives are reconstructions of events, not faithful recapitulations of what happened. 'Oral sources', he argues, 'tell us not just what people did, but what they wanted to do, what they believed there were doing, and what they now think they did' (1991, 50). They are always 'variable and partial' because 'memory is not a passive depository of facts, but an active process of creation of meanings' (1991, 51–2). Labov (1972) argues that a key strategy used by narrators to index their stance is evaluation, and this gives a narrative its significance. Thus, attention should be paid to the ways in which participants frame, evaluate and interpret their experiences rather than simply treating them as factual accounts.

The Analysis

During the interviews, participants tell a number of stories of their own and their families' experiences. These can be organized into four thematic strands: in the first, the participants recount *their parents' stories of life under apartheid*—stories which point to experiences of discrimination and oppression. In the second, they tell stories about *the kinds of things their parents told them about other races* when they were growing up—stories which can be viewed as evidence of the intergenerational transmission of racial beliefs and attitudes. The third category, which comprises the bulk of the stories, encapsulates *their own experiences* of being at the receiving end of racist behaviour (or what they interpret as racially motivated behaviours), both in institutions as well as in informal everyday encounters. Lastly, there is a small though significant set of stories which indicates *an aspiration for some kind of postracial future* and points towards ways in which these participants attempt to transcend the historical divisions.

Parents' Narratives of Life Under Apartheid

In all interviews, participants locate their knowledge of apartheid in their parents' stories of racial oppression. For example, in Bianca's group, several of the participants recall how their parents lost their homes under the infamous Group Areas Act of 1950 which declared certain areas for 'whites only' and resulted in the removal of millions of black, coloured, and Indian people from their homes. Other participants tell stories which recount the indiscriminate violence of apartheid, like being beaten for not having a passbook, the identity document black South Africans were required by law to carry to regulate their movement in white areas. In story (1) below, one of the participants recalls how her parents were beaten up by the *boere* (a reference to white Afrikaner males, often also used for the apartheid police) who came into the historically coloured area of the Bo Kaap to take out their frustrations when the *Bokke* (a reference to the Springbok national rugby team and a symbol of Afrikaner pride) lost a match.[3]

(1) Shamielah: My my mommy grew up in Bo Kaap and she say when when the boer when the Bokke lost their matches then the boers would come and hit them with with the with the what (laughs) it is with the whips and the ropes because they would be so angry because their teams lost (laughs) [*Bianca*]

Note that Story 1 is told with a certain amount of hilarity as indicated by the laughter, certainly not as something painful or difficult to recollect. Here narrative becomes a means to transform painful memories by turning them into humorous anecdotes, and through laughter, to distance oneself from the trauma of the past.

The stories in this category, then, carry the memories of their parents and indicate how race in apartheid South Africa was all pervasive. They also provide the backdrop for the second group of stories, namely those which point to their parents' negative and suspicious attitudes towards other races, especially whites. The participants use these narratives to express their own complex positioning in the present. As Portelli (1991, 50) reminds us, oral narratives tell 'us less about events and more about their meaning'. Thus, these stories are windows onto the narrators' own subjectivities and positions.

Intergenerational Transmission of Racial Attitudes and Prejudices

In all the interviews, participants recount how they became aware of race through the stories of their parents which generally perpetuated racial suspicions of 'the other', although they generally position themselves as having moved beyond their parents' attitudes. Within these stories, the discourses of the past clash with their lived experiences in the present, and the participants use these stories to negotiate the faultline between their racialized inheritance and the desire for a postracial future.

In story (2), Bongani, who identifies as black, went to a multiracial school (the Model C type) and learned to mix with other races from a young age. In this story, he sets this experience against the attitude of his parents whom he recalls as inducting him into their racially suspicious ways of thinking:

(2) Bongani: You see when we grow up neh ah (.) our parents tell us that 'no (.) ah (.) don't ever trust a white man (.) don't ever' (.) you see that's always stuck on my mind but (.) I go to school with them they are my friends (2.0) and I trust them but that voice (.) sticks in my mind 'you never trust a white man' I don't know why. [*Chad*]

This extract represents a small story within a small story: the first, compressed into the quoted words of his parents, is embedded within the second, Bongani's own account of his relationship with white school peers. The layered structure of the narrative becomes a means for Bongani to negotiate his position in the current context: it enables him to acknowledge his parents' history while simultaneously disaligning from their views. In other words, the second story acts as a frame to disable the racial suspicions of the first. However, it is significant that he hesitates for two seconds before the affirmation, 'and I trust them', as though this statement contains residual doubt. And indeed, as story (3) below indicates, these interracial friendships were often somewhat superficial.

Race as a Lived Experience

In all interviews, participants speak about race as a lived social reality and tell stories in which they either witnessed or were at the receiving end of racist behaviours. Many of the stories which make up this category are not stories of overt racism; rather they 'otherize softly' (Walker 2005a) and the exclusion is coded and implicit. For example, in contrast to Bongani's assertion in Story (2) above, Dan, a fellow participant, recounts not being able to be real friends with white children at his multiracial school because they 'tended to have that same mentality that their parents had':

(3) *Dan:*   like they would be your friend but they would still NOT BE
              YOUR FRIEND in in in in terms of like ==
    Andile: == ja ja ==
    Dan: == really like, the way they would be with their other white
              friends [*Chad*]

Andile's affirmation shows that Dan's sentiment is a shared one: the friendships with white children lacked depth and integrity and were underpinned, they suggest, by inherited racial suspicions.

Despite UWC's history as a non-racial institution and more than three decades of integrated admissions, racism is still experienced on campus as very real. In another story of 'otherizing softly', Tsepho recounts how the administrative personnel fail to help him adequately, an experience he interprets as racially motivated:

(4) Tsepho: we experience it [racism] sometimes er uhm they [the administration] just need to explain to you a few things and then they send you back and when it comes to people of their kind that is that is coloured of course they explain and help that person. [*Dineo*]

The use of the present tense in this small story suggests that this is something he habitually experiences, and his claim to speak on behalf of presumably black students, indicated by the use of the inclusive pronoun, *we*, suggests that this is a shared experience. Whereas tensions between black and coloured people in the Western Cape have a long history exacerbated during the apartheid years by legislation which privileged coloured people over black, experiences such as Tsepho's are perhaps also indicative of a sharpening of the racial polarities post-1994 in a context of affirmative action and high unemployment.

Palesa also complains of preferential treatment for coloured students on campus. She recounts how one of the student residences, Liberty, which is more 'modernized', 'beautiful' and 'organized', is mostly occupied by coloured students, whereas the 'more ghetto' residence of Ruth First is home to many black students. She then recalls a story about a coloured student, referred to here as 'this other child':

(5) Palesa: I remember this other situation this other child they wanted to move her from Liberty to Ruth First she cried actually she fainted and then they had to put her back in Liberty. [*Dineo*]

In this story, Palesa uses narrative action to express her stance: she does not need to explain the feelings of horror she attributes to the young student who was placed in a 'ghetto' residence with black students; rather her reference to her crying and fainting does the evaluative work for her. Here, once again, we see the potential of narrative to express a range of positions without the speaker having to state them explicitly or claim them as his or her own.

Not only do the stories in this category show that all participants are acutely aware of race and their own racialized positions, they also show that all participants share experiences of discrimination (or perceived discrimination) on the basis of their race. Even though most of the participants in this data fall into categories officially designated for redress (with the exception of the two white males), they fear that their chances of admission to tertiary programs or future employment will be negatively affected. For example, in the following extracts, the participants discuss the racial quotas used by an historically white university to regulate admissions. Not only are they misinformed about the quotas, but they construct their own racial group as *the* most discriminated against. Note, however, that Joshua (Story 8) later evaluates his exclusion from UCT as having a positive outcome.

(6) Dineo (black female): They are practising that at UCT and that **they are not supposed to have more like more than 20 percent black** they are supposed to have 20 percent black and then maybe 40 white and the remainder coloureds. [*Dineo*]

(7) Adeline (coloured female): But the majority there there by UCT (.) maybe (laugh) **I don't see a lot of coloureds** there I see a lot of Indians I see a lot of blacks and I see a lot of whites! [*Bianca*]

(8) Joshua (white male): Well ja my race might have held me back at UCT when I WAS REJECTED LIKE TWICE FOR UNDERGRAD (. . .) so I think in that way **I was definitely uhm at a disadvantage because of my race.** [*Janette*]

These same fears extend to their perceived job prospects. Palesa (in *Dineo*), for example, believes that her chances are curtailed by the fact that 'normally they would look at the white people first' even when the white applicants are less qualified. She cites as evidence her father's experience of working on the mines where he, a plumber, was called in to fix a water problem that his supervisor, who was white, could not. She frames this story as part of a structural inequality which persists where 'most of the people that are high up there [on the mines] it's whites and they don't even have a certificate and most of the black people neh the they are low like for example our dads our dads'. Although 15 years into democracy at the time of her interview, and within a context of workplace affirmative action, she perceives this inequality as structurally entrenched.

For many coloured students, affirmative action represents just another form of (reverse) discrimination as it promotes black applicants above those identified as coloured. In Charlene's interview, Bernadette tells the story of a friend and colleague who was overlooked for a permanent position at the bank even though she was more experienced. Note how in this small story, as in Bongani's story (2), the racializing position is carried by the quoted words of another and has the effect, as above, of enabling the narrator to contrast two voices, her own and her friend's against that of the manager's and the new official discourse of black empowerment.

(9) Bernadette: And then we asked our manager look what can she do right for next time to make sure she gets the position 'sorry we had to choose someone who's black' that was his exact words 'sorry we have to choose someone who is black'. [*Charlene*]

She later adds:

(10) Bernadette: So for me the biggest fear is going into the working world finding myself either not white enough to make it to the top position or not black enough to make it to the top position. [*Charlene*]

In this category, then, there are a number of stories that speak to participants' lived experience of racism and their fear of being discriminated against on the basis of their race. They are often used to provide 'experience-based evidence' for claims, thereby making them difficult to dispute (De Fina and Georgakopoulou 2012, 98). Data from our larger study show clearly that white students on the historically white campus also fear racially based discrimination as a consequence of affirmative action (Bock and Hunt 2015;

see also Walker 2005a). Thus, across a number of campuses and racial demographics, young South Africans fear discrimination and construct their own racial group as *the* most discriminated against. This, I would argue, is a point of intersection that needs attention and work on a national scale if it is not to have the effect of further entrenching old racial divisions and animosities. In the next section, this chapter explores the small but significant group of stories which point to moments when the participants experience the potential for social transformation.

The Desire to 'Move On' into a Postracial Futurity

The desire to 'move on' and leave the past behind is another sentiment common to all the interviews, perhaps as a result of the fears referred to above (also in Bock and Hunt 2015; Pattman 2007; Walker 2005a). When asked whether they thought it was important to learn more about the past, most of the students responded that whereas it was important not to forget, it was time to 'move on', as indicated by the extracts in (11) below. The last quotation in the list is the source for the title of this chapter: here Clint expresses his passionate desire to disengage from the emotionally charged history of race:

(11) *Ayesha:*   You can forgive (.) but you don't even have to sometimes (.) forgive you just need to **move on** [*Bianca*]

   Grace: I don't like to be associated with it [apartheid] as much because like uhm it it feels like we're going back to the past all the time and I hate that you know what I mean like you need **to move on** (. . .) I'm sick and tired of hearing from black and white and whatever I just wanna get done with the crap and I just wanna you know I want to **set the colour aside** I don't want that anymore [*Lebo*]

   Palesa: Right now **it's just taking our souls back** [*Dineo*]

   Clint: WHY CAN'T IT JUST BE A NORMAL THING? **WHY CAN'T RACE JUST BE NORMAL?** [*Janette*]

So whereas these participants acknowledge the importance of remembering the past, they also express a desire to be free of it. They suggest various means of disentangling themselves, including interracial marriage: 'maybe a black person marries a white person and a bloody blah marries the other thing and so ja I think that's the only way to end it' (Palesa, in *Dineo*).

   In the project of social transformation, academic learning also has a role to play, both in terms of deconstructing the essentialized nature of the racial categories and by encouraging debate on how racial histories are more entangled than any of the master narratives have allowed us to understand (Nuttall 2009). For example, in the following extract, the evolutionary story of the shared genetic ancestry allows Bongani to reimagine all people as belonging to one human race:

(12) Bongani: You see I don't believe in race. Sometimes I wonder why the government ah ah forms (.) us to to to write your race there. I don't believe in race I believe that we all one and then (.) you know mos ah (.) what is this (.) 'Out of Africa' theory, I believe in that theory so we are all one. [*Chad*]

Here Bongani questions the value of the official practice which requires all South Africans to self-identify racially on all official forms. Note also that this is the same participant who claimed somewhat hesitantly that he trusted his white school friends (Story 1). He is clearly searching for ways to transcend the inherited binaries of black and white and the stories he tells are his ways of imagining a postracial futurity.

Most significantly, however, a number of participants point to the importance of social integration as a way to break the apartheid mould. Andile, for example, speaks of the highly successful World Cup 2010 when, for one month, South Africans of all races were united in their support of 'the game':

(13) Andile: If you see the youth of South Africa, they are mingling, they are mingling together like for example this World Cup everyone was (. . .) united in the spirit of *ubunye* and all of it. [*ubunye* translates as 'we are one'] [*Chad*]

Such examples are, however, few and far between, as the participants acknowledge: Carla, for example, asks 'how many people in the Caf[eteria] do you see sitting together in multiracial groups?' and Neels, one of the two white participants, argues that people should make more effort to get to know each other because that is where 'the whole apartheid thing (. . .) is still lingering we haven't learnt anything from each other' [*Lebo*].

However, several stories within the corpus are given as evidence of the transformative potential of social interaction. Interestingly, these stories emerge in the multiracial focus groups and are embodied in the experiences of the two white male participants, Neels and Joshua. Being part of a small minority of white students at UWC has enabled them to break with their inherited socialization patterns and to form friendships across the racial divides. Neels, who describes himself as from a conservative white Afrikaans background with a father who was a general in the former apartheid defence force, relates how his family have stopped telling racist jokes in front of him because 'they know how I feel'. Joshua, who self identifies as white and Jewish, shares how he appreciates the racial diversity of UWC after being in a school which he describes as a 'bubble' because the majority were 'white': 'I felt like I didn't belong in that bubble so I was uncomfortable and I was so grateful to come here [to UWC]'.

Later he tells a story of how, whilst attending a birthday party at the home of a coloured friend, he had the strange experience of suddenly finding himself the outsider, not because he was one of the two white people present, but because of his religion:

(14) Joshua: I went to a friend of mine's birthday party and uhm she's coloured and we (.) there were like two of us who were white and uhm but what was really interesting was that uhm it wasn't a coloured event it was a Christian event so my friend who's Christian was completely chilled (.) was so comfortable (.) was used to everything and I'm not saying I wasn't chilled but I didn't know what was happening (.) suddenly everyones' heads were down when they were praying and I (.) it caught me off guard. [*Janette*]

This small story is a reminder that identities are multifaceted, something which the focus on race often eclipses. It also reminds us that new alignments (and disalignments) across racial barriers are possible on the basis of other shared social characteristics, such as religion or gender. In this small story, the evaluations (e.g., 'what was really interesting', 'I didn't know what was happening') point to the significance of the event and its potentially transformative meanings.

Pattman, Wale, and Walker also explore the importance of social interaction as a way of moving forward but note the deeper underlying structures of entrenched racial privilege and power. It is noticeable that, with one or two exceptions, the participants in this study do not raise structural racism as an issue. Nor do they reflect on their own racializing talk. Clearly, part of moving forward is also becoming aware of the ways in which discourse reproduces racist attitudes and positions, and all South Africans need to engage with the structural nature of racism and the inherited patterns of privilege and disadvantage (Soudien 2013). But, as suggested by these participants, part of moving forward must also involve meaningful social engagement with people from across the racial divides.

Conclusion

The small stories in this data capture the concrete nature of experience and give tangible form to the feelings and attitudes the participants are trying to articulate. While some stories serve to reinforce and perpetuate existing power relations and racial stereotypes, others reveal moments of awareness or change. As recounted in their stories, these 'potentially transformative' moments occur through academic learning, when they witness integrated public events, like the World Cup, or are part of meaningful social interactions which unsettle the inherited discourses on race and suggest new ways of relating as fellow human beings. As Nuttall argues (2009, 1, 12), these entanglements imply a 'human foldedness', a return 'to the concept of the human'.

The 'small story' analytical lens allows the analyst to hold this complexity with its multiple layers and to capture and reflect on the ambiguities, contradictions, and silences of racial positioning in any given moment. It helps build an understanding of how race is understood, reproduced, and challenged in discourse. Understanding 'how racism works and . . . how it is insidiously inserted into the everyday' is central, Soudien (2013, 34) argues, to the project of 'anti-racism' which entails 'a commitment to the idea that all human beings have within them the capacity to surpass the cages of their histories and to be full human beings'.

In this chapter, I have argued that small stories analysis can help build this knowledge by providing a lens onto the tangled web of race and by showing how racial positions are discursively reproduced. Whereas some discourses reproduce inherited hierarchies and stereotypes, others allow participants to find spaces and interstices—to explore the 'folds' of their entanglement—and to imagine themselves and their fellow South Africans in new and different ways.

Acknowledgements

This research was made possible by funding from the National Research Foundation of South Africa. Opinions, findings, conclusions, and recommendations expressed in the article are those of the author and the NRF does not accept any liability in this regard.

My sincere thanks to research assistants Chanel van der Merwe, Cleo Cupido, Hunadi Mokgalaka, Janine Harry, Lerato Makhale, and all their participants who contributed to this project.

Notes

1 The term 'coloured' in South Africa is used to refer to people of complex heritage arising out of a history of colonialism and slavery. Although, under apartheid, they were granted some privileges above those classified 'black', they had no meaningful democratic rights and were excluded from the privileges and resources reserved exclusively for those classified 'white'.

2 I am aware that my own subjectivity as a white, middle-class, female South African is written into the analysis in complex ways. I have, however, worked at the university where this data was gathered for 18 years and discussed this analysis with students and colleagues from across the demographic spectrum in an attempt to understand the many sensitive issues. All failings to do so, however, remain my own.

3 Transcription conventions: short pause (.); longer pause (2.0); latched statements (==); elided material (. . .); emphasis (CAPS); bolding highlights the part of the extract relevant to the analysis.

References

Bamberg, M., and A. Georgakopoulou. 2008. 'Small Stories as a New Perspective in Narrative and Identity Analysis'. *Text and Talk* 28 (3): 377–96.

Bock, Z. 2014. 'Negotiating Race and Belonging in Post-Apartheid South Africa: Bernadette's Stories'. *Working papers in Urban Language and Literacies, Paper 144*. Retrieved from https://www.academia.edu/9499575/WP144.

Bock, Z., and S. Hunt. 2015. '"It's Just Taking Our Souls Back": Apartheid and Race in the Discourses of Young South Africans'. *Southern African Linguistics and Applied Language Studies* 33 (2): 141–58.

Bonilla-Silva, E. 2003. *Racism Without Racists: Color- Blind Racism and the Persistence of Racial Inequality in the United States*. Lanham, MD: Rowman and Littlefield.

Bundy, C. 2014. *Short-Changed? South Africa since Apartheid*. Auckland Park, SA: Jacana Media.

De Fina, A., and A. Georgakopoulou. 2012. *Analyzing Narrative: Discourse and Sociolinguistic Perspectives*. Cambridge: Cambridge University Press.

Dolby, N. 1999. 'Youth and the Global Popular: The Politics and Practices of Race in South Africa'. *European Journal of Cultural Studies* 2 (3): 291–309.

Erwin, K. 2012. 'Race and Race Thinking: Reflections in Theory and Practice for Researchers in South Africa and beyond'. *Transformation* 79: 93–113.

Georgakopoulou, A. 2007. 'Thinking Big with Small Stories in Narrative and Identity Analysis'. In *Narrative: State of the Art*, edited by M. Bamberg, 145–54. Amsterdam: John Benjamins.

———. 2015. 'Small Stories Research: Methods, Analysis, Outreach'. In *The Handbook of Narrative Analysis*, edited by A. De Fina and A. Georgakopoulou, 255–71. Oxford: Wiley-Blackwell.

Kerfoot, C., and B. O. Bello-Nonjengele. 2016. 'Game Changers? Multilingual Learners in a Cape Town Primary School'. *Applied Linguistics* 37 (4): 451–73.

Labov, W. 1972. *Language in the Inner City*. Philadelphia: University of Pennsylvania Press.

Lefko-Everett, K. 2012. 'Leaving It to the Children: Non-racialism, Identity, Socialisation and Generational Change in South Africa'. *Politikon* 39 (1): 127–47.

McKinney, C. 2007. '"If I Speak English, Does It Make Me Less Black Anyway?" "Race" and English in South African Desegregated Schools'. *English Academy Review* 24 (2): 6–24.

Nuttall, S. 2009. *Entanglement: Literary and Cultural Reflections on Post-Apartheid*. Johannesburg: Wits University Press.

Pattman, R. 2007. 'Student Identities, and Researching These, in a Newly "Racially" Merged University in South Africa'. *Race, Ethnicity and Education* 10 (4): 473–92.

Population Registration Act 30 of 1950. Pretoria: Government Printers. Retrieved from http://www.disa.ukzn.ac.za/webpages/DC/leg19500707.028.020.030/leg 19500707.028.020.030.pdf. (Accessed 30 November 2012).

Portelli, A. 1991. *The Death of Luigi Trastulli and Other Stories: Form and Meaning in Oral History*. New York: State University of New York Press.

Posel, D. 2001. 'What's in a Name? Racial Categorisations under Apartheid and Their Afterlife'. *Transformation* 47: 50–74.

Robins, S. 2015. 'Back to the Poo That Started It All'. *Cape Times*, 9 April. Retrieved from http://sbeta.iol.co.za/news/back-to-the-poo-that-started-it-all-1842443.

Seekings, J. 2008. 'The Continuing Salience of Race: Discrimination and Diversity in South Africa'. *Journal of Contemporary African Studies* 26 (1): 1–25.

Soudien, C. 2013. ' "Race" and Its Contemporary Confusions: Towards a Restatement'. *Theoria* 136, 60 (3): 15–37.

Statistics South Africa, Quarterly Labour Force Survey. July 2014. Retrieved from http://beta2.statssa.gov.za/?page_id=737andid=1. (Accessed 12 December 2015).

Wale, K. 2010. 'Policing Racial Boundaries: University Students' Interpretations of Race Relations in South Africa'. *MMG Working Paper 10–10.* Retrieved from http://www.mmg.mpg.de/publications/working-papers/2010/wp-10–10.

Walker, M. 2005a. 'Rainbow Nation or New Racism? Theorizing Race and Identity Formation in South African Higher Education'. *Race Ethnicity and Education* 8 (2): 129–46.

———. 2005b. 'Race Is Nowhere and Race Is Everywhere: Narratives from Black and White South African University Students in Post-Apartheid South Africa'. *British Journal of Sociology of Education* 26 (1): 41–54.

Part II
South-North Entanglements

4 Moving North, Navigating New Work Worlds, and Re-Mooring

Language and Other Semiotic Resources in the Migration Trajectories of East Timorese in the UK

Estêvão Cabral and Marilyn Martin-Jones

Introduction

This chapter provides an account of insights emerging from sociolinguistic research in progress with young men and women from the South East Asian nation of Timor-Leste who are currently living and working in Northern Ireland, in the towns of Dungannon, Cookstown, and Portadown, in County Tyrone. Our research complements and extends a prior study of language practices and language values that was carried out in the town of Dungannon, with two Timorese families (Da Costa Cabral 2010). The research questions that provided the starting point for our project are as follows: What have been the migration trajectories of the Timorese currently working in Northern Ireland? What are the local conditions of employment and settlement? How are the Timorese migrants navigating these conditions and re-mooring in this particular context? What language resources and funds of knowledge do they have? How are they positioned in relation to the local labour market and/or Irish institutions with these resources and funds of knowledge? And, beyond the worlds of work and local institutions, what new spaces of solidarity and conviviality are being created by the Timorese within their local life worlds? How are they drawing on different linguistic and semiotic resources as they construct new identities and a sense of belonging within these diasporic spaces? And how do they represent their origins and their relationship to the nation of Timor-Leste?

The orienting theories for this transdisciplinary research come from the fields of multilingualism, the sociolinguistics of globalization, and the study of migration and contemporary thinking about mobilities, particularly the unequal terrain of south-north mobilities. In the next section of this paper, we touch on new lines of theory-building in these different fields and we foreground the concepts that are most relevant to our research. In the third section, we provide a brief account of the recent history of Timor-Leste and the ways in which the current contours of linguistic and cultural diversity in Timor have been shaped by this history. In the fourth section, we trace the broad temporal and spatial dimensions of transnational population movements from Timor-Leste, focusing in on recent Timorese migration to Northern Ireland. In the fifth section, we describe the research approach adopted in our study. In the sixth, seventh, and eighth sections, we address the first five of the eight questions set out above, drawing on initial insights from the ethnographic work that we have done so far. Then, in section nine, we present a more detailed analysis of the ethnographic, textual, and photographic data that we have gathered so far. Here, we address the last three of the eight questions above. Our focus is on the creation of new spaces of solidarity and conviviality, on the linguistic and semiotic resources being drawn upon in local situated processes of meaning-making and identification and on diverse and multi-layered ways of representing what counts as being Timorese.

Changing Global Conditions and Epistemological Shifts in the Sociolinguistics of Multilingualism

In most of the twentieth century, the dominant concern in the sociolinguistics of multilingualism was with the mapping of patterns of language use in local 'communities'—communities that were constructed as stable, homogeneous, and bounded entities. Pratt (1987, 60) was the first to call for a decentring of the notion of 'community' and to argue for a move towards a 'linguistics of contact' which would focus on 'modes and zones of contact between dominant and dominated groups, between persons of different and multiple identities, speakers of different languages'. By the late twentieth century and the early part of the twenty-first century, a broad epistemological shift had taken place across the social sciences, away from 'sedentarist approaches' (Hannam, Sheller, and Urry 2006, 5) and towards a new concern with mobility, deterritorialization, globalization, and the intensification and diversification of transnational population movements.

This turn to mobility has also been evident in the work of sociolinguists engaged in research on multilingualism from an ethnographic perspective (e.g., Blommaert 2010; Heller 2007, 2011; Heller et al. 2016). Calls have been made for a fundamental rethink of both theory and method in this area of research. As Heller (2007, 6) has put it: 'Tools of enquiry refined when the focus was on boundaries, stability and homogeneity require refashioning for addressing movement, diversity and multiplicity'. Blommaert (2010, 5) has called for the development of a 'sociolinguistics of mobility . . . which focuses not on language-in-place, but on language in motion'. New conceptual compasses have also been forged. For instance, Heller (2007, 2011) and Duchêne and Heller (2012) have employed the notion of 'trajectory'. Heller (2007, 342) argues that designing a research project around the trajectory of social actors involves 'rethinking sociolinguistic ethnography in ways more oriented to processes and practice than to community and identity'. It also provides a way of taking account of the intersecting dimensions of time and space, and of moving away from synchronic accounts. In addition, it enables us to capture some of the complexity of contemporary transnational movements, including those that involve extended sojourns in different countries and, hence, access to diverse language resources and funds of knowledge.

As the mobility paradigm has been developed across the social sciences, there has been growing divergence of views. In one strand of work (e.g., Brenner 2004; Cresswell 2002; Hannam, Sheller, and Urry 2006; Urry 2007), there has been a critique of research where there is an exclusive focus on mobility and of 'deterritorialized approaches that posit a new 'grand narrative' of mobility, fluidity, or liquidity as a pervasive condition of postmodernity or globalization' (Hannam, Sheller, and Urry 2006, 5). These researchers have argued that an account of mobilities is incomplete without reference to moorings. They argue that 'forms of detachment or 'deterritorialization' . . . are always accompanied by rhizomic attachments and reterritorializations of various kinds' (Hannam, Sheller, and Urry 2006, 3).

Aligning ourselves with this strand of work, we take the view that, in our endeavours to provide as full an account as possible of the lived experience of migration among different groups of social actors, we need to keep both mobility and mooring/re-mooring within our sights. We need to capture the historical specificity of particular migration trajectories and, at the same time, we need to capture the situated ways in which mooring and re-mooring occur, along with the ways in which new forms of social organization and new social activities come to be imbued with meaning. Studies of migration, within the disciplines of anthropology and cultural studies (e.g., Ahmed et al. 2003; Brah 1996; Fortier 2000) have sustained this dual focus. They have provided accounts of dislocation and displacement, while also throwing light on the social and cultural processes involved in 'regrounding' (Ahmed et al. 2003).

Locating our research in Northern Ireland within the new sociolinguistics of multilingualism, we combine this duality of focus with an account of the ways in which language and other semiotic resources (Kress 2010) are drawn upon in the process of re-mooring, in the creation of spaces of solidarity and conviviality in local life worlds, in the construction of new identities and new forms of belonging, and in diverse representations of what it means to be Timorese, well beyond the borders of Timor-Leste.

At the same time, we are keenly aware of the need for our research to take account of the fact that south-north migration is bound up with global asymmetries of power and with the major economic shifts taking place in late capitalism. As Adey (2006, 85–6) has pointed out: 'Mobility, like power, is a relational thing' and it is unevenly distributed. The mobility of some social actors needs to be viewed in relation to the immobility of others, and moving north or west, from the global south, rarely involves retaining the same positioning with the social hierarchy. As Duchêne and Heller (2012, 15–16) remind us: 'The landscape is uneven, unbounded and fluid and . . .

social actors occupy different (and differently advantageous) positions with respect to access to the resources that circulate across it'.

For this reason, our research spans the different social spaces traversed by the young Timorese migrants participating in our study. In this chapter, our main focus is on the spaces of conviviality that they are creating within their local life worlds, but in the broader project we are also taking stock of their lived experience of day to day social life in the small town settings in which they find themselves and their experience of accessing different workplaces. We also include the ways in which they are positioned within these workplaces, depending on the language resources and funds of knowledge available to them.

The Political and Sociolinguistic History of East Timor: Regional Diversity and the Imposition of Different, Centralizing Regimes of Language

The population of Timor-Leste has been linguistically and culturally diverse ever since pre-colonial times. Hajek (2000) notes that estimates regarding the number of languages spoken across the country vary from 15–20, depending on how different local varieties are classified. The most widely spoken language is Tetum. It is spoken as a regional language in several districts. It is also used as a language of wider communication. According to the 2004 National Census (Direcção Nacional de Estatistica 2006, 80), 86 percent of the population of Timor-Leste indicated an ability to speak Tetum, while only 25 percent claimed it as their first language. Several other languages, associated with specific regions of Timor-Leste, were claimed as a first language by significant numbers of speakers. These languages include Fataluku and Makasai, which are widely spoken in eastern districts of Timor-Leste, and Mambai, which is spoken in central districts.

The current contours of linguistic and cultural diversity in Timor-Leste also need to be understood with reference to the chequered political and social history of this small nation in South East Asia, and to the regimes of language that have been imposed on the population at different points in time. The territory of the eastern half of Timor was colonized by the Portuguese in the early sixteenth century, but it was not until the nineteenth century that the Portuguese began to exert greater military and political control. From then onward, until 1974, Portuguese was the sole official language. It was also the medium of instruction in the schools, which were, for the most part, run by the Catholic Church. The role of the Church in the development of schooling in the colony and, in particular, the cultivation of a Portuguese-speaking elite,[1] was consolidated with the signing of a Concordat, in 1940, between the Vatican and the Portuguese government. In this way, as Smythe (2004, 35) has observed, 'the church . . . became the principal agent of Portugal's 'civilizing mission".

In 1974, after the Carnation Revolution[2] in Portugal, a process of decolonization was initiated. The East Timorese began forming political parties and preparing for elections. However, this process was interrupted in 1975 by the brutal invasion of the territory by Indonesian troops, under the orders of the military government in Jakarta (Budiardjo and Liong 1984; Taylor 1999). The Indonesians remained in the east of the island of Timor, as an occupying power, for a further 24 years. Portuguese was replaced as an official language with Bahasa Indonesia and, over time, the state education system was expanded, with Bahasa Indonesia as the only medium of instruction. Thus, from 1975 to 1999, a whole generation of East Timorese only had access to education through the medium of Bahasa Indonesia.

During the long years of the Indonesian occupation, FRETILIN[3]—the pro-independence political party—led a nationalist struggle for independence on three main fronts: an armed front in the mountains of East Timor, a clandestine front in the urban areas, and a diplomatic front outside East Timor. As we have shown, in previous publications (Cabral 2013; Cabral and Martin-Jones 2008), in the context of this struggle, the cultural value and significance of both the Portuguese and Tetum languages changed considerably. As the official language of the East Timorese Resistance to the Indonesian occupation, Portuguese took on a new symbolic and strategic value, in opposition to Bahasa Indonesia. This ideological shift is similar to that which took place in South Africa when English, a former colonial language, came to be redefined as 'People's English' (Peirce 1990, 108), in opposition to Afrikaans.

At the same time, the massive social upheavals brought about by the Indonesian invasion and occupation, and the subsequent dispersal of peoples speaking different regional languages, led to the rapid spread of Tetum as a language of wider communication. During this period, the Catholic Church also became a key institutional base for the use and development of written varieties of Tetum. For example, the Catholic liturgy was translated into Tetum, church services were held in the language, and church choirs began to sing in Tetum (Smythe 2004).

Following political upheavals in Indonesia and increasing international pressure regarding the situation in East Timor, 30 August 1999 saw the organization of a UN-sponsored referendum on the political future of the territory. The East Timorese voted overwhelmingly in favour of Independence.[4] This historic vote was followed by continual turbulence and conflict as the Indonesian troops withdrew, leaving a pro-Indonesian militia to wreak havoc. A transitional UN administration (UNTAET) was eventually established with the brief of paving the way towards Independence. On 20 May 2002, Timor-Leste became the first new nation of the twenty-first century. Under the Constitution of the new nation, Portuguese and Tetum became co-official languages and all other languages were designated as 'national languages . . . to be protected and valued by the state' (Constituent

Assembly 2002, Constitution of the Democratic Republic of Timor-Leste, section 3, 16).

The implementation of the national language policy of this new nation has been taking place in a global age, and, as a consequence, the contours of linguistic diversity in Timor-Leste continue to be shaped in complex ways. Under the terms of the Constitution, English and Bahasa Indonesia are designated as 'working languages' and both are still widely used in international trade and diplomacy and in non-governmental organizations. Bahasa Indonesia is still widely used in local commerce and East Timorese who are able to afford to access international media, to view sports programs or films, do so through Indonesian media channels.

The Transnational Movement of Timorese

The first major outward movement of Timorese came in the wake of the Indonesian invasion and occupation. Individuals and whole families moved, as refugees, with the assistance of the International Red Cross, from Timor to build a new and more tranquil life in another country. Most moved to Australia or Portugal. Some also fled to countries which had also been colonized by Portugal, such as Mozambique or Macau. In the 1990s, during the final phase of the struggle against the Indonesian occupation, a significant number of students sought refuge in foreign embassies in Jakarta, Indonesia, as a consequence of student-led demonstrations in East Timor and in Indonesia (Fernandes 2011). Most of these students eventually made their way to Portugal, where they received financial support for several years to continue their studies.

Since Independence, there has been a new transnational pattern of labour migration. A significant number of young Timorese have been leaving Timor-Leste in search of work in Europe. On Independence, new postcolonial entanglements (Nuttall 2009) were created as Portugal made it possible for all Timorese born before 20 May 20 2002 to apply for Portuguese citizenship and, thus, to the right of residence and employment in Portugal, and elsewhere within the European Union (EU). This political and legal arrangement was designed to alleviate the high level of unemployment among young people in the urban areas of Timor-Leste in the years immediately following Independence.

Many of those who take up this entitlement to apply for Portuguese citizenship seek work in countries in the EU, other than Portugal, notably the United Kingdom (UK), particularly since the recent economic downturn in Portugal. There are no official statistics on the numbers of Timorese currently living and working in the UK, but according to informal estimates, the overall number is circa 10,000. Their remittances (to family members in Timor-Leste) are highly significant: in 2008, it was estimated that remittances to Timor-Leste amounted to $5 million (US dollars) a year (Shuaib 2008).

There have been two overlapping routes into employment in the UK for these young migrants from Timor-Leste: First, some have followed the long established labour migration routes from mainland Portugal, and from Madeira, into the rural sector. This has led to the clustering of East Timorese migrant workers in small towns and in rural areas of England (e.g., in Devon and Lincolnshire) and Northern Ireland (in County Tyrone), where factories linked to food production have been established (e.g., factories designed for the processing and packaging of poultry and other meat). Other Timorese have moved into urban areas (e.g., Bristol, Oxford, Peterborough, and Northwich, near Manchester) and have found work within the service sector (e.g., supermarkets, department stores, online shopping/packing services). Whether they are based in rural or urban areas, they occupy precarious positions with the local economy and are part of what Standing (2010) refers to as the growing 'global precariat'. They are generally recruited by employment agencies and are expected to work to 'flexible schedules'.

Research in Progress in Northern Ireland

Thus far, we have made two field visits to Northern Ireland: in October 2014 and in June 2015. We have conducted participant observation in different public settings, e.g., in the Catholic Church in Dungannon and in local sports events. We have also used still photography and we have gathered different kinds of texts and artefacts, including digital texts (e.g., postings on Facebook). In addition, we have also carried out extended interviews, of a semi-structured nature, with 14 Timorese men and women living and working in Dungannon and in Cookstown. The interviews were carried out primarily in Tetum, with the interaction sometimes involving the blending of Tetum and English or Portuguese. All the interviews were audio-recorded. Seven were individual interviews and the others were joint interviews. They focused on the interviewees' migration trajectories and on their lived experiences of re-mooring in this Northern Irish context.

Diverse Origins, Trajectories, Language Resources, and Funds of Knowledge

From our participant observation and our interviews, it is becoming clear that there is considerable diversity among the young Timorese currently living and working in Dungannon and Cookstown. They come from different districts of Timor-Leste and they speak different national languages (e.g., Fataluku, Makasai, and Mambai), as well as Tetum. Since they are all between the ages of 20 and 45, they have all received their education, either solely or partly, through the medium of Bahasa Indonesia.

They all had some modest material resources when taking the decision to move north—enough to cover the cost of the long haul flight to Europe and their living expenses while seeking employment. Take, for example, the following five cases from among those we have interviewed thus far: The first is a young man who had worked in an Indonesian bank during the Indonesian occupation and, then, after Independence, he had worked with a non-governmental organization (Interview with MFB, June 2015). The second case is that of a male nurse who had worked for Médecins Sans Frontières (MSF) during the three-year UN administration of East Timor and had then gone on to work for the national health service after Independence (Interview with CX, June 2015). The third case is that of a young woman who had worked as a civil servant under the first government of Timor-Leste and who had been trained in accountancy (Interview with JFA, October 2014). The fourth case is that of a young man who had been a driver for a government department after Independence (Interview with DA, June 2015). And the fifth case is that of a young man who had been employed as a porter in a warehouse (carrying sacks of rice) and also as a construction worker (Interview with XA, June 2105).

Some of our interviewees had spent some time in Portugal—as students—before moving to Northern Ireland. They thus had a working knowledge of Portuguese. For example, one interviewee had been one of the students who had sought refuge in an embassy in Jakarta in the 1990s. He had subsequently been given safe passage to Portugal (Interview with HA, June 2015). The young woman mentioned above had spent two years in Portugal receiving her training in the field of accountancy. Another interviewee, a former seminarian, had been working as a translator for UNTAET from 1999 to 2001 and had then won a scholarship to study in Portugal at the University of Coimbra for five years (Interview with FDJ, June 2015).

Two of those we interviewed in June 2015 had been among the very first groups to arrive in Dungannon, in 2001 and 2002, directly from Portugal. They had found work through an employment agency in Portugal (Joint interview with RS and HA, June 2015). Another interviewee had worked in England before moving over to Northern Ireland and had therefore had prior exposure to English in the workplace. All three of these young Timorese spoke English with some ease and fluency.

However, all of those who had arrived within the last few years had come directly from Timor-Leste to join friends and family who were already working in Northern Ireland. Most of this group spoke rather little English and virtually no Portuguese. They spoke a regional Timorese language and they all spoke Tetum. As in Timor-Leste, Tetum had become the main language of wider communication in this Irish context.

Local Conditions of Settlement

Whereas there has been a significant pattern of labour migration to England since the mid-twentieth century, large-scale migration to Northern Ireland is a much more recent phenomenon. Northern Ireland only began to see an increase in inward migration at the beginning of the twenty-first century. Two main political developments lay behind this increase in migration: First, the culmination of the Peace Process on 2 December 1999, and the subsequent change in the political economy of this region of the UK, including inward investment in infrastructure. Second, the accession of different nation-states in Eastern Europe and the Baltic to the European Union, between 2002 and 2008. This expansion of the European Union facilitated labour migration from Poland and from the Baltic States (Corrigan, Mearns, and Thorburn 2015).

The small number of migrants arriving in Northern Ireland in the second half of the twentieth century had, for the most part, settled in urban areas such as Belfast, rather than in small towns like those where our study is based. The local population in towns such as Dungannon, Cookstown, and Portadown had relatively little experience of 'incomers'. For this reason, when Timorese came to Dungannon in the early part of the twenty-first century, they encountered considerable small town hostility to 'incomers' and frequent use of racist language. They also had considerable difficulty in understanding the local variety of Irish English (Interview with RS and HA, June 2015).

However, those who indicated that they had experienced this early hostility also noted that there had been change over time as other groups of migrants had also arrived, from Poland, Portugal, and the Baltic States. A local non-governmental organization had also made a difference: the South Tyrone Empowerment Project (STEP) had been established to provide assistance to local groups of migrant origin, in finding appropriate housing, in dealing with local authorities and with legal issues and with interpreting and translation in bureaucratic encounters and in health care settings. During our field visits, there were some visible signs of a change of ethos in the public domain, at least. There were books for children in different languages in the public library and a multicultural festival had been organized by the Dungannon town council.

Most of the rental accommodation available in Dungannon, Cookstown, and Portadown is in houses. There are few apartments. The cost of renting a whole house is high, so, multiple occupancy is the norm for single people. Some of those who are married also share with family members or friends from Timor-Leste.

Local Conditions of Employment

The Timorese arriving in Dungannon, or other local towns, eventually find work in one of the factories in the region. The largest one—Moy Park— is based in Dungannon. It specializes in chicken processing and packaging (e.g., for sale in supermarkets). Formerly an Irish company, it was taken over by a Brazilian corporation in 2010 (Interview with FDJ, June 2015). This development highlights the increasingly globalized nature of this aspect of food production. Two smaller factories in Cookstown specialize in the packaging of pork and of cheese for the retail sector (Interview with DA, in

Tetum, June 2015). There is also a rendering plant in the area that prepares animal feed (Joint interview with RS and HA, June 2015).

Two local employment agencies act as the gatekeepers for those seeking work. Whilst those who arrived in the first groups of Timorese found work right away, and even had their passage from Portugal paid for (Interview with RS and HA, June 2015), those who have arrived in recent years have found that it takes about five to eight months to get a full-time position. There has been increasing casualization of employment so, initially, newcomers are offered part-time work on an ad hoc basis. Describing the insecurity and the anxiety experienced by him and his colleagues, over an eight-month period, due to the precarity of their situation, one of our interviewees gave the following account: 'Ne'ebé ami telefone ami tau deit iha ulun leten, ami toba iha telefone leten . . . kualker tempu deit [sira] liga ona' (We slept with our phones above our heads . . . they could call us at any time) (Interview with CX, June 2015).

For those who do receive a full-time position, the working hours are long. They work 12-hour shifts, but overtime is no longer paid, since the pattern now alternates each week. They work for five days one week and just two days the following week.

The ability to speak English is increasingly used by employment agencies to select employees. Thus, for example, there is an initial screening process in which applicants are interviewed in English before being given an application form. Those who have some capability in English move into positions of greater responsibility in the workplace (e.g., taking on supervisory duties or assisting veterinary staff with poultry inspection) (Interview with FDJ, June 2015). A linguistic hierarchy of the kind describe by Duchêne, Moyer, and Roberts 2013) is clearly being created through these recruitment and workplace practices.

Creating New Spaces of Solidarity and Conviviality beyond the Workplace

In this section, we turn to the ways in which the young Timorese we interviewed were re-mooring within their local life worlds, away from their respective workplaces. Here, we see them exercising agency in the creation of different spaces of solidarity and conviviality. Two forms of social activity, beyond the home and the workplace, were providing a new focus for them. These activities were contributing to the construction of multifaceted Timorese identities, and diverse linguistic and semiotic resources were being drawn upon in the construction of these identities and forms of belonging.

The 'Core Group'

The first set of activities were those undertaken by a group that called itself the 'Core Group'. This group had already established a Timorese choir and a dance troupe, called Fitun Timor (Timor Star). The choir was linked to the Catholic Church and it included both men and women. It was founded by the former seminarian mentioned earlier. He told us that his main motivation in founding the choir was to 'help people vary their activities . . . to make their lives more meaningful' (Interview with FDJ in English, June 2015).

We focus briefly here on the founder of the group, since he played a significant leadership role, drawing on his extensive language resources and funds of knowledge. He had received his education in Timor at a Catholic school and had learned both English and Portuguese, as well as Bahasa Indonesia. He also spoke Tetum and Mambai. He did a wide range of voluntary work in Dungannon, assisting Timorese with the writing of formal letters in English and doing translations of official documents. He also worked as an interpreter/translator for STEP and for the local authority on an occasional basis (about once a week).

He had plans to build up the 'Core Group' as a formally constituted community organization, with the assistance of STEP, with a view to making the Timorese presence more visible within this region of Northern Ireland. In the interview with us, he also talked about the idea of arranging events to coincide with key religious festivals and to commemorate key events of political significance in the history of Timor-Leste. He mentioned two events in particular: First, 12 November, which is the anniversary of a massacre in 1991, at Santa Cruz cemetery, Dili, of students attending a funeral of a student activist (Interview with FDJ, June 2105). This was the first atrocity by Indonesian troops to be have been filmed by the international media. Second, the award of the Nobel Peace Prize, in 1996, to Bishop Belo (the Bishop of Dili at the time) and to José Ramos Horta, the spokesperson for the East Timorese Resistance.

As a former seminarian, the founder of the 'Core Group' had been able to forge links with the Catholic Church in Northern Ireland. He had made arrangements for the choir to contribute to Sunday services, at St. Patrick's Church in Dungannon, on the first Sunday of every month. In addition, he had also arranged for them to perform in the Cathedral in Armagh.

The choir sang primarily in Tetum, like many church choirs in Timor-Leste, but they were also adding hymns and religious music in Portuguese and English to their repertoire, because of their new commitment to performing in local religious settings. They were led on the piano by the choir founder. He was also hoping to encourage the singing of Timorese folk songs in Tetum. He told us that he wanted to 'make people think about their origins through the music' (Interview with FDJ in English, June 2015).

The dancers in the Fitun Timor group were all women. The musicians who accompanied them were all men, including the founder of the Core Group, who played the guitar. Just before our second field visit to Northern Ireland, they had performed traditional Timorese dance at the multicultural festival organized by the Dungannon Town Council. During the festival, photographs of the group were posted on Facebook. These photographs showed the women wearing Timorese *tais* (traditional woven cloth worn on ceremonial occasions).

Both the choir and the Timor Star dance troupe were constructing a Timorese identity based primarily on symbols of cultural heritage. The Facebook photograph in Figure 4.1 below showed the women in the troupe wearing the traditional Timorese *tais*. The music that they danced to was also traditional Timorese music. Choirs are a salient part of traditional religious life in Timor-Leste, where a very high proportion of the population is Catholic. The Dungannon choir was singing in Tetum, though they were broadening their repertoire in this new context to include English and Portuguese. The 'Core Group' had plans to widen the scope of their activities so as to reach a wider range of audiences, representing Timorese-ness in ways based primarily on cultural heritage. They also saw the role of their organization as a means of bringing Timorese together through the observance of Catholic festivals and through commemoration of key national events.

Figure 4.1 Performance at Dungannon Multicultural Festival by the Fitun Timor Dance Troupe (Posted on YouTube by a Member of the Troupe)

The Timorese Football Teams and Clubs

In June 2015, we learned that there were nine Timorese football teams in the Dungannon/Cookstown area. They are listed in Table 4.1 below:

The names of the teams and clubs indexed the identity of the players in different ways. The players in FC Tahi Calu and FC Moko United were mostly Fataluku speakers, from Lospalos, in the Eastern region of Timor-Leste and the names of their teams signified a regional identity. Similarly, the regional identity of the players in FC Matebian was indexed in the name of their team: They were mostly from the Baucau area, also in the east, and most of the players spoke Makasai. The Young Crocs team was organized

Table 4.1 The Names of the Timorese football Teams in Dungannon and Cookstown

Name of team	English translation	Languages used in the name and the acronym
FC[5] Lao Rai United	FC Travellers United	English, Tetum & English
FC Estrela Oriente	FC Eastern Star	English & Portuguese
Fitun Unidade (based in Cookstown)	Star United	Tetum & Portuguese
FC Tahi Calu	FC Rough Sea[6]	English & Fataluku
FC Moko United	FC Sons United	English & Fataluku
The Young Crocs	-	English
AS Bidau	AS[7] + Name of a neighbourhood in Dili, Timor-Leste	
FC Matebian	FC + Name of a mountain in the east of Timor-Leste	
Ramkabian	Compound name, including three mountains in Timor-Leste: Ramelau, Kablake, and Matebian	

for Timorese boys, aged 14–19, who were growing up in Northern Ireland. The name of their team signified their orientation to English.

The six other teams included a mix of adult players, originating from different districts of Timor-Leste.[8] In these football clubs, members were represented as being Timorese and as having a shared national identity. When we conducted a joint interview with the two organizers of the Ramkabian club, they explained that they had included reference to three different mountains in Timor-Leste as a way of emphasizing inclusivity, dealing with difference, and the building of solidarity. One of the organizers outlined the aims of the club. Blending Portuguese with Tetum as he spoke, he pointed out that one of the aims was: '*Criar amizade que [é] forte*, laos ba iha neé deit maibe iha fatin hotu-hotu' (Creating friendship that is strong, not only for this [club] but everywhere) (Interview with RS and HA, June 7, 2015—all Portuguese words are shown in italics).

FC Lao Rai United was also represented in a similar way. One of the organizers said that he saw the football tournaments as giving an opportunity for Timorese from different districts of Timor-Leste to get to know one another. He also pointed out to us that this football club took care of the welfare of its players well beyond matters pertaining to football. For example, if someone needed help to pay for a return trip to Timor-Leste (e.g., for a family funeral), club funds were contributed towards the cost of the air-fare. All those associated with the club paid £10 each per month towards the running of the club. The organizer also noted (in English) that all the football clubs had grown in importance and had become 'better organized in the last few years' (Interview with MFB, June 5, 2015). Two of the players in the Lao Rai club had been in the national team of Timor-Leste before migrating to Northern Ireland and had brought a professional touch to their activities.

Our interviews with club organizers gave us a window on the amount of organization that went into the clubs. As with the founder of the 'Core

Figure 4.2 The Logos for Three of the Football Teams—Posted on Facebook by Members of the Teams

Group', those who took on a leadership role around football were able to communicate in English with some ease and fluency. The club managers had to raise funding for the team and for the tournaments. They also had to book pitches for the tournaments and hire Irish referees. In addition, they had to arrange local sponsorship. A local law firm sponsored Ramkabian and a local taxi firm in Cookstown sponsored Fitun Unidade. The sponsorship funded the purchase of football shirts and jackets for the players, along with medals and cups for the football tournaments. Each of the clubs had its own colours and logo, giving it a distinctive identity. We include in Figure 4.2 above the logos for FC Lao Rai United, Ramkabian, and the Young Crocs.

All these logos incorporate images that link them to Timor-Leste. This includes: The map of Timor-Leste in the logo for FC Lao Rai United; the dominant image of the crocodile[9] in the logo for the Young Crocs; the star in the national flag and the colours—red, yellow, black, and white—of the flag that appear in the logos for the Ramkabian and Young Crocs teams.

Colour was used symbolically in other ways too: In the design of the football shirts, the jackets and even the ribbons for the medals and the cups—all incorporated the red, yellow, black, and white of the national flag. FC Lao Rai United had also commissioned the weaving of a Timorese *tais* in yellow, black, and white with the name of the club incorporated into it. This *tais* is shown in Figure 4.3 below.

The football tournaments in Dungannon are scheduled to coincide with dates of national, political significance in Timor-Leste. They are held in and around 30 August (the anniversary of the Referendum in 1999) and 20 May (the anniversary of Independence). In Figure 4.4 below, we include a photograph of the cup won by Fitun Unidade in the 2014 tournament of 20 May, along with the medals won by individual players. The date of the tournament is engraved on the base of the cup.

Figure 4.3 A Black, White, and Yellow *tais* with the Name of FC Lao Rai United

(Photograph by Estêvão Cabral)

Figure 4.4 The Cup and Medals Won by Fitun Unidade During the 20 May Tournament in 2014. Photographs by Estêvão Cabral.

Reflections on these Diverse Re-Mooring Practices

The diverse re-mooring practices that we have described in the section above have their origins in social and cultural life in Timor-Leste, past and present, but they are also being shaped in new ways in different contact zones in the Irish context. Narrowing our research lens and focusing on the linguistic and semiotic resources being drawn upon in different re-mooring activities gave us revealing insights into the broader social significance of these activities and into the complex and multi-layered processes of identification at work in this migration context. If we compare the current re-mooring practices of the Core Group and the football clubs, along with the range of activities they aspire to in the future, we see that there were significant differences in their ways of representing what counts as being Timorese and, at the same time, there were some overlaps.

The Core Group (the church choir and the Fitun Timor dancers) were primarily orienting to emblems of cultural heritage: To folk song, to choral music of a religious nature and to traditional forms of dress (e.g., the *tais*). In contrast, the football clubs were constructing Timorese identities in a more complex and varied nature, relating to both the present and the past. Occasional visual symbols of heritage (e.g., the *tais* and the crocodile) were interwoven with contemporary symbols of national identity (e.g., the colours of the flag) and, at the same time, with the language and symbols of international football league culture. As we saw in Table 4.1, the actual naming practices were creative, multilingual, and quite hybrid in nature. Whereas some of the names of clubs asserted a regional identity using particular languages, names of places, or landmarks, others espoused an inclusive and/or national identity, using compound names and Tetum or Portuguese, the national official languages. English was present in all the names prefixed by the acronym FC, echoing the wider conventions of football leagues in the Anglophone world.

Despite this diversity in the team-specific practices of identification, the scheduling of the tournaments around dates of national significance in Timor-Leste foregrounded the shared national identity of the players. The tournaments brought all the clubs together in sports events so that, in this Irish context, they could be seen as part of one diasporic 'community', with its origins in the nation of Timor-Leste. Of particular significance is that details of these tournaments were regularly posted on Facebook and viewed by friends and family members in Timor-Leste and across the diaspora, in other regions of the UK, in Portugal, and in Australia. These regular postings were part of wider digital practices and uses of mobile technology across the transnationally connected Timorese diaspora.

There were some overlaps with the Core Group in that the members of this group had aspirations to move beyond their current activities in music and dance and to become a formally constituted community organization, backed by the local STEP (the local NGO). One of their motives was to bring the Timorese in South Tyrone together to commemorate key events in the recent political history of Timor-Leste.

So, in the different re-mooring practices unfolding in this Irish context, we see multi-layered processes of identification at work among the Timorese: At one level, we see a collective orientation to the new nation that has been constructed out of a long history of struggle—a struggle that is still within the living memory of all the adults in Northern Ireland today—and, at another level, we see other processes of identification linked to personal interests in sport or cultural inheritance or linked to the construction of gendered identities[10] or to the construction of identities based on region of origin.

From what we have gleaned thus far, it is clear that the particular migration trajectories, communicative repertoires, and funds of knowledge of some Timorese in this setting in Northern Ireland has positioned them in ways that enable them to take a lead in setting up group activities of a distinctive nature, whether it be a football club with a particular ethos, or cultural groups oriented to particular aspects of Timorese cultural heritage. So, for some, there is considerable scope for individual agency and voice in the process of re-mooring and in the construction of particular Timorese identities. However, at the same time, through the process of re-mooring, a strong sense of shared history and belonging, tied to a new and distant nation, is also emerging.

Concluding Comments

Our aim in this chapter has been to make a contribution to the new sociolinguistics of multilingualism and mobility, focusing in on one particular transnational population movement from the global south to the north and west. The case of the Timorese migrants in Northern Ireland throws the following points into sharp focus: First, the importance of moving away from purely synchronic description and analysis and of taking account of the historical specificity of migration movements, of the particular nature of the south/north entanglements involved and of the ways in which memories of key moments in past political struggles, along with emblems of national identity, contribute to the forging of a sense of solidarity and belonging.

Second, the case of the Timorese migrants in Northern Ireland demonstrates the value of adopting the notion of trajectory as a conceptual compass: It enables us to foreground three processes: (1) the ways in which educational backgrounds, combined with migration trajectories, shape the communicative repertoires, language resources, and funds of knowledge available to migrants; (2) the ways in which migrants are positioned with regard to the navigation of new work worlds depending on the linguistic resources and funds of knowledge available to them; and (3) the ways in which individual migrants, with particular linguistic repertoires and resources, are able to assume local leadership roles.

And, finally, the dual focus on mobility and on the processes and practices involved in mooring makes it possible to counter-balance our accounts of detachment and dislocation with vivid and revealing insights into the situated ways in which moorings and re-moorings occur, foregrounding the agency of those involved. In addition, close attention to the linguistic and other semiotic practices of different groups enables us to build an understanding of the complex ways in which forms of re-mooring activity come to be imbued with social meanings.

Notes

1 Only 20 percent of the population had access to schools by 1975 (Taylor 1999).
2 The Carnation Revolution in Portugal was led by military officers who had fought in the long-drawn out colonial wars in Africa (e.g., in Angola, Guinea-Bissau, and Mozambique). The aims of the Revolution were twofold: (1) To bring to an end a long period of Fascist dictatorship; and (2) to initiate the process of decolonization in Portuguese colonies.
3 Frente Revolucionária de Timor-Leste Independente (Revolutionary Front for an Independent East Timor).
4 78.5 percent of the population voted in favour of Independence (Fernandes 2011).
5 Although the acronym here comes *before* the name and follows the word order used in the names of football clubs in the Portuguese league, according to one of the club organizers, it actually stands for the English words: 'Football Club'.
6 Literally 'Male sea'. This name could be read as a geographical reference to the South East of Timor-Leste, where the tides are known to be stronger. It also has a masculine connotation since, in Fataluku (as in Tetum), a 'calm sea' is described metaphorically as 'female sea', while a 'rough sea' is described as a 'male sea'.
7 AS is an acronym commonly used in the Italian football league (as in AS Milan), but according to one of our interviewees, it stands for the Portuguese word Associação (Association).
8 Whereas their name, AS Bidau, refers to a neighbourhood of Dili, the players actually had mixed backgrounds.
9 The image of a crocodile is often evoked in Timor-Leste since the land is said to have the shape of a crocodile.
10 Our focus thus far has been on football clubs for men and boys, but we have recently learned that there is also a woman's football team in Dungannon.

References

Adey, P. 2006. 'If Mobility Is Everything Then It Is Nothing: Towards a Relational Politics of (Im)Mobilities'. *Mobilities* 1 (1): 75–94.
Ahmed, S., C. Castaneda, A. M. Fortier, and M. Sheller, eds. 2003. *Uprootings/Regroundings: Questions of Home and Migration*. Oxford: Berg.
Blommaert, J. 2010. *The Sociolinguistics of Globalization*. Cambridge: Cambridge University Press.
Brah, A. 1996. *Cartographies of Diaspora: Contesting Identities*. London: Routledge.
Brenner, N. 2004. *New State Spaces: Urban Governance and the Rescaling of Statehood*. Oxford: Oxford University Press.
Budiardjo, C., and L. S. Liong. 1984. *The War against East Timor*. London: Zed Books.
Cabral, E. 2013. 'The Development of Language Policy in a Global Age'. In *Bilingual Education and Language Policy in the Global South*, edited by J. Arthur Shoba and F. Chimbutane, 83–103. New York: Routledge.

Cabral, E., and M. Martin-Jones. 2008. 'Writing the Resistance: Literacy in East Timor 1975–1999'. *International Journal of Bilingual Education and Bilingualism* 11 (2): 149–69.

Constituent Assembly. 2002. *The Constitution of the Republic of Timor-Leste*. Dili: República Democrática de Timor-Leste (RDTL).

Corrigan, Karen P., A. J. Mearns, and J. Thorburn. 2015. *From Home to Here: Stories of Migration Old and New*. Belfast, UK: Nicholson Bass.

Cresswell, T. 2002. 'Introduction: Theorizing Place'. In *Mobilizing Place, Placing Mobility*, edited by G. Verstraete and T. Cresswell, 11–32. Amsterdam: Rodopi.

Da Costa Cabral, I. 2010. *From Dili to Dungannon: A Case Study of Two Bilingual Migrant Families from East-Timor*. Unpublished MA thesis, University of Birmingham, UK.

Direcção Nacional de Estatística (National Statistics Directorate). 2006. *National Priority Tables: Census of Population and Housing, 2004*. Dili, Timor-Leste: República Democrática de Timor-Leste (RDTL), Direcção Nacional de Estatística and United Nations Population Fund (UNFPA).

Duchêne, A., and M. Heller, eds. 2012. *Language in Late Capitalism: Pride and Profit*. New York: Routledge.

Duchêne, A., M. Moyer, and C. Roberts, eds. 2013. *Language, Migration and Social Inequalities*. Bristol, UK: Multilingual Matters.

Fernandes, C. 2011. *The Independence of East-Timor*. Brighton: Sussex Academic Press.

Fortier, A. M. 2000. *Migrant Belongings: Memory, Space, Identity*. Oxford: Berg.

Hajek, J. 2000. 'Language Planning and the Sociolinguistic Environment in East Timor: Colonial Practice and Changing Language Ecologies'. *Current Issues in Language Planning* 1: 400–15.

Hannam, K., M. Sheller, and J. Urry. 2006. 'Editorial: Mobilities, Immobilities and Moorings'. *Mobilities* 1 (1): 1–22.

Heller, M. 2007. 'Bilingualism as Ideology and Practice'. In *Bilingualism: A Social Approach*, edited by M. Heller, 1–22. Basingstoke, Hants.: Palgrave Macmillan.

———. 2011. *Paths to Post-Nationalism: A Critical Ethnography of Language and Identity*. Oxford: Oxford University Press.

Heller, M., L. A. Bell, M. Daveluy, M. McLaughlin, and H. Noël. 2016. *Sustaining the Nation: The Making and Moving of Language and Nation*. Oxford: Oxford University Press.

Kress, G. 2010. *Multimodality: A Social Semiotic Approach to Communication*. London: Routledge.

Nuttall, S. 2009. *Entanglement*. Johannesburg: Wits University Press.

Peirce, B. N. 1990. 'The Author Responds'. *TESOL Quarterly* 24 (1): 105–12.

Pratt, M. L. 1987. 'Linguistic Utopias'. In *The Linguistics of Writing: Arguments between Language and Literature*, edited by N. Fabb, D. Attridge, A. Durant, and C. MacCabe, 48–66. Manchester: Manchester University Press.

Shuaib, F. 2008. *East Timor Country Report*. Canberra, Australia: Department of Foreign Affairs and Trade. Retrieved from http://aid.dfat.gov.au/Publications/Documents/etimor_study.pdf. (Accessed 9 March 2014).

Smythe, P. 2004. *The Heaviest Blow: Responses within the Catholic Church to the East Timorese Issue*. London and New Brunswick: Transaction.

Standing, G. 2010. *The Precariat*. London: Bloomsburg.

Taylor, J. G. 1999. *East Timor: The Price of Freedom*. London: Zed Press.

Urry, J. 2007. *Mobilities*. Cambridge: Polity Press.

5　South-North Trajectories and Language Repertoires

Kasper Juffermans & Bernardino Tavares

Introduction

As a result of relatively affordable technologies of long-distance travel and communication, we live more than ever in an age of mobility and transnational flows (Appadurai 1996). Never before have so many people been able to connect with so many people across such long distances, through physical travel or digital communication. So, twenty-first century migrants are no longer just émigrés and immigrants but typically transmigrants, i.e., mobile persons going back and forth and sustaining multiple engagements and relationships between homelands and new homes. 'The life a person lives as a migrant,' however, Graw and Schielke (2012b, 10) note, 'is often but half of his or her reality, and yet the other half remains often invisible to an outside observer, and often seems also less of a concern for national politics which, in turn, influences the distribution of research funding.' Whereas Vertovec (2010, 86) may be right or wrong in stating that 'more people are now moving from more places, through more places, to more places' (Czaika and de Haas 2014 argue against this), people are now evidently in a state of 'involuntary immobility', i.e., aspiring to migrate but practically incapable to do so (Carling 2002).

Flows of people, texts, and meanings across the globe and globalization and mobility have emerged as major themes in the study of language in society. Work on language and globalization generally points at the relativity of functions, meanings, and uses of language in the increasingly mobile, shifting, and intercultural contexts of daily interaction and encounters. It emphasizes change and fluidity rather than stability and fixity of language and communication, and sees globalization both as a cause of homogenization of language and culture and a source of diversification of linguistic and cultural practices, i.e., as a two-way process that is simultaneously localizing the global and globalizing the local.

But whereas sociolinguistics has recognized power and social class issues in human mobility, from asylum seekers and migrant workers to elite forms of tourism, the new sociolinguistics has perhaps insufficiently engaged with those that are excluded from these flows, with those that don't travel well but remain invisible in global ethnoscapes and transcultural flows. Sociolinguistics arguably struggles with the 'not-there', the 'absent presences', with that which and those that are 'left out' (Kulick 2005). Resonating with arguments in the anthropology of mobility (Carling 2002; Graw and Schielke 2012a), this chapter introduces a notion of desire or aspiration in studying language and migration. Between migrant and non-migrant identities, there are migrant identifications and imaginations which are articulated in local language practices and interactions.

This chapter outlines two conceptual tools that are useful in a sociolinguistics of globalization that considers mobility within a context of growing mobile inequalities—trajectories and repertoires—and illustrates their potential on the basis of data from an ongoing project on language and migration between Lusophone West Africa and Europe.

Repertoires

Repertoire belongs to the classic toolkit of sociolinguistics. Formulated in its most general terms, a repertoire is the totality of linguistic-semiotic resources available in a given space to individuals or a community in local communicative practices. Rymes (2014) explains that repertoire was initially a radical concept in linguistics meant to challenge purist orthodoxies and destabilize linguistic definitions of language as self-evident, *sui generis* entities. Gumperz (1964) coined the term at a time when scholars of language developed an interest in the social life of language and began to conduct fieldwork in addition to philological methods. It is important to note that fieldwork—in India and Norway for Gumperz—is at the root of the development of sociolinguistics as a discipline. Repertoires describe the range of languages circulating in a community that people strategically draw upon in their transactions on the market place, involving not necessarily full competence in each of the individual languages, but also minimal forms of competence.

Rymes explains that Gumperz' work remained by and large concerned with language: 'he never expanded that concept to include other features of interaction that are beyond language' (7). Gumperz' notion of repertoire was also concerned with the 'speech community' as a whole or with individuals as members of that community. Under globalization communities are becoming more and more complex and diverse, up to the point where the usefulness of a notion as community itself, like language, is being questioned and rethought. Community is commonly conceptualized now either as a myth or historical invention, i.e., as 'imagined communities' (Anderson [1983] 1991) or as more or less flexible, transient networks of members engaged in shared activities, i.e., as 'communities of practice' revolving around *doing* rather than *being* (Lave and Wenger 1991).

Han (2013), for instance, draws on the notion of repertoire in her study of African migrant traders' communication and language choices in Guangzhou (China). For her, language repertoire also includes literacy practices and emergent forms of multilingualism. Drawing on Blommaert's (2008) *Grassroots Literacy*, she proposes the term grassroots multilingualism to show how individuals develop their linguistic repertoire locally without formal instruction. For Han, a linguistic repertoire is 'the totality of the different degrees of knowledge and functionality of all of the linguistic varieties learned in a person's life trajectories' (86). Borrowing Bourdieu's notion of capital, she stresses that people's life trajectories are shaped by the accumulation of material and symbolic (including linguistic) capital. For instance, a (Francophone) Guinean storeowner in Africa Town in Guangzhou self-reported that he could speak a little English and had learned a little Chinese from friends in Guangzhou but could use colloquial Mandarin quite effectively in his business transactions.

Independently of each other, Busch (2012) and Blommaert and Backus (2013) have recently revisited the concept of repertoire, situating it not primarily within communities, as Gumperz did, but within individuals. One's repertoire reflects the spaces and networks one navigates and bears the traces of one's biography. Repertoires are dynamic and constantly changing: As one proceeds through life and encounters new individuals or participates in new networks and institutions, one is socialized into new registers, styles, genres and varieties which supplant and supplement previously acquired ones (Blommaert and Backus 2013). A difference in Busch' treatment of repertoire from that of Blommaert and Backus is that for Busch, desire or future potential is as important in the formation of multilingual subjectivities as the traces of one's individual or collective past: 'a linguistic repertoire may not only include what one has but also what one does not have, what one was refused but is still present as desire' (509).

Language desire is developed in more detail by Takahashi (2013) as an alternative for the more simplistic notion of motivation in second language learning. Other than motivation, desire is 'socially and historically constructed at the intersection between individual practices and macro-discourses' (153), thus located not only within but also around the individual learner. Takahashi's study explores the language learning efforts and frustrations of Japanese women studying in Australia, in terms of their desire for creating a new lifestyle and transforming their identities. Their desire is seen against the background of a more general Japanese desire (*akogare*) for English and Western countries as well as for personal (romantic) relationships with Western men. Repertoires (whether of language, identity, etc.) are therefore as much indexes of people's past as of their present and future actions and identifications. The notion of trajectory is meant to capture the changes over time in one's repertoire as movement between past, present, and future. This brings us to our second conceptual tool.

Trajectories

The notion of trajectory is a recurrent theme across the humanities and social sciences from applied linguistics, migration studies, and anthropology to education and occurs in collocation with themes as diverse as 'life', 'text', 'learning', 'migration', 'family', 'work', 'career', 'home ownership', 'population', 'integration' and 'policy'. The notion is, however, often only little theorized and taken as a common sense metaphor for movement across time and space.

In its most general sense, a trajectory can be defined as 'the path that a moving object follows through space as a function of time' (Wikipedia entry: *trajectory*, Dec 2014–Jun 2016). Such a moving object may be an apple falling from a tree, a planet moving in an orbit around its sun, or a human being commuting to work. We are concerned here neither with trajectories at the astronomical scale of planets nor at the microscopic scale of daily micro-movements, but with trajectories at the scale of the lifespan. The notion of trajectory is straightforward to imagine, but in this straightforwardness lies a danger of seeing trajectories linearly as movement from A to B (or a sequence of movements between A and B) without understanding the complexity of relations and the inequalities between A and B (Blommaert, Collins, and Slembrouck 2005). Such lines, of course, are rarely straight lines, and are entangled in complex and often unpredictable ways with other trajectories:

> because of the often instantaneous, spontaneous, improvised and random nature of the lines that unfold through individual biographies, and because of the equally unplanned ways in which these individual biographies get caught up and become entangled in other lines and networks of physical and mental contact with other people and other discourses, practices and ideas, the line of one's life is rarely a straight line forward.
>
> (De Boeck 2012, 81)

In medical sociology *trajectory* has been used in reference to 'a course of illness over time plus the actions taken by patients, families and health professionals to manage or shape the course' (Corbin and Strauss 1992). An illness trajectory consists of various phases or episodes a patient lives through, from diagnosis to recovery or death in the case of terminal illnesses. De Saint-Georges and Filliettaz (2008) applied this notion to learning and interaction in vocational training and defined *situated trajectories of learning* as the 'temporal organization of collective activities aimed at creating the conditions within which learning can take place' as opposed to the cognitive processes underlying the course of learning, which—like the course of illness—we have little control over (de Saint-Georges and Filliettaz 2008). They emphasize that 'trajectories are . . . not fixed in their structure but evolve as part of social and interactional dynamics'.

In a longitudinal study of students transitioning to secondary education in Germany, Budach (2014) critiqued the idealized secondary education trajectories of the late-modern nation-state. Since the beginning of industrialization and the rise of the nation-state, she explains, formal education was gradually reconceived from heterogeneous, freely developed trajectories of individual *Bildung* through voyage, discovery, and experience, to homogenized and rationalized 'straight lines without any detour or aberration and at fast pace' in the service of the labour market. Whereas the former is flexible and unpredictable and can be compared to 'wayfaring' (backpacking is a more contemporary term), the latter can be compared to a package holiday, the modalities of which are pre-set in terms of locale, duration, and activities. Budach shows how consequently language learning is valued very differently in primary and secondary education, from a flexible tool of learning and social inclusion into a rigid target of assessment and social distinction. The notion of trajectory, loosely theorized as a metaphor for how individuals pass through educational institutions and curricular content over time, serves to explain how learning experiences and outcomes are shaped by different cultures and environments of learning, and 'managed' by parents, schoolteachers, and learners themselves. Like Corbin and Strauss (1992) and de Saint-Georges and Filliettaz (2008), she leaves room for a degree of agency distributed across multiple actors and institutions within biological and historical conditions.

For de Costa (2010), learner trajectories are key to understanding the structural and agentive forces that shape adult English second language education. De Costa draws on Bourdieu's concepts of capital, habitus, and field to explain the language and literacy development of one Hmong-speaking Laotian refugee to the U.S. Capital, understood as participants' (and the host society's) investment in language learning in view of increasing the individual's linguistic, cultural, and economic resources, is in itself not sufficient to conceptualize learning. It needs to be 'situated', in Lave and Wenger's (1991) sense, in habitus formation and transformation—i.e., the durable but not eternal skills, dispositions, values, and tastes a learner embodies—as well as in the social field of English language teaching in America. De Costa paints an image of an agentive language learner that is neither free of its own biography and wider ideological and political agendas, nor determined by it.

Migration researchers have argued for a trajectory perspective of migration, i.e., for seeing migration as a dynamic process unfolding over time. This process is managed by immigration and emigration regimes as well as individual agentive strategies in response to changing regimes. Ho (2011), for instance, describes the experiences of Singaporean highly-skilled transnationals in London in terms of 'accidental navigators' and 'self-initiated global careerists' and emphasizes the dynamics of migrant strategies, subjectivities, and categories over time. Their migration experience, she points out, is often sliced into episodes with shifts in visa status and social positionings (118). Grillo (2007, 204–5) has criticized postmodernists for merging 'different states of in-between-ness' and for celebrating cultural hybridity while overlooking social class in analyses of transmigration. One of these postmodernists, for Grillo, is Appadurai: 'What Appadurai says is sometimes astonishingly naïve: 'Everyone has relatives working abroad' (1996, 171). How true! We are all transnationals now, but some more than others, and certainly in different ways.' Carling's (2002) aspiration/capacity framework shares many of these concerns, but complements and complicates the picture with involuntary immobility as a state of being.

A trajectory approach to migration and language attempts to make sense of the practical and cognitive challenges, structural and agentive forces, and the changing subject positions in individual projects of (trans)migration, *after*, *during*, and *before* migration.

Our Research Context and Participants

Let us now move to our specific research context. Our project, which is funded by the FNR, Luxembourg, explores sociolinguistic trajectories and repertories of both aspiring and accomplished migrants from a multi-sited perspective both in the South (Cape Verde and Guinea-Bissau) and in the North (Luxembourg). We will here report on our work in the South, focusing on mobilities in the making and on migrants before they become visible as migrants from the viewpoint of the states in the North to which they aspire to travel.

The two countries of fieldwork, both in Atlantic West Africa, are intimately linked historically. Colonized by Portugal, Guinea-Bissau and Cape Verde gained their Independence in 1974 and 1975 through a long joint struggle led by the PAIGC (*Partido Africano da Independência de Guiné-Bissau e Cabo Verde*). The party's founder and leader until his assassination in 1973, Amilcar Cabral, was of mixed Cape Verdean and Bissau-Guinean descent and is still regarded as the father of both nations. Both countries are presently member states of the Community of Portuguese Language Countries and have many cultural and linguistic commonalities, including a mutual migrant presence, and largely mutually intelligible national languages (Cape Verdean and Guinean Creole). Their political and economic situations, however, are quite distinct. Since Independence, Cape Verde has been relatively stable and peaceful, whereas Guinea-Bissau has known successive coups d'état, military governments, and a civil war (1998–99). This reflects on their contrastive economic situations, with Cape Verde representing one of the more prosperous West African states and Guinea-Bissau being identified among the world's least developed countries (cf. Human Development Index) and as a fragile or failing state (Bybee 2011).

We've conducted parallel fieldwork—Bernardino in Cape Verde and Kasper in Guinea-Bissau—for about six months between January 2014 and March 2016. Bernardino is a native of Cape Verde but had been living outside of Cape Verde (mainly in Portugal) for seven years prior to the start of the project, when he moved to Luxembourg with his family. He is from Santiago Island but his fieldwork concentrates on the islands of Santo Antão and São Vicente (Mindelo). Kasper grew up in the Netherlands and Belgium and has been a regular visitor to West Africa (especially The Gambia, see Juffermans 2015) since 2001, but began learning Creole only at the start of this project.

Our fieldwork consisted of observations of and conversations about (foreign) language learning in function of migration, mobility, and travelling—which in Creole is denoted by the same word, '*bias/viaji*'. After initial contacts and friendships were established, we interviewed (and re-interviewed) several dozen young Luso-Africans about their language life and mobile experiences or aspirations. Participants were approached in meeting places for foreign language learners (e.g., language schools) or were suggested on referral through other participants. All interviews were open-ended and only minimally structured and lasted from 15 minutes to over an hour. Bernardino interviewed in Cape Verdean Creole (with occasional insertions of Portuguese and French) and Kasper in English and French (with occasional insertions in Guinean Creole and Mandinka).

Our study takes a narrative approach in analyzing the interview data. The participants' responses are taken as autobiographic accounts (Pavlenko 2007) and are analyzed not as chronological histories but as narrations of multilingual and mobile/immobile selves. Key events and anecdotes are taken to reconstruct their language lives, their mobile experiences and/or desires, and the social worlds in which they are situated. In what follows we explore the language lives and learning histories, (unfinished) travels and further mobile aspirations, and changing social status of three young Luso-Africans.

Three Young Luso-Africans on the Move

Herina (her real name) is in her early twenties and is a housemaid in Mindelo on the island of São Vicente in Cape Verde. In addition to Cape Verdean Creole and Portuguese, she speaks a little French and English. Her closest relatives (parents, brothers, and sisters) are all in Italy. Despite her family's strong transnationalism, she herself epitomizes the figure of the involuntary immobile. She has a long track-record of failures in trying to travel to Europe. She has applied for visas seven times (to the Netherlands, Italy, and France), but she got all of them refused. When asked about the reasons the embassies and consulates gave her for their refusals, she said: '*nau nunka es dize nada, sinplismenti es da kes papel, es ta rikuza vist mas nada*' [no, they never say anything, they simply give the papers back, they deny visa and nothing else].

She has spent a lot of money applying for visas and she is still saving from her low-paid job as well as counting on her family in order to prepare and apply again. She is resilient and determined to move to Italy or anywhere else in Europe. She pointed out: '*N ta prefiri ba pa Italia, tud manera tud jenti ta la*' [I prefer to go to Italy, anyway all my relatives are there]. Family reunion is her migration goal, but since she is adult now it is difficult to get a visa through this mode. Furthermore, her job category (as a housemaid) and her young age position her as a potential over-stayer for the immigration officials. Her experience suggests that failing in getting a visa once makes it even more difficult for the next time and that rejections can turn into a spiral process.

Herina is not naïve about migrant life, and is very aware of the hardship and difficulties many migrants face in this world. But that awareness does not make migration any less desirable for her; in contrary, it makes her mobile aspirations a matter of dignity and a moral endeavour. She pointed out:

txeu jenti ta dize ki emigrason e iluzon purk la bu ta dize ki bu ta ten un vida midjor em termos economico, mas si nu ben spial el ne asin. Purk asves immigrant ta pasa mas difikuldad du ki nos ki ten stadu li . . . asves bu podi trabadja y es ka rikonpensob manera ki es divia	many people say that emigration is an illusion because there you say that you will have a better life in economic terms, but if we come to see it, it is not like that. Because sometimes immigrants face more difficulties than us who have been staying here . . . sometimes you can work and they do not compensate you as they should

She is what Åkesson (2008) termed 'a transnational at home'. She is very informed about life in Europe by friends and relatives abroad. Their stories and experiences are important push and pulls of her mobility. However, she is very aware about the harsh realities of immigrant life in Europe. She pointed out that going to Europe is not about fun but hard work, '*Europa bu ta bai mas e pa ba trabadja, pasa sabi pasa sabi bu ta pasa sabi na bo tera*' [one goes to Europe mostly for working, having fun you have it in your country].

Herina's case shows that a strong family network abroad is in itself not enough to accomplish migration. The case also shows that decisions about migration or non-migration taken by European consular services are far from transparent for applicants such as Herina. For Herina, acquiring the rights to travel is a long and cumbersome journey with many disappointments along the road. Globalization manifests itself to Herina, and many others like her, mostly in terms of its absence or elusiveness (cf. Graw 2012): Europe is extremely visible and present in Herina's life, but Herina herself, with her ambitions and skills set, remains invisible and absent in the North. Schengen's migration regime successfully keeps her out of Europe, in place, denying her access to her family and the European labour market. Her reasons and motivations to travel are simply 'disqualified by law'; the regime considers her—seven times in a row—ineligible, i.e., 'unfit' or 'unworthy of being chosen' (Gaibazzi 2013, 39), and so she remains involuntary and invisibly immobile.

Kode (a pseudonym) from Guinea-Bissau was a student of political science and international relations in his early twenties before the polytechnic institute he studied at collapsed. He is an active member of the English Club at the American Corner of Bissau and he is very determined to move out of Guinea-Bissau. His trajectory of multilingualism shows passion for foreign languages and a relative indifference to local languages:

> You know we have a local language, which is Creole. It is the first language I start learning. I learn it from my parent at home, although we don't learn it at school. We have our first language, which is Portuguese, our official language. [. . .] I speak a little bit of Mandjago of course. Mandjago. That's my ethnic group. But I don't speak it that well. I went to the village just once, for six months. After that I never lived there again. Because in my house nobody speaks it.

Kode decided to study foreign languages and chose English, 'as *the first language of the world.*' He joined a private language school while in sixth grade and made a quick career in learning English and began teaching it at the age of 15, long before he finished his secondary education. Subsequently, Kode taught himself Spanish through an online course and from taking classes with a Cuban man working in Guinea-Bissau, and claims now to speak Spanish 'just like the way I speak Portuguese'. When Kasper first met him in 2014, he was studying a fourth European language, French. Prompted about this, he explicitly connected his foreign language desire with his aspirations for transnational mobility:

> Yes, I decided to join the French community because I know that, all I'm thinking is to go out of out of this country. [. . .] to look for immigration, or to go for study. I know that French is gonna be a tool I will need. If I don't do it here, any day I will need it, I will regret why I didn't do it.

The rest of the two interviews and Kasper's casual conversations with him focused on his efforts and investments in seeking mobility. His desire to leave Guinea-Bissau, he emphasized, needs to be understood against the background of the weak state and lack of educational and professional opportunities for young people in Guinea-Bissau. For Kode, like many young men (and women) in Guinea-Bissau (cf. Bordonaro 2009), going out is an obsession, a necessity for personal development and social upward mobility, as well as a patriotic moral obligation: 'I am doing ever- at all cost to get out of this country, to give better contribution to my country'. Kode's efforts, however, have only resulted in disappointments so far. Three of these disappointments and his understanding of why his efforts failed are given below:

(1) 'When I was a kid, [my aunt] always promised my mum she was going to take me to England, once I finished my high school'. His aunt's promise was a motivation for Kode to excel in school and focus on English. He did

his part, and counted on his aunt to do her part. 'I told her now I speak English'.

> The problem is she has to adopt me as her son. She sent me 200,000 [CFA—about €300]. We make the passport. After, we send documentation to England. We send it to Dakar and they send it to England. After two weeks they say the names came out, but my name didn't come out. [. . .] But what I realize, she didn't have enough money for the three of us. So she decided to help only her sons and not me.

(2) A friend working at the American diplomatic office in Bissau tells Kode about the 'Young African Leaders Initiative', a prestigious program for 'executive leadership training, networking, and skills building' set up by President Obama in the U.S. 'to invest in the future of Africa' (YALI website). His friend said: 'There is opportunity for you to go'. Kode investigated the requirements thoroughly; he corresponded with a Kenyan YALI alumnus he found on the internet; he met with American Embassy staff visiting the American Corner in Bissau and made a good impression with them. He also generously helped others with the application procedure. In addition, he spend 200,000 CFA changing his birth date to meet the program's minimum age requirement of 25. This requires buying a new birth certificate, passport, and school certificates. He is one of three persons shortlisted for an interview, but finally two non-shortlisted candidates are selected. For Kode it is clear that 'corruption' is in play. 'The ambassador was very mad about the situation. They select people that did not meet the criteria. [. . .] They couldn't even speak English. [. .] Before it made me mad, but I said, let me just wait'.

(3) Together with two friends (male and female), Kode applies for a three-month scholarship to India at their consulate in Bissau: 'We did it and we deliver at the same day. After one, two weeks, they called the girl to go. They asked her about the rest of the documentation. But they never called us. That man I know him like the back of my head. His business is for money or girls. He likes small girls. He is very serious by face, but he's a very dangerous guy'.

Corruption emerged as a major theme in the conversations with Kode. Travelling to the UK to meet his aunt required him to get the papers in which his aunt appeared as his mother; the YALI scheme required him to change his birth date. The corruptions Kode engaged in are, other than what he witnessed at the Indian consulate, victimless 'crimes'. He did it only to find his way, as a means of responding to scarce opportunities:

> What I did before is also a corruption. It's just like a crime. [. . .] But why I'm doing it, not to kill somebody, I'm doing it only to find my way. [. . .] I did it because I know this is not a country of opportunity. I found this opportunity, that's why I say okay let me take opportunity since

there is opportunity for me to go, let me do it at all costs, okay exception killing or hurt somebody. And that's why I changed it. Because I know that, maybe there will not be such opportunity like this.

Kode manouevres, or 'navigates' in Vigh's (2006, 54) terms, 'through unstable social terrains', making agentive and creative use of local bureaucracies in order to satisfy the demanding documentary requirements imposed on him.

Kode's case has much in common with that of Herina: It shows that transnational family ties often fail as strategies to travel, that institutional decisions about mobility are obscure and often (perceived to be) unfair. Like Herina, Kode's case also testifies to the immense perseverance and stamina involved in seeking mobile life trajectories. Globalization manifests itself to Kode also in terms of absence but Kode's strategies are more diversified than Herina's, and he also seems to believe more than Herina that he is getting reasonably closer to accomplishing mobility with each attempt. With each attempt, Kode's knowledge and skills about travelling, his mobility repertoire so to speak, grows. As he prepares himself academically for travel opportunities and through language learning in particular, he positions himself better in his own society, which in turn enhances his mobility potential.

Eunice (real name) from Cape Verde is in her mid-thirties and a receptionist at the Cape Verde Multilingual School in Praia. The school offers English, French, German, Spanish, Italian, Arabic, Russian and Chinese language classes for local children and adults and Portuguese and Creole classes for (mainly) foreigners. Besides Cape Verdean Creole and Portuguese, Eunice speaks French and little English, which she learned as part of her high school curriculum.

Her foreign language learning in school was, contrary to Kode, not very passionate but rather obligational. She said she was not very conscious about the value of foreign languages until she began to travel. In high school she developed affection for France in her French classes, but this was more about the Eiffel Tower, the Champs-Élysées, and the map of France than about the French language.

Unlike the previous two participants, Eunice is relatively mobile as she has had the chance to travel to Portugal, France, and the U.S.. She worked as a selling operator at the national telecommunications operator CVMovel for about three years, selling products to local and foreign customers. When she encountered communication problems with tourists or foreign business people, she would pass the telephone to an engineer whose English and French were better than hers. At night, however, she resorted to Google Translate struggling to make herself understood.

While working for this company, she applied for tourist visas to Portugal. The first one she got was in 2007 to visit her grandmother. She kept renewing her one-year Schengen visa every year, and in 2010 she used it to visit her aunt in France. Once in France she was diagnosed with some health problems, and was advised to take appointments with *Médicins du*

Monde which made her postpone her travel back to Cape Verde for almost one year, but she managed to return before her visa expired. Her travel to France motivated her to invest more in learning French, so that when she returned to Cape Verde she took a course at the *Institut française*. At the time Bernardino met her in 2014 and 2015 she regularly watched the news on *TV5 Monde*, listened to French songs, and had French friends living in or regularly visiting Cape Verde.

When asked about the benefits of her travel to France, she answered that besides solving her health problems, '*foi ih aprendi, foi prendi lida ku pesoas di kulturas diferenti, linguas diferenti*' [it was learning to cope with people from different culture, different language], which in turn could be professionally advantageous. She added that she aspires to work for the French or Luxembourgish cooperation agencies in Cape Verde and so French is one of the most important tools to achieve that goal. During her stay in France, some incidents made her even more aware of the importance of learning French. For instance at Charles-de-Gaulle Airport she got embarrassed because she had not specified to her aunt at which terminal she would arrive:

Kantu N bai pa kel uma aeroportu grandi N fla Ave Maria, nton N odja kel sinhor ki ta da informason. N bai N fla sinhor N fla si: bonjour monsieur, e fla si: bonjour madame, N fla si: monsieur je suis perdue comment est-ce que je peux faire pour appeler ma mère [tante]? e fla si: vous avez le numéro? N fla: oui, nton e fla: donnez-moi s'il vous plaît. Nton N dal numeru, e txoma nha tia y nha tia bai na mi. Mas si pur akazu N ka tinha nuson di lingua ja [. . .] si N ka sta konsentradu N ta fikaba prekupadu, ku prekupason, pamodi e un pais ki nunka N baba. Nton senpri N ta fla ma lingua e inportanti.	When I went to that big airport, I said Ave Maria, so I saw the man who gives information, I went and I said sir, I said so: *bonjour monsieur*, and he said: *bonjour madame*, I said so: [in French] 'sir, I'm lost, what can I do to call my mother [aunt]?' and he said 'do you have the number?' I said 'yes', so he said: 'give it to me please.' So I gave him the number and he called my aunt and my aunt came to me. But if I had not had any notion of the language [. . .] if I was not concentrated I would be more worried, with worry, because it was a country I had never been to before. So I always say that language is important.

After her first travel to Portugal but before her visit to France, she applied for a visa to the U.S. in 2008. She filled the application form on the internet portal of the U.S. Embassy in Cape Verde and later went personally to the embassy with her salary statement. She was granted a B2 visa valid for five years, allowing her one or more visits of up to six months. She only used it in 2013 just before it expired. Similarly to her incident at the airport in Paris, at the airport in Boston she experienced some embarrassment when a border police asked her whom she was going to visit. She didn't know how to say *madrinha* [godmother] in English. Reflecting on that, she said that now before travelling, she will prepare a list of vocabulary that she may need the most during her stay abroad. Acquiring a visa to the US is relatively accessible to Cape Verdean professionals with a well-paid position, and professionals like Eunice commonly apply for it even without concrete travel plans. Having an American visa sticker in one's passport is believed to be an asset for acquiring visas to other countries, too.

Eunice's case shows that mobility does not always (often not) emerge as a result of language learning, but that travelling on the other hand may lead to a greater awareness of and need for foreign languages. At the same time, Eunice's expanding repertoire (she became fluent in French) made her aspire to travel and get to know the world even more. Unlike Kode, her language repertoire follows rather than anticipates her movements. Eunice's trajectory suggests that getting a visa once makes it easier to get another one. In this respect, travelling is like money: The more one has of it, the easier it becomes to acquire even more of it.

Discussion and Conclusion

By means of conclusion, the map below visually summarizes the failed attempts and successful South-North travels discussed above. The map is relatively global in scale, because so are the (attempted) travels of Herina, Kode, and Eunice. A smaller-scaled map in which the geographies of Cape Verde and Guinea-Bissau would be more visible, would make the projected destinations disappear from the map. Making their (aspired) northward, westward, and eastward movements visible reduces the visibility of their countries of origin to mere dots on this global map.

Herina, Kode, and Eunice are three young Luso-Africans located in their countries of origin, differently positioned vis-à-vis their mobility. Unlike Eunice, Herina and Kode are not (yet) transnationally mobile but rather 'transnationals at home' (Åkesson 2008). Herina's mobile desire and strategies to find transnational mobility are mainly based on her family network with individuals already living in Italy. Her relatively low social-economic status in Cape Verde, as a housemaid, and her limited education severely restricts her chances at finding mobility. Repeatedly, her applications for visas are denied by the authorities. Kode in Guinea-Bissau has relatives in the UK (and elsewhere), but he mainly seeks educational opportunities to travel. Opaque and unfair selection procedures prevented him from travelling to the U.S. and India. These series of disappointments do not make Kode to give up, but rather to try harder, to invest more in his multilingual repertoire by learning French as a fourth European language. Herina, however, is getting tired of the constant rejections. While we prepared this chapter for publication, she informed Bernardino of an eighth rejection (to Portugal this time), and wrote '*ja N ti ta perde speransa*' [I am losing hope already] and that she's been thinking of travelling '*di verso*' i.e., through bribing or in the clandestine way.

We've contrasted these two cases of involuntary immobility with that of Eunice, who is older and through her work better positioned to find mobility. Her successful travels to France and beyond illustrate the violence that's done by Europe's restrictive immigration policies on Herina and Kode, i.e., excluding them from an experience and denying them progress in their personal and educational development. Contrasting Kode's with Eunice's case also illustrates the limits of acquisition of linguistic capital for migration. Language learning helps, but is by no means enough (for Kode) and often (for Eunice) not even necessary to find mobility. A cynical conclusion to draw here is that corruption works better.

The notion of desire in relation to repertoires and trajectories is necessary in understanding language in/and mobility and allows for a nuanced and complex understanding of agency. While we have little choice over what languages we are socialized in, or the places we are born in, we can, to some extent, take actions to influence or manage our linguistic repertoire as well as the places to which we move. It is clear from the above cases that few of these decisions are solely individual and that migration requires serious investment. It is also clear that all of these 'choices' depend on prior choices and opportunities and broader material, cognitive, and socio-political conditions. Understood in this way, trajectories follow the 'arrow of time' (Prigogine 1997), i.e., the past is irreversible and affects although not completely determines the future course of the trajectory.

The three cases presented here have shown that South and North are intimately connected. Even if these connections are not always experienced as physical interactions and movements back and forth, they are very real and intense in the form of imagination, desire, or aspiration. For each solid line on a map like that of Figure 5.1, there are many more dashed lines of unfulfilled itineraries. This work of imagination, the personal investments in northward mobility and their disappointments in the South remain largely

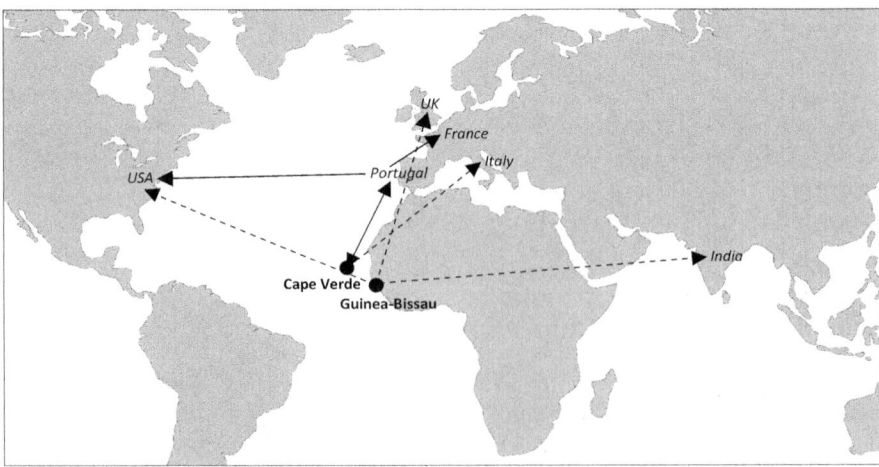

Figure 5.1 Failed and Effective South-North Trajectories

invisible and are disenchantingly absent from debates about migration in the North. What these debates and policies seem to be unable or unwilling to grasp is that the southern object of desire is not migration to the North as a linear and one-off path from A to B, but travelling in the form of realizing interaction between A and B for personal, family, and national development. The ever more restrictive migration regimes in the North may intend to control and curb migration, but in doing so oppress all forms of travel, which cynically encourage illegal and often tragic passages over sea as well as perverse forms of corruption and fraud. Beginning to understand South-North travel also in terms of adventure and journeying (Sarró 2009) and as attempts to escape immobility and global inequality and seek personal and national development, is sorely needed to disentangle discourses of South-North mobilities. Acknowledging the deep and sharp mobile inequalities between cosmopolitan citizens (mobile haves) and involuntary immobile subjects (mobile have-nots) in today's globalizing world, and understanding mobility as another 'site of struggle' (recall Stroud's 2001 discussion of linguistic citizenship) could help in transforming current South-North injustices.

References

Åkesson, L. 2008. 'The Resilience of the Cape Verdean Migration Tradition'. In *Transnational Archipelago: Perspectives on Cape Verdean Migration and Diaspora*, edited by L. Batalha and J. Carling, 269–83. Amsterdam: Amsterdam University Press.

Anderson, B. [1983] 1991. *Imagined Communities: Reflections on the Origin and Spread of Nationalism*, Second Edition. London: Verso.

Appadurai, A. 1996. *Modernity at Large: Cultural Dimensions of Globalisation*. Minneapolis: University of Minnesota Press.

Blommaert, J. 2008. *Grassroots Literacy: Writing, Identity and Voice in Central Africa*. London: Routledge.

Blommaert, J., and A. Backus. 2013. 'Superdiverse Repertoires and the Individual'. In *Multilingualism and Multimodality: Current Challenges for Educational Studies*, edited by I. de Saint-Georges and J.-J. Weber, 11–32. Rotterdam: Sense.

Blommaert, J., J. Collins, and S. Slembrouck. 2005. 'Spaces of Multilingualism'. *Language & Communication* 25 (3): 197–216.

Bordonaro, L. I. 2009. 'Sai fora: Youth, Disconnectedness and Aspiration to Mobility in the Bijagó Islands (Guinea-Bissau)'. *Etnográfica* 13 (1): 125–44.

Budach, G. 2014. 'Educational Trajectories at the Crossroads: The Making and Unmaking of Multilingual Communities of Learners'. *Multilingua* 33 (5–6): 525–49.

Busch, B. 2012. 'The Linguistic Repertoire Revisited'. *Applied Linguistics* 33 (5): 503–23.

Bybee, A. N. 2011. *Narco State or Failed State? Narcotics and Politics in Guinea-Bissau*. Fairfax, VA: School of Public Policy, George Mason University.

Carling, J. 2002. 'Migration in the Age of Involuntary Immobility: Theoretical Reflections and Cape Verdian Experiences'. *Journal of Ethnic and Migration Studies* 28 (1): 5–42.

Corbin, J. M., and A. Strauss. 1992. 'A Nursing Model for Chronic Illness Management Based upon the Trajectory Framework'. *Research and Theory for Nursing Practice* 5 (3): 155–74.

Czaika, M., and H. de Haas. 2014. 'The Globalization of Migration: Has the World Become More Migratory?' *Internaional Migration Review* 48 (2): 283–323.

De Boeck, F. 2012. 'City on the Move: How Urban Dwellers in Central Africa Manage the Siren's Call of Migration'. In *The Global Horizon: Expectations of Migration in African and the Middle East*, edited by K. Graw and S. Schielke, 59–86. Leuven: Leuven University Press.

de Costa, P. 2010. 'From Refugee to Transformer: A Bourdieusian Take on a Hmong Learner's Trajectory'. *TESOL Quarterly* 44 (3): 517–41.

de Saint-Georges, I., and L. Filliettaz. 2008. 'Situated Trajectories of Learning in Vocational Training Interactions'. *European Journal of Psychology of Education* 23 (2): 213–33.

Gaibazzi, P. 2013. 'Visa Problem: Certification, Kinship and the Production of "Ineligibility" in the Gambia'. *Journal of Royal Anthropological Institute* 20: 38–55.

Graw, K. 2012. 'On the Cause of Migration: Being and Nothingness in the African-European Border Zone'. In *The Global Horizon: Expectations of Migration in African and the Middle East*, edited by K. Graw and S. Schielke, 23–42. Leuven: Leuven University Press.

Graw, K., and S. Schielke. 2012a. *The Global Horizon: Expectations of Migration in African and the Middle East*. Leuven: Leuven University Press.

———. 2012b. 'Introduction: Reflections on Migratory Expectations in Africa and beyond'. In *The Global Horizon: Expectations of Migration in African and the Middle East*, edited by K. Graw and S. Schielke, 7–22. Leuven: Leuven University Press.

Grillo, R. 2007. 'Betwixt and Between: Trajectories and Projects of Transmigration'. *Journal of Ethnic and Migration Studies* 33 (2): 199–217.

Gumperz, J. J. 1964. 'Linguistic and Social Interaction in Two Communities'. *American Anthropologist* 66 (2, 6): 137–53.

Han, H. 2013. 'Individual Grassroots Multilingualism in Africa Town in Guangzhou: The Role of States in Globalization'. *International Multilingual Research Journal* 7: 83–97.

Ho, E. L.-E. 2011. 'Migration Trajectories of "Highly Skilled" Middling Transnationals: Singaporean Transmigrants in London'. *Population, Space and Place* 17: 116–29.

Juffermans, K. 2015. *Local Languaging, Literacy and Multilingualism in a West African Society*. Bristol: Multilingual Matters.

Kulick, D. 2005. 'The Importance of What Gets Left Out'. *Discourse Studies* 7 (4): 615–24.

Lave, J., and E. Wenger. 1991. *Situated Learning: Legitimate Peripheral Participation*. Cambridge: Cambridge University Press.

Pavlenko, A. 2007. 'Autobiographic Narratives as Data in Applied Linguistics'. *Applied Linguistics* 28 (2):163–88.

Prigogine, I. 1997. *The End of Certainty: Time, Chaos, and the New Laws of Nature*. New York: Free.

Rymes, B. 2014. *Communicating beyond Language: Everyday Encounters with Diversity*. London: Routledge.

Sarró, R. 2009. 'La aventura como categoría cultural: apuntes simmelianos sobre la emigración subsahariana'. *Revista de Ciências Humanas* 43 (2): 501–21.

Stroud, C. 2001. 'African Mother-Tongue Programmes and the Politics of Language: Linguistic Citizenship versus Linguistic Human Rights'. *Journal of Multilingual and Multicultural Development* 22 (4): 339–55.

Takahashi, K. 2013. *Language Learning, Gender and Desire: Japanese Women on the Move*. Bristol: Multilingual Matters.

Vertovec, S. 2010. 'Towards Post-Multiculturalism? Changing Communities, Conditions and Contexts of Diversity'. *International Social Science Journal* 61 (199): 83–95.

Vigh, H. E. 2006. 'Social Death and Violent Life Changes'. In *Navigating Youth, Generating Adulthood: Social Becoming in an African Context*, edited by C. Christiansen, M. Utas, and H. E. Vigh, 31–60. Uppsala: Nordic Africa Institute.

Part III
Northern Perspectives

6 Conflicting Agendas in Swedish Adult Second Language Education

Inger Lindberg and Karin Sandwall

The Swedish language program for newly arrived adult immigrants (sfi) is under constant political debate and expected to serve many masters. The program appears to be "Nobody's darling" (Lindberg and Sandwall 2007; Swedish National Agency for Education 1997) and is persistently criticized for its alleged low quality and lack of efficiency. Recently, its role as a labour market tool to ensure employment as rapidly as possible—in accordance with the so-called work strategy (*'arbetslinjen'*)—has gained priority over other longer-term goals of equitable career opportunities, personal and professional development. This is a situation that resembles that of Australia, the US and several countries in Europe (see e.g., Burns 2006; Burns and Roberts 2010; Simpson 2011). A political agenda in accordance with the work strategy paired with an increased government 'competition' policy, reflected in the tendered delivery of sfi, has contributed to conflicting agendas in terms of the role and responsibilities of the Swedish language program.

In this chapter, we will address entanglements in terms of roles and responsibilities and orders of visibility as reflected in the Swedish integration and labour market policies, discourses, and practices with regards to the basic Swedish language program for adult immigrants from a socio-political perspective. In the light of a recent study by Sandwall (2013a), we will specifically focus on ambivalent views on the role of language skills for social integration and the complex aspects of L2 learning and use in Swedish work-life. Finally, we will look ahead and discuss present and future challenges for sfi with regard to the entanglements of power and interests inherent in its development and delivery. First, however, we will give a short background on immigration to Sweden, the development of the basic Swedish language program for newly arrived immigrants (sfi), and the Swedish Language Act.

Background

Immigration to Sweden

Since the World War II, immigration to Sweden has gradually increased, changing the country from a relatively homogeneous society to one of considerable ethnic and linguistic diversity. In 2015, more than 20 percent of Sweden's 10 million population has a migrant background. From the 1970s onward, humanitarian migration and family reunification have consistently outnumbered all other forms of migration to Sweden due to a continuous flow of refugees resulting from armed conflict or crises all over the world.

In 2014, 81,300 refugees applied for asylum in Sweden, which was an increase of 50 percent compared to 2013. In 2015, unprecedented numbers of asylum seekers mainly from Syria, Eritrea, Somalia, Afghanistan, and Iraq found their way to Europe to escape conflicts, violence, and highly repressive governments. Along with Germany, Sweden has proportionally taken by far the greatest responsibility for this European migration crisis with an estimated number of 170,000 asylum seekers expected by the end of the year. The extent of recent immigration to Sweden due to the recent refugee crisis, and the great ethnic and linguistic heterogeneity of the migrant population compared to many other countries in and outside Europe, are important factors to bear in mind when reflecting on the challenges currently facing integration, labour market policies, and the organization of the basic Swedish language program for immigrants in Sweden today.

Swedish for Immigrants (sfi)

The Swedish language program for adult immigrants has been running for more than 50 years. It is state-funded but provided by the municipalities either as part of the municipal adult education program or tendered by private organizations. Participants are ensured free basic language tuition, with no legal limitation on hours of provision up to a level corresponding to level B1 as described in the Common European Framework of Reference (Council of Europe 2001) and are also offered financial support while studying. Due to the recent acceleration of the refugee crisis in Europe, sfi had more than 125,000 participants in 2014, which is a threefold increase since 2000 and the highest number so far (Swedish National Agency for Education 2015a). However, a well-supported estimation would be that in 2019–20 the number of participants will have doubled—as will the number of sfi teachers needed (personal communication, Ministry of Education).

Initiated in the mid-1960s, sfi tuition was for a long time carried out as a preliminary pilot activity in private study associations, with no formal curriculum or requirements for teachers. It was not until 1986, after several years of political deliberations, that sfi finally became a permanent education program with a formal curriculum and some modest teacher qualification requirements. The 1986 syllabus was accompanied by considerable efforts at a national level in terms of the implementation of functional and communicative language teaching influenced by research in applied linguistics and second-language learning and teaching.

Coordinated initiatives in terms of teacher training which have had any significant impact on the professional field, however, have decreased since

1994 when sfi was integrated into the national goal-based curriculum for the public school system, partly due to restrictions in the government's right to interfere with municipal issues and to the professional freedom of teachers to implement curricula and other steering documents according to local needs and contexts. All syllabuses within the Swedish public school system—including the sfi syllabus—since 1994 are criterion-referenced and lack direct specifications with regard to content or method (see also Lindberg and Sandwall 2007; Sandwall 2010). According to the current syllabus (SKOLFS 2012, 13), the goal for sfi is to provide learners with basic Swedish language skills. 'Participants must be given the opportunity to develop their ability to communicate in Swedish—orally and in writing—in everyday situations, social settings and working life. Swedish for immigrants must also prepare learners for further studies' (SKOLFS 2012, 13). The program should be flexible and organized so as to facilitate the combination of sfi studies and employment, work placement, or other education. In addition, the program, since 2009, aims at giving adult immigrants who cannot read or write the chance to acquire these skills, an important complement to the program, considering the fact that more than 20 percent of sfi students have less than seven years of schooling prior to entering the program (Swedish National Agency for Education 2015a).

In accordance with a directive of the European Council and Parliament (2004) and the Swedish Public Procurement Act (SFS 2007, 1091),[1] sfi has continuously become open for public procurement in which candidates—to a large extent private profit-seeking organizations—compete for the tendering of sfi for periods of two to three years. In this process, short-term economic considerations run the risk of clouding important regards for professionalism and quality among competing bids within municipalities strained by poor finances. Experience shows that tendering often entails a fragmented provision, lower teacher/student ratio, less regard for teacher qualifications, and reduced opportunities for in-service training. According to official statistics, the mean student/teacher ratio in sfi programs run by the municipalities was 22.1:1 compared to 45.5:1 in tendered programs 2014–15 (Swedish National Agency for Education 2015c). During the same period, 78 percent of the teachers employed by the municipalities had a formal teacher education compared to 67 percent of the teachers employed by tenders (Swedish National Agency for Education 2015b).

Negative effects on sfi as a result of an increased delivery of the program by actors in search of quick-fix solutions in order to make bigger profits and speed up the learning process may have contributed to a stagnation of sfi as a professional field. Just to mention one recent example, representatives for one of the biggest private tenders offering sfi, financed by a major venture capital firm, recently put forward a suggestion to do away with the requirements for specific teacher training to teach Swedish as a second language as a solution for the lack of qualified teachers which represents an obstacle to taking advantage of the increasing numbers of refugees for profit gains (SvD 2015a, b).

Even though many promising local initiatives aimed at orienting provision to individual language needs in terms of work and other societal contexts have been taken, such actions, if not informed by relevant research findings and proven experience, do not contribute to a more principled and professional development of the field.

The Language Act

Since 2006, the sfi program has also been endorsed by an official language policy, which, among other things, states that 'everyone has a right to language: to develop and learn Swedish, to develop and use their own mother tongue and national minority language, and to have the opportunity to learn foreign languages' (Swedish Government's Proposition 2005/06) a policy later reinforced by a Language Act (SFS 2009a). The purpose of the language policy and the Language Act was to specify the position and usage of the Swedish language and other languages in Swedish society and was intended to both protect the Swedish language in relation to the increasingly strong position of English and at the same time promote language diversity[2] in Sweden and secure the individual's access to language.

Since the Language Act states everyone's right to equal opportunities to acquire and use the Swedish language, it is of great relevance to sfi as far as its role, scope, and content is concerned. But the Language Act also raises issues of language matters on a broader level, such as how new varieties of Swedish moulded in linguistically heterogeneous contexts should be regarded. The negatively marked status of non-native speakers of Swedish in general and of non-native varieties of Swedish in particular (Fraurud and Bijvoet 2004; Lindberg 2009) bear evidence of a widely spread linguicism (Lippi-Green 1997/2012; Phillipson 1992; Stroud 2004) in line with which the intelligence, competence, or other character traits of an individual are judged according to his/her language or distinctive language features. It remains to be seen whether instances of linguicism can be addressed and counteracted with support from the Swedish Language Act in order to tackle stigmatization of local languages and dialects in educational settings that leads to unequal distribution of power and resources.

Sfi in the Service of Many Masters

The Work Strategy

The sfi language program is also part of the official Swedish integration policy (The Swedish Government Offices 2009) built on equal rights, obligations, and opportunities for all, regardless of ethnic or cultural background. In recent times, there has been a tendency to downplay aspects of diversity and mutual responsibility for integration in favour of a stronger emphasis on labour market entry and employment, confirmed in the current version of the policy. 'More people in work and more entrepreneurs' encapsulates the ideology of the so-called *work strategy* (arbetslinjen), the number one beacon of the centre-right coalition government in power in Sweden between 2006 and 2014. The same policy is also embraced by the centre-left coalition currently in government and has in fact been supported by all governments since the Social Democrats took power in Sweden in 1920 (Junestav 2004). Still, it is fair to say that the centre-right government in power 2006–14 implemented the most extreme interpretation of the strategy so far.

As stated by Lappalainen (2011), to many politicians, *integration* equals integration into the labour market as measured by immigrants' employment rate. The mantra 'work is the (only) key to integration' is being repeated by politicians, almost regardless of political affiliation. Instead of dealing with complex issues of inequities and discrimination, politicians seem to have a common interest in delimiting and reducing the question of integration to an area where they feel comfortable and where they can score political points—i.e., employment policy—where 'they don't have to think too much about how to influence employers and unions' (Lappalainen 2011, 82, our translation). Labour market integration is a measurable dimension but by no means the only trajectory of social integration. Demands on the individual to accept any job can, according to Lappalainen (2011), be viewed as a survival strategy for the individual but never as an acceptable level of ambition for an integration policy.

Nevertheless, to increase employment in the migrant population, politicians in Sweden and other countries in Europe, according to Lappalainen (2011), keep focusing on immigrants and measures targeted at improving their individual assets such as language education, conversion of foreign exams, and traineeships. There is, however, a strong reluctance to focus on measures targeting structural discrimination vis-a-vis actors with power and privilege in a position to react, i.e., employers, unions, politicians, and civil servants. Since integration, as pointed out by Ray (2002), builds on sustained mutual interaction between newcomers and the societies that receive them, it is of great importance to deal with the complexities inherent in these interactions directly to ensure policies and programs responsive to the on-the-ground realities of migration. Sweden has seen a rise in anti-immigrant politics during the last 10 years when the Sweden Democrats (SD), a far-right party with a nationalist and anti-immigrant platform, has received increased support: from 5.7 percent of the votes in their initial parliamentary participation in 2010, they recently polled 19.9 percent of the votes in the latest survey by Statistics Sweden 2015 (SCB 2015). Considering this political development and the fact that Sweden had the highest gap between native and immigrant employment rates among OECD countries in 2009–10, ethnic discrimination and xenophobia cannot be ruled out as major obstacles for integration. The strong belief among those in power that a job is the one and only key to integration may very well be the problem, since Sweden in spite of all the efforts in this direction, tends to fail at getting immigrants into the workplace.

The strong allegiance to the work strategy by the governments in power has had a strong impact on sfi, caught in the crossfire between the role and responsibilities of a language program on the one hand, and of a labour market tool for rapid employment on the other. In this clash between different ideological formations of discourse concerning the liability of sfi, the strong impact of the work strategy in current politics runs the risk of jeopardizing the individuals' rights to language in terms of equal career opportunities and active participation in society in accordance with the Language Act (Lindberg and Sandwall 2007; Rosén and Bagga Gupta 2013).

As the most indisputable and substantial component of integration policies for newcomers in Sweden, sfi is frequently made a convenient scapegoat for political failures in current integration and labour market policies, not least in terms of unsuccessful efforts of raising the employment rate among migrants (Dahlström 2004). For instance, a documented widespread ethnic segregation and discrimination in the labour market (cf. de los Reyes 2008; Fredholm-Blomst 2014) is repeatedly explained with reference to alleged language deficiencies of migrant applicants due to poor language training rather than structural discrimination. Still, there is no empirical support for an association between language proficiency and employment. In the same vein, uncontested claims that immigrants do not make an effort enough to learn Swedish constitute a frequent element in the dominant discourse on integration. In an interview on national radio in 2008, Jan Björklund, Minister of Education in the former centre-right government, made his opinion in this respect quite clear saying:

> All students can, if they make an effort, reach the goals within three years. But today some may be tempted to be enrolled for some more years without making any progress since they get subsidies. We want to take away this temptation, we want people to make an effort to finish their sfi studies and find a job and stand on their own two feet.
>
> (Björklund 2008, our translation)

Again, there is little empirical support for the assumption that adult immigrants in sfi show poor motivation in general or compared to students in other educational programs, nor for the claim that dropout rates in sfi outnumber those in other study programs. On the contrary, according to official reports and recent studies within Swedish second language research (cf. Ahlgren 2014; Bigestans 2014; The National Agency for Education 1997; SCB 2009), most immigrants show evidence of a strong urge to learn the language of the new country and seem to be willing to make big sacrifices to be able to eliminate or at least diminish the language barriers which stand in the way of their integration in the new country. Thus, in spite of strong research support for the fact that adult second language learning takes a lot of time and effort especially in migration contexts, as pointed out by Hyltenstam and Milani (2012), the dominant sfi discourse often finds legitimacy in common sense or 'folk ideologies' rather than in research-based knowledge.

Sticks and Carrots

A focus on individual effort and motivation also sends messages of the need for sticks and carrots to increase motivation.

In order to improve program outcomes and speed up employment among sfi participants, a somewhat unconventional measure was taken by the former centre-right government in the form of a pilot bonus system project "to test whether financial incentives may help participants to learn Swedish faster, and thereby improve their chances of obtaining a job" (Swedish Government's Proposition 2008/09, 156). The bonus was offered to newly arrived immigrants who completed their sfi studies with a pass grade within twelve months. Depending on exit level, the students taking advantage of the bonus system could earn up to 12,000 Swedish crowns (approx. € 1,300) if completing their sfi studies within a year. The initial proposal was subject to massive critique for being built on an assumption that sfi learners do not make a strong enough effort to learn Swedish and therefore need economic incentives and for discriminating against less advantaged learner groups with limited education (Lindberg 2009, 2010) but was nonetheless initiated in 2009 (SFS 2009b). Two years later, very few immigrants had taken advantage of the bonus. Still the bonus system was made permanent only to be abolished in 2014 after an evaluation carried out by the Institute for Labour Market and the Education Policy Appraisal showing that the system had had a limited effect on sfi outcomes. The final bill for this questionable experiment is estimated to 200 million crowns.

Sfi as a Provider of Linguistic Tools for Employment

Torn between the partly incompatible roles of being a qualified language program promoting integration and active participation in society, and enhancing rapid employment to minimize the number of people dependent on social assistance, sfi has had a hard job trying to serve all its masters. As Rosén (2013) has pointed out in an analysis of the various discourses that framed the development of the sfi program from the 1980s to the early 2000s, the roles of sfi are becoming increasingly blurred in the dominating discourse underpinning current work and marketization policy since Swedish language proficiency and integration are expected to appear automatically as a result of the employment of the individual.

In her analysis, Rosén (2013) reveals an interesting shift from a worker-oriented to a work-oriented discourse from the 1980 to the 2006 curriculum which coheres with the increased emphasis on the work strategy and focus on the individual in the recent implementation of the integration policy. Whereas the 1980 sfi curriculum emphasized language skills that would enable newcomers to exercise their rights and duties in the workplace as well as in other spheres of society, in 2006 the emphasis was on the responsibility of sfi and the individual newcomer to develop competencies to support their employability. In line with a focus on 'vocational Swedish' and rapid employment in recent years, Swedish municipalities have also started to request educational providers to include practical work placements in their program, even in very early stages of sfi.

The assumption that rapid employment (including unqualified, low-paid, and temporary jobs) is equivalent to successful integration is also underpinning the priority that the current government is giving to introducing so called 'fast tracks' to employment for newcomers. 'Fast' in this case supposedly holds promise for direct access to employment, avoiding 'unnecessary detours' (such as an extensive basic language tuition). Hence, the Minister of Employment (also responsible for integration policy, Swedish citizenship, and minority policy) has invited labour market parties to consultations concerning 'how much Swedish [immigrants] are supposed to study, how vocational Swedish is to be described' (Swedish Ministry of Employment 2015, our translation). The minister's choice of consultants in this venture reveals the interpretative prerogative of laymen among political actors and the marginal role of language education research and language expertise plays in political decisions concerning migrant language learning issues. As the Minister argues (Aktuellt i politiken 2015): 'Everybody knows how much easier it is to learn Swedish at the workplace.' (our translation).

The proposal is, however, in accordance with increased demands for a strong focus on work-related language skills in sfi. To what extent such tailored programs lead to employment and/or to faster language development is, however, far from evident (Swedish Agency for Public Management 2009; Swedish National Audit Office 2008). Still, many providers now organize sfi in ways that specialize in different areas of the employment sector and include practical work placements in the curriculum by way of a tuition often marketed as 'vocational Swedish', a concept that is seldom defined or specified. In most cases, however, it seems to refer to specific vocabulary and phrases related to the accomplishment of separate rather elementary work-related tasks rather than to the multifaceted language demands associated with the complex institutional discourses of different working contexts (cf. Burns 2006; Cooke 2006; Holmes and Stubbe 2003). The importance of needs-based, socially relevant, and work-oriented language tuition is hardly a question of debate. Still, there is no doubt that the call for more work-adapted language training is often based on naïve and unrealistic views of possible shortcuts to speed up entrance to the labour market and improve employment rates in line with common sense arguments rather than on informed knowledge. The requests for 'vocational Swedish' thus tend to downplay the need for basic and general language skills at beginner and intermediate levels as a foundation for the development of further and more specialized language skills. Furthermore, such limited understanding of the concept runs counter not only to research on institutional discourse of different working contexts mentioned above, but also to the Language Act referred to earlier in this chapter (Lindberg 2009; SFS 2009a) and the national syllabus of sfi (SKOLFS 2012, 13).

Entanglement and Orders of Visibility: Work Placements as Part of Sfi

In the following, a recent study on sfi tuition and the provision of work placements within sfi will serve as a convex lens or a focal point to illustrate previously discussed entanglements of power in macro and micro perspectives.

In search of empirical support as to the extent to which early work placement enhances sfi students' language learning, Karin Sandwall (2013a, b) carried out a multiple case study from a critical perspective in order to explore and analyze students' opportunities for interaction and language learning at work placements in early stages of sfi. Data for the study were gathered from four students enrolled in sfi who were observed and audio- and videotaped at various work placements (at a preschool, a clothes shop, a grocery store, and as a church caretaker, respectively) lasting for periods between seven and 20 weeks. Additional data comprised field notes from observations at work placements and in school and interviews with teachers, coaches (employed by the providers), and tutors. In addition, interviews and stimulated recall sessions with students in their mother tongues were carried out with the help of interpreters.

Qualitative and quantitative analyses of the recordings were supported by a computer program categorizing data into *transactional* and *relational* interactions (see, e.g., Gumperz 1964; Koester 2006), and relevant subcategories found to be relevant to each workplace. The computer program also performed a quantitative assessment of the time spent on each category.

The quantitative analysis of the data shows that students participated in interaction to an extremely limited extent at their work placements. The interactions could, for the greater part, be described as transactional and situated with interactants focusing on the accomplishment of the workplace task at hand rather than on the interaction as a possibility for language training. Moreover, interactions were to a high degree dominated by tutors and fellow workers, restricting the four students' spoken contributions to between 30 seconds and 2 minutes on average each day for each student at their respective workplaces, and decreasing over time (see below).

In the analysis which aimed at making visible the sayings, doings, and relations that dynamically shape and are being shaped within each workplace practice (cf. Kemmis and Grootenboer 2008), the results were accounted for in relation to three central factors that influenced students' opportunities for interaction and language learning: Interaction, workplace tasks, and relations.

The qualitative analysis of the data was carried out from an ecological perspective following van Lier (2004), and suggests an array of other factors that contributed to the students' scarce opportunities to interact and learn Swedish at their work placements, including some rather unexpected ones. Contrary to the well-established finding in second language research that scaffolding has a positive effect on language development, the fact that the interactions were situated and mediated by various *affordances* (Gibson 1979; van Lier 2004) actually reduced the students' need to use and expand their linguistic resources. As a matter of fact, meaning-making was scaffolded by the situated nature of the interaction to the extent that extended verbal exchanges were made redundant and unnecessary. To the detriment of students' opportunities for improving their Swedish, the use of limited vocabulary and syntax supported by gestures and numerous contextual references was often enough to serve the communicative needs of many workplace interactions.

The analysis also confirms that both students and tutors gave priority to the goals and continuity of the practices going on in the actual workplace—a fact which further contributed to the limitation of extended opportunities for interaction. Workplace talk was primarily viewed as an instrument to support workplace tasks; talk occurred when it was necessary for getting the job done—not for practising Swedish. Therefore, as soon as students were acquainted with the tasks—mostly "simple" and solitary workplace tasks—no further interaction was needed.

The students' goals and their imagined communities of practice, as well as their social and professional identities, appeared to be important for opportunities for interaction and learning (cf. Kanno and Norton 2003; Norton 2001). The analysis further suggests that this also influenced students' opportunities to consider themselves—and to be so considered by others—as members of the social and professional communities of practice at their work placements (cf. Lave and Wenger 1991). The students' position at their work placements might be described as marginal with very limited opportunities for learning (cf. Wenger 1998). Here, arguments can be made that the interactants' perceived affordances were dependent on more or less invisible power relations influencing students' as well as mentors' investment in sayings, doings, and relations (Kemmis and Grootenboer 2008; Norton Peirce 1995).

In the interviews, the students, the tutors, and teachers as well as workplace coaches stated that the students did not improve their ability to communicate in Swedish as a result of their work placements. Moreover, at the end of the placement period, all involved parties gave evidence of a strong feeling of failure and disappointment at the fact that the high expectations of employment and language development had not been met. The students blamed themselves for their inability to learn the language and some also felt disappointed and exploited since they did not get a job in spite of their hard work at their work placements.

The teachers also referred to a tightrope walk between the partly incompatible goals of the work strategy and the sfi syllabus, a dilemma never discussed with school management or the municipality's representative. As questioning the sfi-work placement system could jeopardize the provider's chances of winning the upcoming tender and ultimately their own job, the teachers considered themselves trapped within the tendering system. The conflicting goals of sfi and the system of competing short-term providers thus made teachers suppress views that did not sit comfortably with the policy of the municipality, rather than promote a critical and constructive discussion of the system in use.

Despite the students' limited opportunities to participate in interaction and language learning at their work placements, Sandwall points to an untapped potential for interaction and learning at work placements within the sfi program. She proposes a way of working where (semi-)authentic interaction at work placements is taken as a point of departure for the content of tuition. The model is aimed at bridging the gap between formal classroom language training and the communicative needs that the students need to face in their everyday life at the workplace and elsewhere (Sandwall 2013a). Based on the opportunities and limitations for learning in schools and at work placements, the model makes use of designed tasks to increase opportunities for active participation in both contexts and for integration of (in-)formal learning within and between them.

In conclusion, Sandwall argues that the urgency with which the system of work placements within sfi was carried out in the municipality shows a strong commitment to the work strategy and to the acknowledgement of sfi as primarily a labour market instrument. In accordance with a neoliberal ideology, the system of work placement puts all the responsibility on the individual—student, teacher, or mentor at the workplace—disregarding not only the complex nature of integration but fundamental research findings with regards to second language learning as well as the steering documents of sfi. Moreover, the study illustrates that a complex variety of conditions need to be met for learning to occur at a workplace. Contradictory to what is often argued by advocates for rapid employment as key to language learning, an employment or a work placement does not automatically lead to the development of second language competence relevant for working life (also Newton and Kusmierczyk 2011).

Conclusions

In this chapter we have touched upon a number of entangled and conflicting agendas at play in the implementation of sfi. Underpinning these agendas rtly incongruous views on the role and responsibility of the program, what can be described as a tug-of-war between actors with detrimental effects on the development of sfi. National initiatives to improve the program have so far been limited in scope, lacking in coherence or a common ground between sectorial policies and other actors involved. Due to short-sighted policies, municipalities, in the hope of financial gains, opt for quick-fix solutions to speed up labour market entry and improve employment statistics, rather than settling for long-term investments for quality in language education with benefits for the individual as well as for society. The low status of the program leaves the door wide open for a continuous discrediting of sfi as scapegoat for current integration policies failing to achieve their objectives.

Instead of viewing the different roles of sfi as conflicting and incompatible, we argue for a long term, consistent, and sustainable agenda for sfi through which different roles of the program can be reconciled and unified in order to prepare students for active participation in their daily life in the society at large as well as in the workplace. As shown earlier, the program needs to empower students to cope with situations of exclusion, discrimination, and dominant discourses of power equating foreign background and non-native varieties of Swedish with deficiency and inferiority.

The agenda is based on three foundations: A model for conceptualizing tuition, teacher training, and an agreement among actors to start pulling in the same direction. The first foundation is a model for the development of sfi as an arena with two interacting spaces—*an affirmative learning space* and *a critical learning space* (Svendsen Pedersen 2007, also Sandwall 2013a). In accordance with recent research and proven experience (e.g., the model proposed by Sandwall 2013a), the program within an imaginary *affirmative space* takes advantage of work placements and authentic interaction at workplaces as a starting point for planning teaching for labour market entry and active participation in workplace communities of practice.

To fulfill requirements in line with the intentions of the Swedish Language Act and the Education Act,[3] and for preparing students for manifestations of discrimination and linguicism, the program also needs to offer a space for *critical learning*. Within the critical learning space, teachers' and students' collective experiences, knowledge, and insights can be used to analyze and examine authentic confrontations with hidden codes and manifestations of discrimination and linguicism. As witnessed by voices articulated in the work by Ahlgren (2014); Bigestans (2014); Norton (2001) and others, identity and agency are at risk and threatened where migrants are confronted with prejudice and unfair treatment in the workplace and other social settings in society. Within this learning space, various socio-pragmatic aspects of language use can be made explicit and discussed from a critical perspective to promote students' possibilities of active participation on their own terms in different current, imagined, and future communities of practice (Kanno and Norton 2003; Norton 2001; van Lier 2004).

As for the second foundation for the agenda, the Swedish government has recognized the lack of qualified sfi teachers and recently allocated resources for in-service training and a campaign to attract more sfi teachers (Swedish Ministry of Education 2015). Such measures are welcome but are, in our view, better regarded as band-aids than a stable base for long-term sustainable development as long as a basic education for training sfi teachers is missing. Regular extensive teacher education tailored for the specific conditions framing the sfi program is top priority for the development of sfi as a professional field. In addition, there is a strong need for recurrent in-service programs to satisfy the continuous need for professional development for active teachers. What is currently required in terms of formal education for sfi teachers by the Swedish qualification regulation (SFS 2011, 326, 33§), i.e., a teacher's degree and 30 credits in Swedish as a second language,[4] is apparently insufficient for teachers, given the important commitment to 'provide students with linguistic tools for communication and active participation in everyday situations in society and in their working lives'.

As for the third foundation, we argue that the entangled and dynamic, though often blurred, formations of power and their intersections affect the program's possibilities to perform its task in a major way. As argued earlier in this chapter, discourses and power relations of different orders of visibility play a decisive role for the implementation and recognition of the sfi program as a qualified language education for social integration. According to the Swedish Educational Act, sfi tuition should be based on research and proven experience (SFS 2010, 800). So, we would argue, should government and municipal measures taken. This would rule out uninformed political initiatives like the costly bonus system previously referred to and introduce consultations with professional expertise as regular routine when it comes to adjusting sfi programs to the needs of specific areas of the labour market and discussions of the allocation of sufficient resources. Evidently, a language program informed by relevant research and proven experience (as outlined above) presupposes qualified teachers who can draw on research with relevance for L2 adult language learning and teaching in different contexts to tailor their own courses according to different learner groups in accordance with applicable steering documents.

Moreover, we argue that actors within the field must take responsibility for raising the level of the official debate and refrain from discrediting sfi on flimsy grounds, blaming the individual for political failures, and offering quick-fix solutions against better judgements. Instead they must support a development of sfi guided by professional wisdom and best available empirical evidence and value the insights of both researchers and practitioners. This would mean taking the full complexity of the issues into account and put an end to the current tug-of-war in order to recognize how different actors can contribute to the formation of a new agenda for sfi.

Finally, it is worth repeating that integration is not a question of immigrants acquiring keys, i.e., learning the majority language or finding a job.

Many immigrants in Sweden find themselves locked into low entry jobs in spite of high L2 and professional skills. Young adults with full control of the Swedish language, born and raised in Sweden by immigrant parents, experience repeated discrimination in their daily lives when applying for jobs, being caught in unwarranted ID controls, or when prevented from taking a taxi home after a night out. This situation was poignantly brought to light by the Swedish novelist and playwright Jonas Hassen Khemiri in an open letter to the former Swedish Minister for Justice and later featured in *The New York Times* (Khemiri 2013). As pointed out by Ray (2002), integration and second language learning comes about (or not) in everyday encounters between people: This is a concern for all members of a society, for the majority as well as for minority members. Equally, sfi is a language program of considerable concern not only for immigrants but for the society as a whole. Therefore, our vision for sfi is a program with consistent rather than conflicting agendas.

Notes

1 The Swedish Public Procurement Act regulates the purchasing by public sector bodies and certain utility sector bodies of contracts for goods, works, or services.
2 Sweden has become an increasingly multilingual country, primarily due to immigration but also to the official recognition of five national minority languages confirmed by law in 1999 to the status of national minority languages (Framework for Protection of National Minorities 1999).
3 The program must contribute to students' opportunities to 'strengthen their positions in working life and in society' and 'promote his/her personal development' (Educational Act 2010, 800, chapter 22, 2§).
4 30 credits, typically six months of full-time studies.

References

Ahlgren, K. 2014. *Narrativa Identiteter och Levande Metaforer i ett Andraspråksperspektiv.* Doktorsavhandlingar i språkdidaktik 4, Institutionen för språkdidaktik, Stockholms universitet.
Aktuellt i Politiken. 2015. '100-Klubben Hjälper Nyanlända': 2015–10–12: Socialdemokraternas Nyhetstidning'. Retrieved from http://www.aip.nu/default.aspx?page=3andnyhet=42056. (Accessed 14 December 2015).
Bigestans, A. 2014. *Utmaningar och Möjligheter för Utländska Lärare Som Återinträder i Yrkeslivet i Svensk Skola.* Doktorsavhandlingar i språkdidaktik 5, Institutionen för språkdidaktik, Stockholms universitet.
Björklund, J. 2008. *Uttalande i Ekot, P1, 2008–02–18.* Retrieved from http://sverigesradio.se/sida/artikel.aspx?programid=83andartikel=1901208. (Accessed 16 December 2015).
Burns, A. 2006. 'Surveying Landscapes in Adult ESOL Research'. *Linguistics and Education* 17: 97–105.
Burns, A., and C. Roberts. 2010. 'Migration and Adult Language Learning: Global Flows and Local Transpositions'. *TESOL Quarterly* 44 (3): 409–19.
Cooke, M. 2006. ' "When I Wake Up I Dream of Electricity": The Lives, Aspirations and "Needs" of Adult ESOL Learners'. *Linguistics and Education* 17: 56–73.

Council of Europe 2001. *Common European Framework of References for Languages: Learning, Teaching and Assessment.* Retrieved from http://www.coe. int/t/dg4/linguistic/source/framework_en.pdf. (Accessed 4 July 2015).

Dahlström, C. 2004. *Nästan Välkomna: Invandrarpolitikens Retorik och Praktik.* Sweden: Statsvetenskapliga institutionen, Göteborgs Universitet.

de los Reyes, P. 2008. *Etnisk Diskriminering i Arbetslivet—Kunskapsläge Och Kunskapsbehov.* Landsorganisationen i Sverige. Retrieved from http://lo.webshop. strd.se/ftp/pdf/566–2470–4.pdf. (Accessed 14 December 2015).

European Council and Parliament. 2004. *Directive 2004/17/EC.* Retrieved from http://eur-lex.europa.eu/LexUriServ/LexUriServ.do?uri=OJ:L:2004:134:0001:01 13:en:PDF. (Accessed 14 December 2015).

Fraurud, K., and E. Bijvoet. 2004. 'Multietniskt Ungdomsspråk och Andra Varieteter av Svenska i Flerspråkiga Miljöer'. In *Svenska Som Andraspråk—I Forskning, Undervisning och Samhälle,* edited by K. Hyltenstam and I. Lindberg, 389–417. Lund: Studentlitteratur.

Fredholm-Blomst, S. 2014. 'Assessing Immigrant Integration in Sweden after the May 2013 Riots'. *The On-line Journal of the Migration Policy Institute.* Retrieved from http://www.migrationpolicy.org/article/assessing-immigrant-integration-sweden-after-may-2013-riots. (Accessed 16 December 2015).

Gibson, J. 1979. *The Ecological Approach to Visual Perception.* Boston, MA: Houghton Mifflin.

Gumperz, J. 1964. 'Linguistic and Social Interaction in Two Communities'. *American Anthropologist* 66 (6): 137–53.

Holmes, J., and M. Stubbe. 2003. *Power and Politeness in the Workplace: A Sociolinguistic Analysis of Talk at Work.* London: Pearson Education.

Hyltenstam, K., and T. Milani. 2012. 'Flerspråkighetens Sociopolitiska och Sociokulturella Ramar'. In *Forskningsöversikt om flerspråkighet,* edited by K. Hyltenstam, M. Axelsson, and I. Lindberg, 17–152. Vetenskapsrådet, 5. Stockholm: Vetenskapsrådet.

Junestav, M. 2004. 'Arbetslinjer i Svensk Socialpolitisk Debatt och Lagstiftning 1930–2001'. Doktorsavhandling, Uppsala: Uppsala Universitet, Ekonomisk-Historiska Institutionen.

Kanno, K., and B. Norton. 2003. 'Imagined Communities and Educational Possibilities: Introduction'. *Journal of Language, Identity and Education* 2 (4): 241–9.

Kemmis, S., and P. Grootenboer. 2008. 'Situating Praxis in Practice: Practice Architectures and the Cultural, Social and Material Conditions for Practice'. In *Enabling Praxis: Challenges for Education,* edited by S. Kemmis and T. J. Smith, 37–62. Rotterdam: Sense.

Khemiri, J. H. 2013. 'Sweden's Closet Racists'. *The New York Times,* April 20. Retrieved from http://www.nytimes.com/2013/04/21/opinion/sunday/swedens-closet-racists.html?_r=0. (Accessed 30 June 2015).

Koester, A. 2006. *Investigating Workplace Discourse.* London: Routledge.

Lappalainen, P. 2011. 'Kommentar'. In *Reglering eller Diskriminering—Vad Hindrar Etablering?* edited by P. Skedinger and M. Carlsson, Fores Studie 2011, 14, 79–86. Retrieved from http://fores.se/wp-content/uploads/2011/11/72036069-Reglering-eller-diskriminering-Vad-hindrar-etablering-FORES-Studie-2011–4. pdf. (Accessed 30 June 2015).

Lave, J., and E. Wenger. 1991. *Situated Learning: Legitimate Peripheral Participation.* Cambridge: Cambridge University Press.

Lindberg, I. 2009. 'I det Nya Mångspråkiga Sverige'. *Utbildning och Demokrati* 18 (2): 9–37.

———. 2010. 'Bonuspengar och Snabba Klipp i Sfi'. *Alfa* 2010: 1.

Lindberg, I., and K. Sandwall. 2007. 'Nobody's Darling? Swedish for Adult Immigrants: A Critical Perspective'. *Prospect* 22 (3): 79–95.

Lippi-Green, R. 1997/2012. *English with an Accent: Language, Ideology and Discrimination in the United States.* New York: Routledge.

Newton, J., and E. Kusmierczyk. 2011. 'Teaching Second Language for the Workplace'. *Annual Review of Applied Linguistics* 31: 74–92.

Norton, B. 2001. 'Non-Participation, Imagined Communities, and the Language Classroom'. In *Learner Contributions to Language Learning: New Directions in Research*, edited by M. Breen, 159–71. London: Pearson Education.

Norton Peirce, B. 1995. 'Social Identity, Investment, and Language Learning'. *TESOL Quarterly* 29 (1): 9–31.

Phillipson, R. 1992. *Linguistic Imperialism.* Oxford: Oxford University Press.

Ray, B. 2002. *Immigrant Integration: Building to Opportunity.* Retrieved from http://www.migrationpolicy.org/article/immigrant-integration-building-opport unity. (Accessed 16 December 2015).

Rosén, J. K. 2013. *Svenska för Invandrarskap? Språk, Kategorisering och Identitet inom Utbildningsformen Svenska för Invandrare.* Doktorsavhandling: Högskolan Dalarna.

Rosén, J. K., and S. Bagga Gupta. 2013. 'Shifting Identity Positions in the Development of Language Education for Immigrants: An Analysis of Discourses Associated with "Swedish for Immigrants"'. *Language, Culture and Curriculum* 26 (1): 68–88.

Sandwall, K. 2010. ' "I Learn More at School": A Critical Perspective on Workplace-Related Second Language Learning in and out of School'. *TESOL Quarterly* 44: 542–74.

———. 2013a. *Att Hantera Praktiken—Om Sfi-Studerandes Möjligheter till Interaktion och Lärande på Praktikplatser.* Doktorsavhandling: Göteborgsstudier i Nordisk Språkvetenskap 20: Göteborg: Göteborgs Universitet.

———. 2013b. 'Starting with Practice: Workplace Related Second Language Learning in and out of School'. In *Adult Second Language Learning outside School*, edited by J. Rymarczyk. Bern: Peter Lang.

SCB. 2009. *Deltagare i Svenskundervisning (sfi).* Retrieved from www.scb.se/statistik/_publikationer/UF0539_2008T02_BR_A40BR0901.pdf. (Accessed 6 July 2015).

———. 2015. *Partisympatiundersökningen.* Retrieved from http://www.scb.se/sv_/Hitta-statistik/Statistik-efter-amne/Demokrati/Partisympatier/Partisympatiun dersokningen-PSU/. (Accessed 16 December 2015).

SFS. 2007:1091. *Lag om Offentlig Upphandling.* Retrieved from http://www.riks dagen.se/sv/Dokument-Lagar/Lagar/Svenskforfattningssamling/_sfs-2007–1091/. (Accessed 16 December 2015).

———. 2009a. *The Swedish Language Act.* Retrieved from http://www.eui.eu/Proj ects/InternationalArtHeritageLaw/Documents/NationalLegislation/Sweden/lan guageact.pdf. (Accessed 16 December 2015).

———. 2009b. *Försöksverksamhet med prestationsbaserad stimulansersättning inom svenskundervisning för invandrare.* Retrieved from http://www.riksdagen.se/

sv/Dokument-Lagar/Lagar/Svenskforfattningssamling/Forordning-2009728-om-forso_sfs-2009–728/. (Accessed 16 December 2015).

———. 2010. *The Swedish Educational Act*. Retrieved from https://www.riksdagen. se/sv/Dokument-Lagar/Lagar/Svenskforfattningssamling/Skollag-2010800_sfs-2010–800/. (Accessed 16 December 2015).

———. 2011. *Förordning om behörighet och legitimation för lärare och förskollärare och utnämning till lektor*. Retrieved from www.riksdagen.se/sv/Dokument-Lagar/ Lagar/Svenskforfattningssamling/Forordning-2011326-om-behor_sfs-2011–326/. (Accessed 4 July 2015).

Simpson, J. 2011. 'Telling Tales: Discursive Space and Narratives in ESOL Classrooms'. *Linguistics and Education* 22 (1): 10–22.

SKOLFS. 2012:13. *The National Sfi Syllabus*. Retrieved from http://www.skolver ket.se/regelverk/skolfs/skolfs?_xurl_=http%3A%2F%2Fwww5.skolverket.se% 2Fwtpub%2Fws%2Fskolfs%2Fwpubext%2Ffs%2FRecord%3Fk%3D1491. (Accessed 16 December 2015).

Stroud, C. 2004. 'Rinkeby Swedish and Semi-Lingualism in Language Ideological Debates: A Bourdieuan Perspective'. *Journal of Sociolinguistics* 8 (2): 162–383.

SvD. 2015a. 'Sänk Kraven när det Gäller SFI-Lärare: Letter to the Editor by Representatives for Academedia'. Retrieved from http://www.svd.se/sank-kraven-nar-det-galler-sfi-larare. (Accessed 16 December 2015).

———. 2015b. 'SFI-lärare: Förakt för Kunskap och Utbildning'. Letter to the Editor. Retrieved from http://www.svd.se/sfi-larare-forakt-for-kunskap-och-utbild ning. (Accessed 16 December 2015).

Svendsen Pedersen, M. 2007. *På Vej Med Sproget—Arbejde, Livshistorie og Sproglæring. Danskuddannelse til Voksne Udlændinge*. København: Ministeriet for Flygtinge, Indvandrere og Integration. Retrieved from http://uvm.dk/~/media/ UVM/Filer/Udd/Voksne/Bibliotek%20voksne%20udlaendinge/111221%20paa_ vej_med_sproget.pdf. (Accessed 16 December 2015).

The Swedish Agency for Public Management. 2009. *Sfi—Resultat, Genomförande och Lärarkompetens: En Utvärdering av Svenska för Invandrare*. Rapport 2009:2.

The Swedish Government Offices. 2009. *Egenmakt mot Utanförskap—Redovisning av Regeringens Strategi för Integration*. Regeringens Skrivelse om Integration 2009/10:233. Retrieved from http://sverigesresurser.se/2011/08/ett-oppet-och-tolerant-sverige-med-en-ny-integrationspolitik/. (Accessed 16 December 2015).

The Swedish Government's Proposition 2005/06. *Bästa Språket—En Samlad Svensk språkpolitik*. Retrieved from http://regeringen.se/sb/d/108/a/50761. (Accessed 4 July 2015).

The Swedish Government's Proposition 2008/09:156. *Sfi-bonus—Försöksverksamhet för att Stimulera Nyanlända Invandrare att Snabbare Lära Sig Svenska*. Retrieved from http://www.regeringen.se/contentassets/25c60442789b43abb 65f5c66f517d4be/prop.-200809156-sfi-bonus—-forsoksverksamhet-for-att-stimulera-nyanlanda-invandrare-att-snabbare-lara-sig-svenska. (Accessed 16 December 2015).

The Swedish Ministry of Education. 2015. *Språkundervisning för Bättre Etablering*. PM 2015–04–11. Retrieved from http://www.regeringen.se/contentassets/ 9c2cf03708b743a68c0a73358767be48/sprakundervisning-for-battre-etablering. (Accessed 4 July 2015).

The Swedish Ministry of Employment. 2015. *Newsletter.* Retrieved from http://newsletter.paloma.se/webversion/default.aspx?cid=10165andmid=299655ande mailkey=a80086c6-dbc0–497e-ace3–65965de6bb5b. (Accessed 4 July 2015).

The Swedish National Agency for Education. 1997. *Vem älskar sfi?Utvärdering av svenskunder visning för vuxna invandrare – en utbildning mellan två stolar.* Rapport 131. Stockholm: Skolverket.

———. 2015a. *PM. Elever och Studieresultat i Utbildning i Svenska för Invandrare 2014.* Retrieved from http://www.skolverket.se/publikationer?id=3484. (Accessed 4 July 2015).

———. 2015b. Pedagogisk personal i skola och vuxenutbildning läsåret 2014/15. Enheten för utbildnings statistik 2015-04-16 Dnr (2015:00459). Retrieved 2016-10-25: http://www.skolverket.se/om-skolverket/publikationer/sok?_xurl_= http%3A%2F%2Fwww5.skolverket.se%2Fwtpub%2Fws%2Fskolbok%2Fwp ubext%2Ftrycksak%2FBlob%2Fpdf3417.pdf%3Fk%3D3417.

———. 2015c. *Skolverkets Officiella Statistik.* Tabell 2: Pedagogisk Högskoleexamen, Anställningsslag och Lärartäthet Läsåren 2002/03–2014/15. Retrieved from http://www.skolverket.se/statistik-och-utvardering/om-skolverkets-statis tik/sveriges-officiella-statistik-1.37616. (Accessed 4 July 2015).

The Swedish National Audit Office. 2008. *Svenskundervisning för Invandrare (sfi): En Verksamhet Med Okända Effekter.* Rapport 2008:13. Retrieved from www.riksrevisionen.se/sv/rapporter/Rapporter/EFF/2008/Svenskundervisning- for-invandrare-SFI-En-verksamhet-med-okanda-effekter. (Accessed 16 December 2015).

van Lier, L. 2004. *The Ecology and Semiotics of Language Learning: A Sociocultural Perspective.* New York: Kluwer Academic.

Wenger, E. 1998. *Communities of Practice: Learning, Meaning, and Identity.* Cambridge: Cambridge University Press.

7   Institutional Constraints on Flexible versus Fixed Multilingualism

The Case of Parallel Language Ideology in Sweden

Lionel Wee

Introduction

Nuttall (2009) describes the notion of entanglement as 'a relationship or set of social relationships that is complicated, ensnaring, in a tangle . . .' (2) and suggests (2001) that it offers a useful way of thinking about 'those sites in which what was once thought of as separate—identities, spaces, histories—come together or find points of intersection in unexpected ways' (11). Writing about the aftermath of South Africa's apartheid era, Nuttall is concerned with the coming or bringing together of relationships that were once kept separate. But once we accept the conceptual value of thinking in terms of entanglements, then it also becomes important to ask how things that might otherwise be intertwined are kept within distinct boundaries.

Neither entanglements nor, for that matter, disentanglements are in and of themselves necessarily good or bad. A state of complete entanglement arguably indicates a situation where anarchy and anomie exist. In contrast, a state of complete disentanglement speaks to excessive control or unthinking adherence to the convention, with little or no room for improvisation or spontaneity.

States of complete entanglement or disentanglement represent ideal types. In reality, states of entanglement or disentanglement are always in flux relative to each other. Entanglements carry with them the potential for transitions towards newer regimes of disentanglements as different social actors attempt to impose their own ideas of normative order. Disentanglements, too, contain within them the capacity for newer kinds of social formations to emerge, conjoining hitherto disparate relationships whose coming together may have once been considered unimaginable. For example, the global spread of English has led to the language being disentangled (to varying degrees) from its traditional institutional and national histories while being entangled (again, to varying degrees) with the institutions and discourses of societies where it is being retained in the aftermath of decolonization or is being eagerly pursued as part of the activity of foreign language learning. It is this sense of entanglement and disentanglement that leads

Widdowson (1994) to argue that English is no longer 'owned' by its traditional native speakers.

In this chapter, I am interested in strategies of disentangling regarding language practices, where the aim is to sustain perceptions of order and control. I want to therefore look at how that which linguistically intersects is kept separate.

The issue of how to theorize about the boundaries between languages has become central to debates about the nature of multilingualism in recent years. The traditional understanding of multilingualism as competence in multiple languages—where this competence is itself understood as the ability to keep the languages apart—has been challenged by Blommaert (2010):

> Multilingualism . . . should not be seen as a collection of 'languages' that a speaker controls, but rather as a complex of specific semiotic resources, some of which belong to a conventionally defined 'language', while others belong to another 'language'.
>
> (102)

Blommaert's argument is that multilingualism can in fact involve the mixing of resources across the boundaries of conventionally defined languages, and furthermore, the knowledge of each language is usually partial or 'truncated' (Blommaert, Collins, and Slembrouck 2005, 199). The tension between the more traditional versus the more recent ways of understanding multilingualism is usefully captured in the distinction between fixed and flexible multilingualism. Fixed multilingualism assumes that different languages ought to be kept separate. In contrast to fixed multilingualism, flexible multilingualism treats the boundaries between languages as porous.

Where the relationship between individuals and organizations is concerned, fixed multilingualism is usually attributed to the language preferences of organizations whereas flexible multilingualism is associated with the language practices of individuals. As I have discussed elsewhere (Wee 2015), insofar as organizations are at all concerned with multilingualism, they tend to construe it in fixed rather than flexible terms. This is because organizations are in the main social actors whose continued legitimacy often depends on them conforming to various regulatory requirements and institutional myths that prevail in their social environment (Meyer and Rowan 1991):

> Many of the positions, policies, programs, and procedures of modern organizations are enforced by public opinion, by the views of important constituents, by knowledge legitimated through the educational system, by social prestige, by the laws, and by the definitions of negligence and prudence used by the courts. Such elements of formal structure are manifestations of powerful institutional rules which function as highly rationalized myths that are binding on particular organizations.
>
> (44)

In the case of language, one powerfully pervasive myth is that languages are stable and discrete, and differently named languages (such as English, Japanese, or Malay) therefore need to be kept separate in order that their systemic integrity not be compromised. The power and influence of this particular language ideology means that any attempt by organizations to challenge or renounce this way of understanding language has to confront the question of why they are embracing a view of language that (as yet) lacks institutional hegemonic force, such as that associated with flexible multilingualism. This contrasting view of language, where the boundaries of linguistic resources imposed by the use of language names can or should be flouted and transgressed is no less ideological. Nevertheless, in comparison with the view of multilingualism as fixed, the construal of multilingualism as flexible currently enjoys far less institutional support and entrenchment.[1] Fixed multilingualism thus can be seen to represent a form of disentanglement and flexible multilingualism a form of entanglement: The latter brings together what has been thought of as separate whereas the former maintains this separation. As we see shortly, the flexible multilingualism associated with the language practices of individuals and the fixed multilingualism found in organizations are typically presented as being in tension, if not actual conflict, with each other.

In what follows, I examine the case of parallel language ideology in Sweden as a way of concretizing my discussion, focusing on educational institutions rather than organizations in general. This is important to keep in mind since different political and socio-economic fields do significantly determine the kinds of language ideologies that prevail and, consequently, what kinds of language practices get official attention or endorsement. I make the argument that, in the field of education, constructing orders of visibility represents one strategy at disentangling otherwise complicated social formations. In this case, the appeal to parallel language ideology in Swedish universities presumes a linguistic reality where fixed multilingualism is the norm vis-à-vis English and Swedish such that faculty and students are themselves uncertain about the legitimacy of engaging in flexible multilingual practices. In contrast, other forms of multilingualism such as, say, Arabic-Swedish bilingual practices, would not be as visible and subject to institutional scrutiny. The consequence, I argue, is a visible ordering of fixed over flexible multilingualism in the case of English-Swedish bilingual practices as a result of assumptions on part of faculty and students about what kind of linguistic practices ought to be considered institutionally acceptable in the context of higher education. Flexible multilingualism is thereby effectively rendered invisible.

Faced with this situation, we might respond by arguing that the institutional context unfairly discourages or even penalizes the use of flexible multilingualism. But as I indicated above, organizations are themselves bound by institutional myths and it is not clear that a language policy that openly encourages flexible multilingualism would not itself result in to protests from faculty, students, parents, political leaders, and other members of the community that the organizations—in this case, universities—have abandoned their educational mission.

I therefore suggest that the more important challenge is to explore pedagogically meaningful ways of relating the two types of multilingualisms. This is because we need to ask how students can be best prepared for a multilingual reality that also includes organizations, since it is an inescapable fact that many graduates will end up working for organizations—which are entities that tend to prefer fixed rather than flexible multilingualism. In this regard, I discuss two possible ways of relating fixed and flexible multilingualisms. One way is to treat flexible multilingualism as a scaffold or bridge towards fixed multilingualism. The other way is to highlight to students the relationship between these two types of multilingualism as a topic for critical discussion, as an issue that does not allow for any easy resolution, but one which the students need to be aware of as they currently negotiate the parallel language ideology in Swedish universities and when they later enter the workplace.

Fixed Multilingualism, Flexible Multilingualism, and Organizations

The distinction between fixed and flexible multilingualism (Blackledge and Creese 2010; Weber and Horner 2012, 108) has been gathering momentum in discussions about the language practices of speakers. With its emphasis on the boundaries between languages, fixed multilingualism is actually based on an ideology of monolingualism, since each language is treated as a self-contained system assumed to have its own internal integrity. The maintenance of this integrity is dependent on each system being kept separate from the others. A good example of fixed multilingualism comes from Canagarajah's (2005, 425) description of the LTTE's (Liberation Tigers of Tamil Eelam) attempt in Jaffna to purge the Tamil language of English elements. This is because, as far as the LTTE is concerned, the Tamil identity is exclusively identified with the Tamil language as a bounded, formal code that must be kept separate from other codes. This is despite the fact that for many of the residents of Jaffna, mixing Tamil and English constitutes a natural part of their language practice (Canagarajah 2005, 426).

In the case of flexible multilingualism, the mixing of linguistic resources conventionally associated with distinct languages is not considered a problem. Flexible multilingualism, however, differs from code-switching (at least as the latter is traditionally understood) in that it does not presuppose bringing together otherwise distinct languages. For example, in their discussion of a conversation between two co-workers using a mix of Japanese and English, Harissi, Otsuji, and Pennycook (2012) reject a code-switching analysis on the grounds that it is premised on 'assumptions about discrete codes' and instead offer an account based on 'more fluid, and potentially poststructuralist, explanation of *resourceful speakers* (using semiotic resources and doing so inventively . . .)' (525–6, italics in the original). Thus, as Canagarajah (2013a) points out, the focus in flexible multilingualism is on:

> the ability to merge different language resources in situated interactions for new meaning construction. Competence is not an arithmetical addition of the resources of different languages, but the transformative capacity to mesh their resources for creative new forms and meanings.
>
> (1–2)

The observation that speakers tend to engage in flexible multilingualism has led to calls in both sociolinguistics and applied linguistics for a better appreciation—particularly in educational and work-related contexts—of the 'fluid multilingual realities of today's world' (Weber and Horner 2012, 117), a fluidity that has been variously characterized as translanguaging (García 2009), polylanguaging (Jørgensen 2008), metrolingualism (Otsuji and Pennycook 2010), and translingual practices (Canagarajah 2013a, b). In this regard, a number of studies (Blackledge and Creese 2010; Garcia 2009; Otsuji and Pennycook 2010) have noted the tensions that arise when speakers' more flexible use of language is contrasted against organizational backdrops, where the institutional norm is either monolingualism or if multilingualism, then fixed rather than flexible. As Otsuji and Pennycook (2010) point out:

> metrolingual language use may have to confront its static nemesis, the fixed identity regulations of institutional modernity: when judgements in law courts, educational systems, asylum tribunals, job interviews or hospital waiting rooms are brought to bear on metrolingual language use, the full discriminatory apparatus of the state all too often works against such fluidity.
>
> (246–7)

It is clear that flexible multilingualism represents a form of entanglement, at least where speakers' language practices are concerned. Language resources otherwise associated with different named varieties and, hence, what are conventionally treated as separate linguistic sites, are brought together in unexpected ways. From the perspective of the conventional boundaries established by the use of different language names (e.g., English versus Japanese), such linguistic entanglements seem to wilfully contravene the notion that such boundaries ought to be respected or at the very least, they seem to simply ignore the idea that such boundaries even exist. Conversely, fixed multilingualism thus represents disentanglement, one where the conventional nature of language boundaries are respected or at least simply acknowledged so that, where transgressions across such boundaries occur—as in the cases of traditional code-switching or code-mixing—they might be accompanied by some metalinguistic acknowledgement on the part of speakers that there is a mixing of language resources.

Despite acknowledgements that fixed multilingualism may still have a place in education (Weber and Horner 2012, 132), there is a tendency to assume that fixed multilingualism unnecessarily or unfairly constrains speakers' language practices (Weber and Horner 2012, 115, citing García 2009). Indeed, as Otsuji and Pennycook (2010) point out:

> Current cultural, social, geopolitical and linguistic thinking is predominated by a celebration of multiplicity, hybridity and diversity. Within this trend, terminology such as multiculturalism, multilingualism and cosmopolitanism are taken as a focus and a desirable norm in various fields including academia, policy-making and education.
>
> on the one hand, the celebration of multiple allows for difference and dynamism providing new possibilities to society and people. On the other hand, its antagonistic view towards pre-given fixed ascriptions of cultural identities—chastised for being essentialist—often fails to acknowledge the contribution that such pre-given identities have in becoming different. That is, one of the driving forces to be different and multiple and dynamic is the interaction between fixed and fluid cultural identities.
>
> (243)

The tendency to celebrate or valorize flexible multilingualism whilst positioning fixed multilingualism as 'evil/bad' has to be balanced against the fact that many speakers work for organizations or are likely to do so upon graduation. As we noted above, organizations in the main tend to prefer fixed multilingualism as opposed to its flexible counterpart. Paraphrasing Prodromou (2008, 249–50), it is critical that we do not ignore 'the realities of political and economic power [in this case, organizational power] in a globalized world'. Neglecting the importance of the ability to communicate without mixing codes risks the danger of offering speakers 'a halfway house' where speakers have 'reduced linguistic capital' (Prodromou 2008). In other words, we need to bear in mind that the multilingual reality that speakers inhabit also includes organizations and their preferred language practices.

With the foregoing in mind, let us now take a look at the case of parallel language ideology in Sweden.

Parallel Language Ideology: Swedish Universities

In 2006, the Nordic ministers for education and culture collectively issued a declaration on the importance of reinforcing the status of the local languages vis-à-vis the growing use of English (Bolton and Kuteeva 2012, 430). The rationale behind this move was an acknowledgement that the English language was gaining wider usage and prestige in both the public sphere of general interactions as well as in more specialized domains such as those of education, especially higher education, and research and development. As Haberland (2014) points out in his discussion of Danish universities:

> In planners' and administrators' views, a close connection has been established between internationalization and the use of English as a medium of instruction. It is assumed that internationalization is simply not possible or thinkable without the use of the English language in teaching. And it does not stop here: with ever increasing transnational mobility of staff and students, English becomes a language of internal communication and is even being considered as a language of administration.
>
> (252)

And rather than aiming to find ways of curtailing the spread of English—a move that the ministers considered neither feasible nor realistic—the policy goal became one of trying to ensure that the local languages continue to find relevance alongside this global language. This, then, is the parallel language ideology, where the intention is not force speakers to have to choose between English and the local languages (a competition between languages in which English was perceived to hold a strong advantage) but instead, to encourage the use of both.

In the specific case of Sweden, for example, the Swedish Language Council (1998, 16, quoted in Kuteva 2011, 6) has mandated that:

> encouragement should be given to educational development work aimed at enhancing students' ability to use Swedish and English in parallel in their subjects. It is unfortunate if separate domains develop, with foundation courses predominantly in Swedish and more advanced courses only in English.

Notice that in the above extract, the Swedish Language Council explicitly wants to discourage situations where Swedish and English become associated with separate domains, since the worry is that English might then be affiliated with the more advanced (and by implication, the more prestigious) courses while Swedish might then be linked only with foundational or basic knowledge. However, if it is the case that Swedish and English are supposed to be used in the similar or comparable domains, one might then infer that in any course, be it a foundation or advance course, it would be expected that both languages might well be present. Even so, this still leaves a high degree of uncertainty over how this ideology ought to be specifically operationalized. This leads Kuteva (2011) to make the following observation:

> two years after the introduction of the Language Act, 2009 (Swedish Government 2009) which established the official status of Swedish

as the country's main language, 'parallel language use' is increasingly regarded as a guiding principle for the dual use of Swedish and English in higher education. However, it seems that this concept was conceived by policymakers and concerns primarily the administrative aspect of the education system, rather than students, teachers, and their language and disciplinary competences (Airey 2009). The full implications of parallel language use remain unclear, and more research needs to be done on how this concept is implemented in practice.

(6–7)

The conception of the ideology, not surprisingly, appears to have been motivated more by administrative and political considerations rather than a proper appreciation of the constraints and limitations that inevitably come into play when the considerations have to do with actual learning, teaching, and disciplinary expectations. As a result, there is a great deal of on-the-ground improvisation and variation.

And especially since the push towards the parallel language ideology has been most keenly felt in the institutions of higher learning, its impact on research and pedagogy remains both controversial as well as a constant source of bemusement for students and faculty. Thus, from the perspective of one student T (personal communication):

> code-switching and code-mixing is not very common . . I, myself, find it embarrassing to have to use English words if I can't think of the Swedish word when I'm speaking Swedish, as I believe it sounds as if I am trying to 'show off' or make a point out of the fact that I know the word in English.
>
> As I remember it, if a teacher wanted to use an English term while speaking Swedish, s/he would preface it with something like 'vilket pa engelska heter X' (= 'which in English would be X'). The only time that Swedish words are used when the discussion is in English is, I would say, to facilitate understanding of a term. For example, '. . . when you write a paragraph—'stycke' in Swedish—you should always try to . . .'

In the above extract, the student cannot escape thinking in terms of separate languages. The student's reluctance to engage in code-switching and code-mixing indicates the entrenched and hegemonic status that fixed multilingualism enjoys in the domain of higher education. And even when code-switching and code-mixing do occur, these appear to in fact take the form of alternations between discrete codes rather than the kind of 'fluid . . . poststructuralist' use of language resources described by Harissi, Otsuji, and Pennycook (2012, 525–6, see above), thus suggesting that any resulting flexibility in multilingual practices is minimal. The correctness of this suggestion is bolstered by the fact that there is also a tendency to highlight the metadiscursive regimes (Makoni and Pennycook 2007) of the different languages, where speakers signal explicitly that they are using words belonging to either English or Swedish, as seen in the teacher's use of the phrase *vilket pa engelska heter X*. This is because the ideological view of languages as bounded entities that need to be kept separate is so pervasive that even those individuals who engage in flexible multilingualism sometimes do so sub-consciously (Otsuji and Pennycook 2010). When such individuals are asked to consciously account for and reflect on their language practices, it is clear that they themselves find it difficult to avoid invoking an order of visibility where language, culture, and identity as viewed as fixed and stable (Blackledge and Creese 2010, 17; Harissi, Otsuji, and Pennycook 2012, 527).

Where teaching materials are concerned, language use is complementary in that the same materials are never in both languages. Some are in Swedish and others in English. In terms of evaluation, some departments apparently allow their students to decide whether they want to write their projects in English or Swedish. T also gives the example of a woman from the UK who was allowed to write her final assignment in English, although the MA course was mainly in Swedish and all the other students wrote their assignment in Swedish. The default appears to be that the teachers decide on the language to be used, and also if the course is taught in Swedish, the exam will mostly likely be in Swedish (and vice versa). There are some instances, however, when students are allowed to choose for themselves.[2]

There are also important disciplinary differences, and a general articulation of the parallel language ideology does not really provide any guidelines on how to navigate these. For instance, in their study of Stockholm University, Bolton and Kuteva (2012) emphasize that:

> Content-based lectures are very common in the Science faculty, and the difference in terms of content transmitted through a lecture in English or Swedish is small . . .
>
> Thus, it appears that transmitting knowledge in English may not present as many challenges as constructing knowledge through discussion in English, a core pedagogical method for the Humanities and Social Sciences.
>
> (438–9)

Bolton and Kuteva (2012) quote faculty members from the School of Business and the Department of Social Anthropology, both of whom express frustration that trying to follow the parallel language ideology has adverse effects on teaching:

> Within humanities and social sciences, where 'meaning' is important it is almost impossible to express oneself clearly in any other language than in one's native language. At the master classes the level of the

discussions can sometimes be very low. The reason for this is to large extent language problems.

(Senior lecturer, aged 51–55, from Sweden, School of Business,
Faculty of Social Sciences)

Teaching, especially lecturing, in English when it is not your native language usually makes for less lively and engaging lessons, which is pedagogically detrimental.

(Reader, aged 56–60, from Sweden, Department
of Social Anthropology) (439)

In other words, where the pedagogical focus is on the transmission of established content, and where many of the technical terms involved are presumably of English origin (as appears to be the case with the Science faculty), then switching between English and Swedish appears to be less problematic. Notice here that the issue of code-switching or code-mixing now seems to be less of a concern, unlike the student's comments discussed above. There is a simple reason for this, namely, that the English origin of the technical terms has become bleached to the point where treating these as 'English' words is really, if one can be forgiven for the pun, just a technicality. Analogous phenomena can be seen in Leeman and Modan's (2009, 335) concerns about the uncritical classification of the word 'Pepsi' as an English word in linguistic landscape studies. It is important to appreciate that this bleaching of the metadiscursive origins of various terms is not necessarily the same thing as the fluid poststructural mixing of resources that notions such as metrolingualism, translanguaging, polylanguaging, etc., are all trying to capture. Rather, the internationalization of technical scientific terms and brand names such as Pepsi means that, even though there is a sense in which they can be described as English words, for many speakers, the regular use of these terms has naturalized them to the point where there is neither any perception of moving across the conventionalized boundaries of named languages nor any creative and transformative 'meshing of resources' (Canagarajah 2013a, 1–2, see above also). Crucially, this therefore means that the prevailing order of visibility is still largely one of fixed rather flexible multilingualism.

In contrast to the kind content transmission common in the Science faculty, discussions in the Humanities and Social Sciences pose a greater problem for attempts at realizing the parallel language ideology. The pedagogical goal here is one of knowledge construction, and neither lecturers nor students necessarily have access to a readily available set of terms with clearly defined meanings and bleached linguistic provenance. This means the participants have to decide at what point in the course of a discussion Swedish (or English) terms are no longer appropriate, then make a strategic decision to introduce English (or Swedish) ones, and where necessary, innovatively coin new terms whilst explaining to the other interactants what they intend to mean by these nonce formations. Here, we come closer to the kind of 'new meaning construction' that Canagarajah (2013a, 1–2) talks about in his description of translingual practices. But we also have to note that it is a fraught process that the participants find frustrating and difficult. This is because there is no clear indication that such flexible multilingualism is being encouraged or even considered acceptable, unlike the kinds of 'safe sites' that Canagarajah has deliberately created in his own classes for his students. Thus, in teaching his own course on second language writing, Canagarajah assigned students the project of producing a 'serially drafted and peer-reviewed literacy autobiography' (2013b, 134). His goal was to get students to be more reflexive about their writing strategies, to encourage them to further explore the strategies for reading and writing translingual texts that they were already employing to various extents (2013b):

> All that I can claim is that I constructed a favourable pedagogical environment, a relatively safe site, to help students practice the strategies they already bring with them. Rather than imposing my own literacy assumptions on students one-sidedly, I provided a context where I could negotiate with them the strategies they were familiar with. This doesn't mean that I didn't influence them in any way, but my teacherly intervention was also open to negotiation, as were the feedback and suggestions of their peers.
>
> (133)

In the absence of any such supportive environment, however, the more established order of visibility prevails, which is one where fixed multilingualism is institutionally more hegemonic than flexible multilingualism.

Therefore, whereas the full implications of parallel language use still remain unclear, the available data suggest that implementation, where it does occur, tends to be in terms of fixed rather than flexible multilingualism.[3] That is, the choice is one code or the other. Where the mixing of codes occurs, this is highly marked and qualified metalinguistically.

Relating Fixed and Flexible Multilingualisms

Though the discussion thus far might open me to charges that I am encouraging a resigned acceptance of the status quo, this is certainly not my intent. Rather, my goal is to highlight the fact that a simple dualism that pits fixed and flexible multilingualism against each other runs the risk of ignoring key issues, such as (1) organizations are themselves ideologically constrained, and (2) especially in the case of universities, the educational mission of preparing students for a world populated by organizations cannot afford to jettison a focus on fixed multilingualism. Therefore, rather than seeing the relationship between the two types of multilingualism as antagonistic,

I want to suggest that it may be more relevant to try to find pedagogically useful ways of connecting them.

It seems to me that there are two possible ways of relating fixed and flexible multilingualisms. One way is to treat flexible multilingualism as a scaffold or bridge towards fixed multilingualism. This is especially important as a pedagogical principle because many students are likely to come from homes and social backgrounds where flexible multilingualism is a norm. And educational systems need to build on this background as a linguistic resource rather than ignore or condemn it (Garcia 2009). This is no easy task because many policy makers, parents, and educators themselves are still uneasy with the idea of allowing the mixing of languages, even if this is meant as a stepping stone towards greater monolingual competence in multiple separate languages rather than an end in itself.

The other way is to highlight to students the relationship between these two types of multilingualism as a topic for critical discussion, raising their metalinguistic awareness of this as an issue and emphasizing that it does not allow for any easy resolution. Nevertheless, it is an issue that the students most certainly need to be aware of as they currently negotiate the parallel language ideology in the university and also later on when they enter the workplace. This would require getting students to examine their own ideological assumptions about language, the language practices that they engage in, and the relationship between the two. It would also require facilitation by educators who have an interest in language, and who have the confidence to engage in critical open-ended discussions about language practices informed by sociolinguistic theorizing.

Such an approach should focus on helping students to develop metaliteracy skills. Literacy is implicated because arguments for flexible multilingualism oftentimes draw on literacy studies to suggest that we need to move away from autonomous literacy towards literacy that is more ideological, situated, and negotiated, in order to give greater space to flexible multilingualism (e.g., Canagarajah 2013a). But because organizations are more likely to impose literacy regimes that are based on fixed multilingualism than to encourage the formation of contact zones where flexible multilingualism might be encouraged, students need to understand where more static and hegemonic literacy regimes are likely to be found, where more fluid contact zones are likely to be found, and what allowances in multilingual practices might be possible in these various regimes and zones. This is where metaliteracy skills, that is, the ability to appreciate and maneuver the social, political, and linguistic dimensions of the intersection between mobility and literacy, become pedagogically important. Students need to understand what the social costs are when they produce different kinds of texts (including multilingual, multimodal texts). They need to be able to make informed/educated decisions when faced with questions such as the following: When and how mobile are various kinds of texts? How might they be received? Are there any costs for those involved in the product or reception of these texts?[4]

By way of closing this section, it is also worth noting that these two options are not mutually exclusive. However, the latter option, in particular, has a greater potential to lead to what Giddens (1987) describes as the double hermeneutic, and hence, open up the possibility for change such that institutional spaces for flexible multilingualism might well grow. And this might, over time, even lead to a change in the orders of visibility so that fixed and flexible multilingualism either exist as co-equals or the latter might even come to be dominant form of multilingualism (see below for further discussion).

Giddens's (1987) 'double hermeneutic' refers to the fact that there is a two-way relationship between lay/everyday concepts and social scientific ones (Wee, under preparation). Unlike the natural sciences where scientists study objects and phenomena (e.g., chemical processes) that lack awareness, the objects and phenomena studied by social scientists (i.e., people, society) can come (via education, the mass media, socio-political debates, etc.) to not only appreciate social scientific concepts such as 'citizen' and 'sovereignty' (Giddens 1987, 20) and more recently, 'diaspora' or 'inflation', but to even use them themselves. As Giddens (1987) puts it:

> the subjects of study in the social sciences and the humanities are concept-using beings, whose concepts of their actions enter in a constitutive manner into what those actions are. Social life cannot be accurately described by a sociological observer, let alone causally elucidated, if that observer does not master the array of concepts employed (discursively or non-discursively) by those involved . . .
>
> unlike in the natural science, in the social sciences, there is no way of keeping the conceptual apparatus of the observer—whether in sociology, political science or economic—free from appropriation by lay actors.
>
> (18–19)

The critical exploration of the relationship between fixed and flexible multilingualisms in the education context creates an awareness amongst students that there is a metaliteracy issue that needs to be addressed. What the double hermeneutic suggests is that this awareness can potentially go on to influence the social behaviour of the students themselves, so that, over time, larger societal changes in attitudes towards flexible multilingualism might result, as these students enter different arenas of social life and, hopefully, bring about institutional changes in the various organizations they inhabit.

The caveat here is that some of the changes wrought by former students— should they go on to become influential lay actors who might shape language policy—might be substantially different from what they were initially taught. But this possibility of the further resemioticization of concepts, even to the point where they are re-interpreted in ways that we as academics might not be comfortable with, is something that we not only have to countenance. It is an unavoidable corollary of the double hermeneutic.

Conclusion: Challenging and Changing Orders of Visibility

I have argued in this chapter for a view of fixed multilingualism as form of disentanglement and that of flexible multilingualism as one of entanglement. And as I suggested at the beginning of this chapter, both entanglements and distanglements exist in states of flux relative to each other, with transitions from one to the other always potentially occurring.

Bearing this in mind, I have also suggested that whereas the current realization of the parallel language ideology tends to assume as a default the legitimacy of fixed multilingualism over its more flexible counterpart, the possibility for change can come about once we think more carefully about how the two forms of multilingualism can be constructively related, that is, how current order of visibility might be challenged and ultimately tranformed.

That having been said, I nevertheless want to conclude by emphasizing that the enormity of the task should not be underestimated, nor the nature of the task misconstrued. This is an important issue because Canagarajah (2013b, 111) has suggested that various scholars, despite being sympathetic to the fact that different languages have their now norms and values, all tend to promote a 'dualistic approach to literacy'. This is an approach where students might be encouraged or allowed to engage in the communicative norms of their minority languages and even mixing these in various ways with the conventions of Standard Written English (SWE), but ultimately, their final submissions have to be cleaned up so that traces of these other languages are erased. Canagarajah (2013b) describes this as a kind of diglossia:

> Home languages are treated as a lower form and SWE is treated as a higher variety. All these approaches have rightly been called *codeswitching* models . . . Not to be confused with codeswitching in sociolinguistics, critical writing scholars adopt this term as a metaphor to refer to the distinction of language norms in diglossic terms, with different spaces or functions assigned to SWE and vernaculars . . .
>
> critical scholars point out that the codeswitching approach still maintains power differences and doesn't go far in envisioning change. For example, teaching students that their community/home languages have their place outside formal written contexts in academic settings conveys to them that their languages are inferior or not acceptable in elite, formal, or high-stakes contexts.

There is evidence to suggest that this bifurcated approach to language norms doesn't satisfy minority students and writers. Young (2004), an

African-American scholar, argues that this separation of codes sup-
presses his voice. He considers it racist to be forced to segregate the
language of his repertoire and asked to write without relevance to all
his identities.

(112, italics in original)

Whereas I have a great deal of sympathy and respect for Canagarajah's
argument, I think it is important that in trying to challenge the current order
of visibility, we be cognizant of what the goal or purpose involved is. If our
goal is to empower students to be freer to manifest their identities, then
creating relatively segregated or isolated safe spaces is certainly feasible. But
if our goal is to prepare students to negotiate a working life where organizations play a significant part, then any attempt to change the order of visibility has to be more circumspect. The linguistic market (Bourdieu 1991)
outside the creative writing classroom is much more unified and entrenched.

This, it seems to me, is a point that Canagarajah (2013b) himself would
not disagree with, when he says that any attempt at wider change has to be
gradual:

By inserting the oppositional codes gradually into the existing conventions, I deal with the same audience and genre of communication but
in my own terms. To be really effective, I need to work from within the
existing rules to transform the game. Besides, I need to socialize the
players into the revised rules of the game. The qualified use of alternate
codes into the dominant discourse will serve to both play the game and
also change its rules.

(114)

In this regard, my discussion of the double hermeneutic can be regarded as
one possible way of trying to gradually change the rules of the game. But it
is also crucial to keep in mind that the game that I have focused on in this
paper is not only about writing essays for creative writing classes where,
arguably, the writer might take umbrage at not being able to bring in 'all his
identities'. Rather, it is also about appreciating that organizations, too, and
not just individuals, have identity concerns of their own (Wee 2015), and it
is important for a competent writer to be able to play that particular game
(i.e., writing for or representing organizations) well.

Notes

1 I am by no means suggesting that there is a neat correlation where flexible multilingualism is only ever associated with individuals and fixed multilingualism with
organizations. Rather, as a general observation, it cannot be denied that formal
organizational settings do tend to discriminate against the use of flexible multilingualism (Otsuji and Pennycook 2010, 246–247; see below).
2 My thanks to Tove Larsson (personal communication) for these observations.

3 This is notwithstanding the fact that there are numerous English loan words in Swedish and Swedish expressions that include English words that are used in everyday conversation, such as 'Det var nice' (= 'It was nice') (Larsson, personal communication).
4 The implementation of this second option, however, is more limited, since teachers of other subjects, such as physics, often do not see language/literacy/discourse as being something that they should concern themselves with (Airey 2012).

References

Airey, J. *Science, Language and Literacy. Case Studies of Learning in Swedish University Physics*. Acta Universitatis Upsaliensis. Uppsala Dissertations from the Faculty of Science and Technology 81. Uppsala: Uppsala University.
———. 2012. ' "I Don't Teach Language": The Linguistic Attitudes of Physics Lecturers in Sweden'. *AILA Review* 25: 64–79.
Blackledge, A., and A. Creese. 2010. *Multilingualism*. London: Continuum.
Blommaert, J. 2010. *The Sociolinguistics of Globalization*. Cambridge: Cambridge University Press.
Blommaert, J., J. Collins, and S. Slembrouck. 2005. 'Spaces of Multilingualism'. *Language & Communication* 25: 197–216.
Bolton, K., and M. Kuteeva. 2012. 'English as an Academic Language at a Swedish University: Parallel Language Use and the "Threat" of English'. *Journal of Multilingual & Multicultural Development* 33 (5): 429–47.
Bourdieu, P. 1991. *Language and Symbolic Power*. Cambridge: Polity Press.
Canagarajah, S. 2005. 'Dilemmas in Planning English/ Vernacular Relations in Post-Colonial Communities'. *Journal of Sociolinguistics* 9 (3): 418–47.
———. 2013a. *Literacy as Translingual Practice*. New York: Routledge.
———. 2013b. *Translingual Practice: Global Englishes and Cosmopolitan Relations*. London: Routledge.
García, O. 2009. *Bilingual Education in the 21st Century: A Global Perspective*. Oxford: Wiley-Blackwell.
Giddens, A. 1987. *Social Theory and Modern Sociology*. Cambridge: Polity Press.
Haberland, H. 2014. 'Epilogue: English from above and below, and from outside'. In *English in Nordic Universities: Ideologies and Practices*, edited by A. Kristina, F. Hultgren, and J. Thøgersen, 251–63. Amsterdam: John Benjamins.
Harissi, M., E. Otsuji, and A. Pennycook. 2012. 'The Performative Fixing and Unfixing of Subjectivities'. *Applied Linguistics* 33 (5): 524–43.
Jørgensen, J. 2008. 'Polylingual Languaging around and among Children and Adolescents'. *International Journal of Multilingualism* 5 (3): 161–76.
Kuteva, M. 2011. 'Editorial: Teaching and Learning in English in Parallel-Language and ELF Settings: Debates, Concerns and Realities in Higher Education'. *Iberica* 22: 5–12.
Leeman, J., and G. Modan. 2009. 'Commodified Language in Chinatown: A Contextualized Approach to Linguistic Landscape'. *Journal of Sociolinguistics* 13 (3): 332–62.
Makoni, S., and A. Pennycook. 2007. *Disinventing and Reconstituting Languages*. Clevedon: Multilingual Matters.
Meyer, J. W., and B. Rowan. 1991. 'Institutionalized Organizations: Formal Structure as Myth and Ceremony'. In *The New Institutionalism in Organizational*

Analysis, edited by W. W. Powell, and P. J. DiMaggio, 41–62. Chicago: University of Chicago Press.

Nuttall, S. 2009. *Entanglement*. Johannesburg: Wits University Press.

Otsuji, E., and A. Pennycook. 2010. 'Metrolingualism: Fixity, Fluidity and Language in Flux'. *International Journal of Multilingualism* 7: 240–54.

Prodromou, L. 2008. *English as a Lingua Franca: A Corpus-based Analysis*. London: Continuum.

Swedish Government. 2009. Language Act (SFS 2009:600).

Swedish Language Council. 1998. *Draft Action Programme for the Promotion of the Swedish Language*. Stockholm: Språkrådet

Weber, J. J. and K. Horner. 2012. *Introducing Multilingualism:A Social Approach*. New York/London: Routledge.

Wee, L. 2015. Under preparation. 'Are There Zombies in Language Policy?' In *Sociolinguistics: Theoretical Debates*, edited by N. Coupland. Cambridge: Cambridge University Press.

Weber, J. and K. Horner. 2012. *Introducing Multilingualism: A Social Approach*. New York/London: Routledge.

Widdowson, H. G. 1994. 'The Ownership of English'. *TESOL Quarterly* 28 (2): 377–89.

Young, A. A. 2004. 'Experiences in Ethnographic Interviewing about Race: The Inside and Outside of It.' In *Researching Race and Racism*, edited by M. Bulmer and J. Solomos, 187–202. New York: Routledge Taylor & Francis Group.

8 Nine Months of Entextualizations

Discourse and Knowledge in an Online Discussion Forum Thread for Expectant Parents

Linnea Hanell & Linus Salö

Introduction

This chapter is concerned with knowledge as an object of sociolinguistic inquiry. Drawing on some key work in mediated discourse analysis, MDA (Jones 2013; Scollon and Scollon 2004), we hold that knowledge is a crucial aspect of the processes whereby people take actions with discourses. We frame this pursuit by dwelling on the interwoven relationship between power and knowledge, aiming at accentuating the ways in which social structures of power stratify knowledge in *orders of visibility*, rendering some types of knowledge, as well as the practices that produce them, more credible, more legitimate—and hence more *visible*—than others. As we shall argue here, however, practices and artefacts arising on the internet reconfigure such old-established orders of visibility, as they potentially change people's access to knowledge, technologically as well as socially.

At the core of our research agenda here are the ways in which historical entanglements of power are manifested in contemporary practices where people increasingly appropriate control over medical knowledge (Briggs 2005). From this vantage point, what we will do in this chapter is pry into issues of knowledge (and thus power) by directing attention to the Swedish online discussion forum *Familjeliv.se*, where matters and experiences of family life are discussed, thereby generating accounts on that topic that can function as means to take actions. More precisely, we analyze a particular forum thread that assembles prospective parents expecting a child in the same month, who produce and simultaneously draw on this thread as a knowledge resource. The objective here is twofold. First, we seek to reach an in-depth understanding of the ways in which the forum thread can function as a knowledge resource. We therefore attempt to disentangle some of the discursive activities that occur in the forum thread, and interpret them in relation to actions concerning pregnancy and parenting, so as to account for how this discourse produces something that can function as knowledge. Second, we aim at bringing to light the ways in which *entextualizations* invoke issues of power in the processes of knowledge production.

Here, we analyze the forum thread data in terms of cycles in which actions, through processes of entextualization, are transformed into pieces of discourse, which in turn are *recentred* in the forum thread, and so made available as knowledge which may inform new actions (cf. Jones 2013). Essentially, the concepts of entextualization and recentring (Bauman and Briggs 1990) are here pivotal for grasping knowledge in a practice approach, as they open up insights into the ways in which knowledge emanates from actions—in fact *is* the outcome of actions—as well as the ways in which knowledge is first and foremost realized as it is applied in concrete actions.

We begin by framing the issue: Power and knowledge in the wired age, after which we introduce Familjeliv.se as a discursive locus. Next, we theorize knowledge and entextualization as research topics and tools. After this, we present data obtained from the forum thread, analyzed through the lens of entextualization. In our discussion, following this, we contemplate our findings regarding knowledge in relation to power and orders of visibility. In the final concluding remarks, we shall argue that knowledge is a phenomenon to be understood in the intersection of discourse and action, and that entextualization mediates this relationship.

The Frame: Power and Knowledge

The assertion that knowledge *is* power is often attributed to the sixteenth century philosopher Francis Bacon. In the work of Foucault, this sententious phrase is pushed to the extent that the two words are framed as inextricably inter-related. Hence, he famously substituted the 'is' with a slash, power/knowledge, claiming that '[i]t is not possible for power to be exercised without knowledge, it is impossible for knowledge not to engender power' (1980, 52). Foucault considers *discourse* to be the chief concept for disclosing the ways in which knowledge on a particular topic is represented through language and practice at a particular point in time and place (Hall 1997, 44). He invokes the notion of *order of discourse* to suggest that 'in every society the production of discourse is at once controlled, selected, organised and redistributed by a certain number of procedures whose role it is to ward off its powers and dangers' (Foucault 1981, 52). Analogically, we argue that there are orders of visibility regarding knowledge in the sense that discourse casts some types of knowledge as more open to negotiation than others. Knowledge, thus, is a stratified construct, interest-laden and historically saturated with power, and, as Hall (1997, 42) notes, some people have more power to speak about some subjects than others. It follows from this position that all types of knowledge are neither equally valorized, nor equally *visible*.

In Sweden and other welfare states alike, knowledge that emanates from official authorities embedded in the power field of the state tends to acquire a value as more credible than knowledge that stems from other practices. On this point, Bourdieu (2000) sees the institutions of the state as holders of the privilege to impose *the* legitimate vision of the world; through the state, they 'have established their viewpoints as the universal viewpoint, after struggles against rival views' (2000, 174). A case in point is provided by the institutionalization of medical knowledge in Sweden, which Johannisson (1997) dates to the late eighteenth century—in other words the point in time where Foucault (1973) placed 'the birth of the clinic.' The development of professionalized medical epistemologies brought about a misrecognition of knowledge emanating from alternative medicine and *folk*-medicine (Johannisson 1997). This struggle yielded an order of visibility where doctors and other health professionals, through institutional support, came to be reinforced as bearers of medical truth. Medical authorities have since provided the Swedish state and its health institutions with what has generally been regarded as valid and reliable health information.

It may be argued, however, that the advent of the internet re-orders some of these entanglements of power and knowledge, as it allows the general public—*the former audience* (Gillmor 2004)—to become active co-constructors of widely visible discourse. For what has become of the internet is not only an *information superhighway*, as it was often pictured in its early days (Besser 1995), that is to say, a channel for information to move between (offline) spaces, but also a range of spaces in themselves where knowledge is produced, negotiated, and applied to concrete circumstances. This technical development has, arguably, resulted in a disarrangement of what might be perceived as the state's monopoly of knowledge (Bourdieu 2014), as public and local authorities are nowadays entailed to co-exist with other, less legitimate producers of entextualized knowledge. An example of such tension is provided by the Swedish website Familjeliv and its popular discussion forum for topics regarding family life.

Locus, Data, and Approach

Familjeliv (literally 'family life') is one of the most frequented websites in Sweden, with around 700,000 unique visitors every week.[1] It is explicitly profiled[2] as a meeting place for women, where users can share tips and support each other around issues regarding family, parenting, and pregnancy. The orientation towards female users is evident in editorial and commercial pictures on the site, which predominantly portray women and children, as well as in written discourse where direct address is often restricted to readers who can breastfeed, are pregnant, have a menstrual cycle, etc. Only one subcategory of the discussion forum, labelled *Pappagrupp* ('Dads' group'), explicitly addresses male users. Apart from the discussion forum, the website also includes a variety of editorial, commercial, and user-generated content. Writing and replying to posts in the discussion forum is reserved for registered users, but reading is open for anyone. The home page of the site can be seen in Figure 8.1.

Familjeliv's discussion forum bears a resemblance to other popular discussion forums in contemporary Sweden in that it has varied content and

Figure 8.1 Home Page on Familjeliv.se
(Screenshot 21 March 2014)

different kinds of threads dealing with topics spanning from acute issues that may be solved within a handful of posts, to more general discussions that may be ongoing for years. However, Familjeliv appears to stand out among the most popular Swedish discussion forums in that it focuses on a particular area of interest (family life), and in that it at the same time commonly houses support groups for people in a certain situation within this area. Every month, for example, a couple of threads are started that assemble people who are expecting a child one specific month. This study deals with one such thread.

The analyzed thread assembles 231 participants[3] who write 11,420 posts over a time span of one year. The title of this thread addresses users who are expecting a child a particular month. The thread immediately reached high activity, with more than 150 posts the first day, and an average of 43 posts a day up until the end of the due month, after which activity rapidly decreased. Author 1 followed the thread in real-time for nine months from the start of the thread to the last reports of birth at the end of the due month. The mere 46 messages posted during three months after the babies were born were analyzed retrospectively. Although the title does not impose such a restriction, all active participants are pregnant women, some with their first child, and some with previous experience of childbearing and parenting. The thread was started eight months before the expected month of birth, meaning that the participants (granted the expected month of delivery was correct) were in pregnancy week three to seven. At the time of writing, the thread is still available online for both reading and posting, but no new posts have been made since three months after the due month.

Procedure

Data generated from this online fieldwork include the thread itself, field notes, screenshots, and extracted sequences of interaction. The observations during fieldwork were consistently oriented towards issues of knowledge, and after finishing up the fieldwork, the data were analyzed in retrospect to find patterns of common activities that constitute the thread as a knowledge resource. Three key activities were identified: exchanging information, providing reports, and contesting knowledge. With these labels, we do not intend to cover the whole content of the thread, not even all parts of the content that relate to knowledge in some way. Rather, it is the activities that seem to be particularly important to constitute the thread as a knowledge resource that are in focus. Furthermore, the labels do not exclude one another, and are not put to work to categorize separate posts: The activity of exchanging information may, for example, well include the activity of providing a report.

Notes on Ethics[4]

The online context poses a range of ethical challenges for sociolinguistic analysis (Varis 2014). First, the kind of discussion forum thread analyzed in this particular case typically includes a large number of participants, making it practically impossible to achieve consent from all. Second, as pointed out in the ethical guidelines from the Association of Internet Researchers (Markham and Buchanan 2012, 6–7), people may uphold clear expectations of privacy even when they appear in public spaces. Supposedly aware that Familjeliv is a highly public setting, the members of this forum have taken some precautions to protect their integrity: Most participants never state their name, and to a varying extent they conceal their identity when they share pictures and talk about where they live.

Nevertheless, we have taken further measures to protect their identities, given that the privacy precautions the participants have taken are intended for the context of the discussion forum. In other words, it is a matter of what Nissenbaum (2010) has termed *contextual integrity*. To recentre their discursive products in this new frame with new regimes of control destabilizes the original privacy considerations of the participating individuals—regardless of the fact that this piece of research is in many ways less public than Familjeliv.

Concretely, the following measures have been taken to protect participants' anonymity. None of the participants have been approached by us, so as to avoid a scenario where some of the participants know of our analytical agenda on this particular thread, while some are not able to consent to it. Because of this disguised analytical work, we have not posted any messages in the thread. The exact title of the thread is not revealed, and the participants' aliases are substituted with randomly selected names. In order to avoid the traceability of the thread by copy-pasting extracts to a search engine, the original Swedish phrasings are not provided. Furthermore, the timestamps appended to the extracts do not respond to calendar months, but to the months passed since the starting of the thread. This corresponds roughly to the participants' pregnancy months, and all participants were meant to give birth at some point during month nine.

Knowledge: A Matter of Discourse and Action

In mediated discourse analysis, the two most basic concepts for theoretical inquiry are action and discourse—what people do and the language that they use in doing it (Norris and Jones 2005; Scollon and Scollon 2004). At heart, we understand the forum thread in this intersection of discourse and action: People engage in discourse as a way of enabling future actions—as well as reporting about, reflecting upon, and reframing previous ones. It is in these relations between discourse and action that knowledge is produced. Therefore, we employ the notion of knowledge to be able to foreground aspects of the way in which conceptualizations of previous actions, through discourse, are used in taking new actions. What we mean by knowledge here, then, is reflections of former actions recentred as a resource for taking a current or future action. For example, when a participant in the thread states that it is good to have a particular ointment by the nursing table, this is fundamentally a reflection of her own history of acting in relation to a baby. This statement is treated as knowledge by another participant who asks for advice for supplying her nursing table, anticipating in turn future actions of caring for her baby (cf. Scollon and Scollon 2004, 18–34). We thereby concur with van Leeuwen (2008, vii) in the supposition that 'all discourses recontextualize social practices, and that all knowledge is, therefore, ultimately grounded in practice, however slender that link may seem at times.' Additionally, we hold that *entextualization* is a concept attuned to specifying how this relationship operates. From this viewpoint, knowledge is a matter of utilizing discourse to construe resources for action. As will be emphasized, this involves processes of entextualizing actions, that is, treating them as objects through the use of discourse, and thus rendering them recentrable, that is, possible to move across times and spaces.

Entextualizing and Recentring

The last few decades of sociolinguistic research have seen a rich array of theoretical endeavours to understand transformational processes whereby discourse changes its form, as it is shuffled across time and space (Bauman and Briggs 1990; Salö and Hanell 2014; Scollon 2008; Silverstein and Urban

1996). The concept employed in this study is entextualization, which was originally defined as 'the process of rendering discourse extractable, of making a stretch of linguistic production into a unit—a *text*—that can be lifted out of its interactional setting' (Bauman and Briggs 1990, 73, emphasis in original). Later studies have been less prone to emphasize linguistic form, and rather consider reified, materialized texts to be only one possible outcome of such processes. For example, adopting a more semiotic approach, Jones (2009) draws on entextualization to account for processes whereby actions become 'frozen,' so as to also include photography. Similarly, Massoud and Kuipers (2008) talk of entextualization as a type of *objectification*, and use it in its broadest meaning as discourse positioned as 'a verbal thing to which we can refer' (2008, 217). Accordingly, they use examples of entextualizations as loosely materialized as a repetition of what another person has said in a conversation.

Applied to processes of knowledge making, we will here use entextualization in order to point to the complex array of embedded processes whereby actions are referred to in discourse and thus rendered fixed and therefore transferable, evoking units ranging from full texts to particular propositions. Of these units, we are here predominantly interested in the latter. Concretely, we argue that the production of a proposition such as 'I put on 30 kg with my first baby' involves a transformational process of making a range of prior actions and events into an experience, which is then given the linguistic form of a proposition. This transformational process is what we call entextualization. The unit produced by this process can then be transferred to a new situation, and recentred in discourse, making it possible to draw on this proposition as knowledge. An example found in the data is that a participant presents the proposition about weight gain as a way of helping another participant anticipate her own weight progress. The production of a piece of knowledge is consequently a discursive process: Actions in a given historical time and place are transferable to a current time and place through discourse that renders those actions disposed to be decentred, entextualized, and recentred. These dynamics are enclosed in Jones's (2013, 30) cyclic model of the relationship between discourse and action (Figure 8.2). Here, action is linked to discourse through processes of entextualization, whereas discourse, in turn, is linked back to action through processes of recentring.[5]

Notably, this is a cycle and not a circle: As Bauman and Briggs (1990, 67) remark, processes of entextualization do not 'simply imply a circular movement from text to context to text.' Rather, the way that discourse travels and is transformed between social spaces is a process carried out by actual social actors taking concrete actions with discourse. Thus, the action that is entextualized into discourse already includes some form of recentred discourses. This way, a particular piece of discourse may be gradually 'solidified' as it is shuffled through numerous processes of entextualizations (Scollon and Scollon 2004, 28). Ultimately, we draw on entextualization in order to point

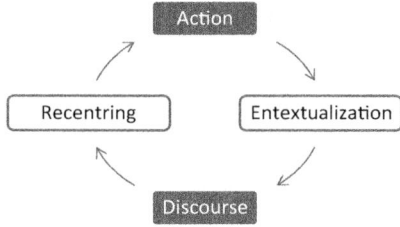

Figure 8.2 The Cycle of Action and Discourse
(Adapted from Jones 2013, 30)

to issues of power linked to the production of knowledge. From this outlook, representations of knowledge found in the interactional data have a trajectory of their own. Like discourse, a given piece of knowledge 'carries elements of its history of use within it' (Bauman and Briggs 1990, 73). Consequently, as the piece of knowledge is recentred in the forum thread, it brings with it aspects of power and authority, which get caught up and entangled with pieces of knowledge of vastly different trajectories.

The Thread as a Knowledge Resource

In what follows, we present three discursive activities that occur frequently in the forum thread, which produce discourse apposite to relate to as a means to take actions.

Exchanging Information

Much of the discourse in the thread relates rather directly to knowledge about pregnancy or infants. The most straightforward examples are sequences of interaction that start off with someone requesting accounts of other participants' experiences or plans on a certain matter. An example of interaction with such a communicative end can be seen in Extract 1.

In this sequence, the thread becomes a resource for picking up non-officialized discourse, that is, for acquiring come-in-handy parenting knowledge that is primarily the product of lived experience and that is seldom entextualized within the practices of public health services. Prior to this sequence, the participant Marie has recurrently mentioned that she has children, and she thus has the capacity of recentring lived experience in the forum thread. As can be seen, Marie also brings pharmaceutical discourse into the interaction, inserting actual product names of some of the medical products she recommends. Notably, what is essentially a range of former actions are here entextualized as propositions such as 'Dialon powder might

Extract 1 Supplying the nursing table

Post no Participant Timestamp	Post
#10794 Emma 8/13 14:01	We also still have the nursing table left to prepare! What kind of supplies will you guys get for it? A soft changing pad (or whatever those mattress thingies are called?) Diapers, wet wipes . . .? Anything else?
#10795 Marie 8/13 14:10	Some kind of ointment from a pharmacy is good, like Idomin, and Dialon powder might be good to have. I never buy wet wipes, I have ordinary dry washcloths . . . Wet wipes only in the diaper bag.
#10797 Isabelle 8/13 14:34	Wipes, ointment from a pharmacy, diapers (cloth + disposable). Then there will be a box for other supplies, like a hairbrush, a pair of nail scissors, a toothbrush until that's needed, cotton, etc. Nursing pads for me will also be by the nursing table!

be good to have.' This transformation includes the process of understanding a range of prior actions as an experience. Transient prior actions are thus made into a unit that can be given the textual form of information, recentred in the thread to the benefit of Emma. In this respect, information is typically intentionally composed entextualizations to be used for constructing knowledge. This kind of information exchange is used extensively throughout the thread, often providing access to experiences and insights that are seldom entextualized in official discourse.

Providing Reports

In addition to this kind of information exchange, the thread is also largely constituted by reports that do not respond to any explicit request. Posts of this kind often seem to have no clear pre-constructed purpose apart from keeping the conversation going. Examples range from accounts of what the participant has planned for the weekend, to briefings about current pregnancy related matters, such as measures and figures recently obtained from a meeting at the maternity clinic. As pointed out by Malinowski ([1923] 1994), interaction of this kind typically fulfills a social function, and he termed it *phatic communion*: 'A type of speech in which ties of union are created by a mere exchange of words' (10). With the emergence of online social life, the notion of phatic communion has experienced a significant revival in social research (e.g., the contributions in Blommaert and Varis 2015), not least as a means for understanding online situations where 'the maintenance of a network itself has become the primary focus' (Miller 2008, 398). These posts are often neither contextualized metadiscursively nor placed sequentially after posts where the same issue has been touched upon, rendering them somewhat contextually detached. They are often left uncommented, but every now and then they constitute what in MDA is referred to as *sites of engagement*, that is intersections in time and space that 'make certain kinds of social actions possible' (Jones 2013, 57). The kinds of social actions made possible, from our analytical position, are additional entextualizations on a similar matter. An example of this is shown in Extract 2, which starts off with a report of one participant's weight gain and

Extract 2 Getting in Control Over One's Weight Gain

Post no Participant Timestamp	Post
#6325 Hannah 4/8 20:39	Oooooooopsss . . . Plus 12 kg in w20 . . . Well well . . I put on 30 and 35 kg during my other pregnancies . . . But I guess I'll have to start thinking about what I eat now . . .
#6336 Josephine 4/8 22:27	[quote #6325] It's hard when you realize that you've kind of lost control over the weight. I'm afraid that the last part of my pregnancy and the delivery will be tough if I put on too much? It makes the babies bigger = harder to squeeze out, right?? Last time I got a c-section because of breech presentation, and I put on 13 kg in total (the baby girl weighed 4530), but this time I've already put on 10 kg. Let's hope the baby's weight isn't proportional to my weight gain ☺
#6339 Hannah 4/8 22:37	With my first I put on 30 kg and out comes a little 2850 gram nugget . . . and that's after a full length pregnancy . . . [quote #6336]
#6367 Sophie 4/9 09:56	[quote #6339] I'm in week 17 and have put on 11kg. I eat healthy food and I get some exercise. Have SPD[6] which keeps me from walking and moving properly, but I use a stationary bike and do the weight training I can manage. If I'm to 'stop' my weight gain I have to go on a strict diet. And I'm not going to do that. Last time I lost all extra weight in 10 weeks without doing anything (didn't breastfeed either) I'm pretty fit and slim 'usually'
#6494 Josephine 4/9 21:41	[quote #6367] It's valuable to hear about what you guys have been through, since it's so much I'm pondering over. Soothing to be able to hear about other people's experiences and interpretations, it puts one's own thoughts in perspective. Good to realize it can be in many different ways. Right, dieting is certainly not something one is advised to do.. I for one am going to try and get some support from a dietician. Of course I know when I'm eating junk and when not, but I need support from someone who can boost me and maybe give me some structure so I can cut down on the junk food . . .

is followed up by other participants who talk about weight gain from the perspective of their own experience.

In the thread, this aspect of linguistic use, where participants provide unrequested reports of this kind, is often shown to be meaningful in establishing sites of engagement where participants can ask questions and in other ways use the thread as a knowledge resource. As can be seen, Hannah's initial report in Extract 2 is not metadiscursively contextualized in any way, but it still initiates a conversation on the introduced topic. In the extract are only some of the contributions to what can be seen as a corpus of weight gain narratives that the participants in the thread build up after Hannah's post, thereby constructing a frame of normality to which other participants can relate (Drentea and Moren-Cross 2005, 931). A key in this project is the entextualization of bodily transformations, measured in grams and pregnancy weeks. Such entextualizations of the body are identified by Jones (2013, 133–8) as crucial for the process he calls *medical imagining*. Weighing her own body, Hannah makes the transient transformation of her body into something measurable, and apparently, this facilitates a comparison between different experiences of pregnancy. As Josephine joins the conversation to give an account of her experience of pregnancy, she entextualizes not only bodily measurements, but also her suspicions and fears about what consequences these transformations might have. Recentring these in the conversation in the form of propositions, she explicitly invites someone to challenge them, by using question marks and the possibly defying 'right??' to which Hannah answers by refuting her conclusions with a more detailed entextualization of the bodily transformations during her first pregnancy.

In the last post of the extract, Josephine concludes the last days' conversation about weight gain with an explicit metapragmatic statement. Expressing gratitude over the opportunity to share other participants' experiences, she explains that the reason these narratives are so 'valuable' and 'soothing' is that they *put her own thoughts in perspective*. In other words, by entextualizing their experiences of bodily transformation, the participants in the thread can juxtapose them, and thus reevaluate the very experience. Thus, beyond creating ties of union, posts like the first one in Extract 2 fill the function of introducing topics of conversation that are central in the thread's capacity to function as a knowledge resource.

Contesting Knowledge

Previous extracts have shown that the forum thread is frequently used to provide insight into private, seemingly trivial experiences. However, the lived experience entextualized in the thread also encompasses the participants' actions in non-private life. Thus, knowledge obtained from institutional settings such as hospitals and maternity clinics is often recentred in the thread, a practice that opens up opportunities for the participants to negotiate the implication of information and recommendations they have received.

Moreover, the participants also juxtapose knowledge obtained from different professional health practices. Extract 3 constitutes an example of this. The conversation is here directed towards thrush infections, and a range of participants have contributed with entextualizations of their experiences of treating this condition. The extract starts with Monica providing an account of the treatment she has been recommended. This report triggers a juxtaposition of experiences that appear to disagree with each other, as Ingrid and Monica have been given contradictory advice from their respective clinics.

As can be seen, Monica mentions parenthetically that her midwife has recommended Canesten ointment. Responding to this, Ingrid reports that

Extract 3 Treating a Thrush Infection

Post no Participant Timestamp	Post
#1837 Monica 1/25 21:21 (truncated)	I've also got a thrush infection as a delightful bonus for my eating of Kåvepenin[7]! Gah! Talked with an MW[8] about it and she recommended Canesten[9] (ointment not pessaries). Not very comfortable about both taking antibiotics for tonsillitis and using all sorts of creams 'down there' this early. Will take antibiotics for two more days, then I hope my thrush infection goes away!
#1839 Ingrid 1/25 21:34	Monica: That's weird, my ob-gyn said the exact opposite! He said Canesten pessaries, but not ointment. And in the information leaflet to Canesten it says they don't recommend the ointment during pregnancy, but only the pessaries. It's so confusing when different 'experts' give different information!
#1840 Monica 1/25 21:39	[quote #1839] Strange! I agree, it's such a mess! Maybe I should go with traditional yoghurt? Though I've never tried that and it seems super scary, but now I don't wanna go on with the ointment in spite of what the MW said. Argh, this makes me slightly crazy . . .
#1841 Ingrid 1/25 21:50	Isn't it weird?? You should think they all had the same information :/ Check around online for household remedies, everything works differently on different people! I for one am not helped by yoghurt, but the solution for me have been zero sweets and that I binge lemon water as soon as I can sense a thrush infection, it's the only thing that works for me. On the other hand, you take penicillin, so maybe yoghurt is exactly what you need if your lactic acid bacteria are all wiped out. But try EATING yoghurt or sour milk for starters, it can actually be enough. I mean, if you're skeptical about messing about with it down there . . .:)
#1842 Monica 1/25 22:01	[quote #1841] Lemon water and yoghurt on the table now! Thanks for awesome tips!

her ob-gyn has recommended the exact opposite: Pessaries, not ointment. Entextualizations originating from Monica's midwife are thus juxtaposed with entextualizations originating from Ingrid's ob-gyn, and the forum thread, as an already established space for interaction between Monica and Ingrid, becomes the site where this contestation is enacted. As can be seen, Ingrid recentres a proposition resourced from the information leaflet, which appears to support her ob-gyn's recommendation of avoiding the ointment during pregnancy. Both Ingrid and Monica express that it is 'strange,' 'confusing', or 'such a mess' that there is no consensus among the group of people that they label as 'experts.' Apparently, they consider Monica's midwife, Ingrid's ob-gyn, and the writer of the information leaflet to be representatives of the same medical authority, who are consequently expected to produce entextualizations in harmony with each other. The outcome of this conflict is that Monica chooses to entirely discount recommendations from medical authorities, and instead follow Ingrid's example of consuming lemon water and yoghurt, a line of action hailing to a register distinctively different from the *expertise* that has apparently exhausted its credibility. Above all, this extract shows an important way in which the forum functions as a knowledge resource, namely that it allows the participants to recentre authoritative knowledge in the thread, and consequently appropriate control over issues concerning their own bodies (cf. Briggs 2005). Notably, in Extract 3 both Ingrid and Monica join an already ongoing discussion of thrush infections. They can, and evidentially do, discuss this topic in professional health care settings as well, but because that is a different site of engagement, the discursive actions unfold in a different manner there. This perspective on action illustrates why the participants asking questions about, for example, thrush infections or weight gain cannot take the same actions in a completely different but supposedly more appropriate context, such as a maternity clinic.

Discussion: Knowledge, Power, and Orders of Visibility

One of the key stakes of contemporary symbolic struggle pertains to the power over the instruments of knowledge (Bourdieu 2000, 186). Discursive representations of knowledge are perforce enmeshed in relations of power, because they are, at heart, vested in the regulation of social conduct in practice (Hall 1997, 47). As this chapter has shown, the forum thread analyzed can be seen as a site of entangled discourses, comprising various actors, activities, places, and relations. It follows from this that the thread encloses a certain tension, engendered due to the fact that it embraces an arena for the display and dissemination of pieces of knowledge, which challenge the state's monopoly. These are pieces of knowledge borne out of a different order of visibility, recentred in the thread as pieces of information for others to use. Many of the topics that arise in the forum thread relate to health, and there is a widespread opinion that online sites with user-generated content are inappropriate as sources for health information (see Powell et al. 2005 for a critical overview). In fact, new parents are occasionally discouraged from using online sources all together. A case in point is found in an interview in the popular parenting magazine *Föräldrar & Barn* ['Parents & Kids'], where a midwife urges pregnant women to 'Google with care' (as the headline puts it), or rather not google at all, and warns them against trusting information acquired from informal online contexts rather than from medical health care:

> The advice she gives to pregnant patients is that they should stop googling all together. —I think they should use their midwife as a sounding board instead. We google too, and there is lots of good information online, but we can evaluate the sources in another way. (. . .) Many people do not dare to have faith in medical staff today. It is so easy to pick up information by reading on the web, you can even get it through your phone, and there is a risk that you trust that information more.
>
> (Perman 2014, our translation)

It is easy to be sympathetic with this health professional, who, as a producer of authoritative discourse, is at pains to defend the market for her competence (Bourdieu 2000, 106). However, our data show that the knowledge that circulates through the forum thread does not exclusively stem from private settings. In the process of entextualizing prior experiences as posts in the forum, authoritative discourse from professionals regularly emanates in the forum thread through the entry point of the participants' individual histories.

In the light of this study, we argue that the fear indexed by the imperative 'Google with care' is based on uninformed assumptions that on the whole exaggerate the potential risks of engaging in online discourse with other laypeople. First, at the level of epistemology, this risk discourse reproduces the idea that some forms of practical knowledge pervert the otherwise pure nature of knowledge (Bourdieu 2000). This reflects what Briggs (2005, 274–5) refers to as *the linearity of dominant ideologies of communication*, that is, 'the idea that knowledge is produced in scientific or other expert sectors, disseminated through other spheres, and then assimilated by publics.' Second, it builds on the assumption that people who engage in discussion forums lack the ability to reflect critically upon their own actions and the propositions they make in discussion forums and similar discursive contexts. Third, it supposes that their engagement in the discussion forum excludes engagement in other practices, and that it thus competes with professional knowledge. As our data show, the discourse that circulates in the forum thread often includes pieces of knowledge obtained from professional health care practices, which are discussed and re-evaluated as they are recentred in the thread. In contrast to the mentioned presuppositions, the participants producing this discourse: (1) Demonstrate an awareness of the origin of the propositions the make, (2) reflect upon and discuss implications of them, and (3), in fact, enhance experiences of encounters with health professionals as they recentre meaningful parts in the conversation of the thread.

Concluding Remarks

This chapter argues that knowledge is a phenomenon to be understood in the intersection of discourse and action, and that entextualization mediates this relationship. In the wired age, a discussion forum functions as a discursive vortex where pieces of knowledge of different orders of visibility converge. Whereas the tools and perspectives of MDA here provide a lens to grasp the ways in which this process operates, the notion of entextualization brings additional specificity to the insights into such matters. From this vantage point, knowledge encompasses, on the one hand, the process whereby a range of past actions are entextualized into a discursive entity that can be moved between spaces and times. On the other hand, it encompasses the process whereby such a discursive entity is recentred as something to draw on in a situation where a new action is taken. This way, the forum thread offers a way of making mundane actions visible, entextualized, and suitable to be employed as knowledge. Ultimately, what people do in the thread is 'secure the right to decontextualize discourse and recontextualize it in different settings' (Briggs 2005, 273), thus enabling themselves to appropriate control over the biologically and socially turbulent experience of pregnancy. Examining the process through which experiences recentred in the posts become *knowledge*, it is evident that knowledge is a fundamentally emergent phenomenon, and rather than having an independent existence of its own, it is what former actions, recentred in discourse, *are used as* (cf. Salö and Hanell 2014, 25). To the extent that the forum thread can function as a knowledge resource, it is thus 'not just a repository of information' (Heaton 2011, 216), that is, a collection of 'facts.' Rather, and in a more complex way, it is discourse that can be utilized, to speak with MDA, as a means to take an action.

Acknowledgements

We wish to thank Anders Björkvall, Mona Blåsjö, Karin Hagren Idevall, David Karlander, and Valelia Muni Toke for reading drafts at various stages of this article. Thanks also go to the two anonymous reviewers and to the editors Caroline Kerfoot and Kenneth Hyltenstam.

Notes

1 See ('ORVESTO Internet' 2014). The current population of Sweden is about 9.5 million people.
2 http://www.familjeliv.se/article/Information/om accessed 28 August 2015.
3 Defined as people who post at least once in the thread.

4 The study design, including the measures reported here, has been approved by The Regional Ethical Review Board in Stockholm (http://www.epn.se/en).
5 Jones uses the term *text* where we use *discourse*, and *recontextualization* for *recentring*. Bauman and Briggs (1990) use the terms *recentring* and *recontextualization* interchangeably. In this chapter, we prefer *recentre* since, in our view, the target is not necessarily a defined 'context.' Furthermore, we prefer to speak of *discourse* rather than *text* in order to regard different modalities of discourse by means of the same label.
6 Abbreviation of *symphysis pubis dysfunction*, a condition commonly associated with pregnancy, which causes pain in the pelvic region. Notably, the Swedish term used, 'foglossning,' is not an abbreviation.
7 Kåvepenin is a prescription-only antibiotic.
8 MW is commonly used in the thread as an acronym for midwife (Swedish *barnmorska—BM*).
9 Canesten is an over-the-counter anti-thrush medicine.

References

Bauman, R., and C. L. Briggs. 1990. 'Poetics and Performance as Critical Perspectives on Language and Social Life'. *Annual Review of Anthropology* 19: 59–88.
Besser, H. 1995. 'From Internet to Information SuperHighway'. In *Resisting the Virtual Life: The Culture and Politics of Information*, edited by J. Brook and I. A. Boal, 59–70. San Francisco: City Lights.
Blommaert, J., and P. Varis, eds. 2015. 'Special Issue'. *Multilingual Margins: A Journal of Multilingualism from the Periphery* 2 (1): 1–100.
Bourdieu, P. 2000. *Pascalian Meditations*. Cambridge: Polity.
———. 2014. *On the State: Lectures at the College de France 1989–1992*. Cambridge: Polity.
Briggs, C. L. 2005. 'Communicability, Racial Discourse, and Disease'. *Annual Review of Anthropology* 34 (1): 269–91.
Drentea, P., and J. L. Moren-Cross. 2005. 'Social Capital and Social Support on the Web: The Case of an Internet Mother Site'. *Sociology of Health & Illness* 27 (7): 920–43.
Foucault, M. 1973. *The Birth of the Clinic: An Archaeology of Medical Perception*. New York: Pantheon Books.
———. 1980. *Power/Knowledge: Selected Interviews and Other Writings 1972–1977*. Edited by C. Gordon. New York: Pantheon.
———. 1981. 'The Order of Discourse: Inaugural Lecture at the Collège de France, Given 2 December 1970'. In *Untying the Text: A Post-Structuralist Reader*, edited by R. Young, 51–78. Boston: Routledge.
Gillmor, D. 2004. *We the Media: Grassroots Journalism by the People, for the People*. Beijing: O'Reilly.
Hall, S. 1997. 'The Work of Representation'. In *Representation: Cultural Representations and Signifying Practices*, edited by S. Hall, 13–74. London: Sage.
Heaton, L. 2011. 'Internet and Health Communication'. In *The Handbook of Internet Studies*, edited by M. Consalvo and C. Ess, 212–31. Oxford: Wiley-Blackwell.
Johannisson, K. 1997. *Kroppens Tunna Skal: Sex Essäer Om Kropp, Historia Och Kultur*. Stockholm: Norstedt.
Jones, R. H. 2009. 'Dancing, Skating and Sex: Action and Text in the Digital Age'. *Journal of Applied Linguistics* 6 (3): 283–302.

————. 2013. *Health and Risk Communication: An Applied Linguistic Perspective.* London: Routledge.

Malinowski, B. 1994. 'The Problem of Meaning in Primitive Languages'. In *Language and Literacy in Social Practice: A Reader*, edited by J. Maybin, 1–10. Bristol, UK: Multilingual Matters, the Open University.

Markham, A., and E. Buchanan. 2012. 'Ethical Decision-Making and Internet Research: Recommendations from the AOIR Ethics Committee (Version 2.0)'. Retrieved from http://aoir.org/reports/ethics2.pdf.

Massoud, L. A., and J. C. Kuipers. 2008. 'Objectification and the Inscription of Knowledge in Science Classrooms'. *Linguistics and Education* 19 (3): 211–24.

Miller, V. 2008. 'New Media, Networking and Phatic Culture'. *Convergence: The International Journal of Research into New Media Technologies* 14 (4): 387–400.

Nissenbaum, H. 2010. *Privacy in Context : Technology, Policy, and the Integrity of Social Life.* Stanford: Stanford Law Books.

Norris, S., and R. H. Jones, eds. 2005. *Discourse in Action: Introducing Mediated Discourse Analysis.* London: Routledge.

ORVESTO Internet. 2014. *Rapporter & Undersökningar—Räckviddsrapporter: September 2014 (ORVESTO®) | TNS-Sifo.* Retrieved from http://www.tns-sifo.se/rapporter-undersokningar/rackviddsrapporter-orvesto/orvesto-internet.

Perman, T. 2014. 'Barnmorskans Råd: Googla Lagom!' *Föräldrar & Barn.* Retrieved from http://foraldrarochbarn.se/barnmorskans-rad-googla-inte/.

Powell, J. A., P. Lowe, F. E. Griffiths, and M. Thorogood. 2005. 'A Critical Analysis of the Literature on the Internet and Consumer Health Information'. *Journal of Telemedicine and Telecare* 11 (suppl 1): 41–3.

Salö, L., and L. Hanell. 2014. 'Performance of Unprecedented Genres: Interdiscursivity in the Writing Practices of a Swedish Researcher'. *Language & Communication* 37: 12–28.

Scollon, R. 2008. 'Discourse Itineraries: Nine Processes of Resemiotization'. In *Advances in Discourse Studies*, edited by V. K. Bhatia, J. Flowerdew, and R. H. Jones, 233–44. London: Routledge.

Scollon, R., and S. W. Scollon. 2004. *Nexus Analysis: Discourse and the Emerging Internet.* New York: Routledge.

Silverstein, M., and G. Urban, eds. 1996. *Natural Histories of Discourse.* Chicago: University of Chicago Press.

van Leeuwen, T. 2008. *Discourse and Practice: New Tools for Critical Discourse Analysis.* Oxford: Oxford University Press.

Varis, P. 2014. 'Digital Ethnography'. *Tilburg Papers in Culture Studies No. 104.*

Part IV

North-South Dynamics in Research and Knowledge Production

9　The Politics of the Margins

Multi-Semiotic and Affective Strategies of Voice and Visibility[1]

Tommaso M. Milani

Introduction

Over the last two years, at least in the academic circles of postcolonial, post-apartheid South Africa in which I move, the expression *theory from the South* has started to echo increasingly more frequently and more loudly in a variety of intellectual spaces, from anthropology to urban studies, and from politics to sociolinguistics. For example, at a symposium titled Language Practices, Migration, and Labour organized at the University of the Western Cape in October 2012, several South Africa-based scholars raised reservations about the applicability and relevance of the notion of 'superdiversity' (Vertovec 2007) to the multilingual and multi-semiotic conditions in contemporary South Africa (see also Deumert 2014). In a similar vein, the question of how cities from the South should be theorized from a non-western perspective loomed large over an inter-disciplinary workshop on urban spaces held at the University of the Witwatersrand, Johannesburg, in April 2013. Far from being isolated instances deployed to set the scene for this chapter, these examples are historical materializations of more long-standing discursive formations that have revolved around the question of developing theoretical tools through which to capture phenomena in postcolonial conditions. Such discussions have received renewed impetus as a result of, and in response to, the relatively recent publication of Raewyn Connell's (2007) *Southern Theory* as well as Jean and John Comaroff's (2012) *Theory from the South*.

Apparently oblivious of each other's work (Comaroff and Comaroff 2012, footnote 1), these three authors reach very similar conclusions, albeit considering very different contexts. Connell indicts the universalizing tendencies of 'western theory', that is, the attempt to present as universal what is in actual fact a theoretical leap made on the basis of very local—European or North American—data. As Edensor and Jayne (2012, 8) have noted, Connell does not ask for a complete rejection of 'western' theoretical concepts, but rather argues for transcending North/South and East/West binaries through the creation of 'dirty theory', a hybrid and messy conceptual entanglement 'which chooses ideas that suit particular situations' (Edensor and Jayne 2012, 8; see also Wodak (2001) for a similar proposal based on Mouzelis' (1995) notion of 'conceptual pragmatism').

Reasoning along similar lines, the Comaroffs (2012) expose the Eurocentric bias of much contemporary scholarship in the social sciences and the humanities, an academic enterprise in which the North is consistently and unashamedly posited as 'the wellspring of universal learning' and the South as 'a place of parochial wisdom, of antiquarian traditions, of exotic ways and means. And above all, of unprocessed data' (1). In their view, we should look instead at the global South as a site which 'affords privileged insight into the workings of the world at large' (47), thus ultimately allowing theory to escape the very North/South dichotomy.

The reading of both books raises more questions than it provides answers: What counts as the South, or the West and the North, for that matter? Is the South a geographical location, a socio-political position, or a heuristic viewpoint? Do Australia and New Zealand count as the South in the same way as, say, Brazil or South Africa do? Do former 'Eastern bloc' countries form part of the South by virtue of their socio-political, post-Soviet conditions? And, why invoke one pole of a binary—South—if the ultimate goal is to outstrip such dichotomy?

The main problem I see with the deployment of the notion of the South, or any other cardinal point for that matter, is that the very act of using this spatial, sociocultural, political, and historical position brings with it the spectre of essentialism, namely the assumption that conditions in the South are *inherently* and *ontologically* different from those in the North, or that data generated in Southern contexts *necessarily* need to be read through non-Northern theoretical heuristic lenses. As post-structuralism has taught us, dyadic thinking is intrinsically reductionist for several reason. It is bound up with processes of epistemological power whereby one element of the binary is recast as better, more suitable, or academically 'cooler' than the other (see also Baker 2008). Moreover, postcolonial scholars have pointed out that binary understandings fail to account for the complex interconnectedness of the elements of a dyad. For example, it would be too simplistic to understand the colonies as geographically far-away spaces external to the metropole. Quite the contrary, colonies and metropoles were mutually constitutive, creating entangled relations of social, cultural, economic, and epistemological interdependency (Cooper and Stoler 1997; see also Nuttall 2009). Finally, dyadic thinking runs the risk of creating allochronic histories. Most cogently expressed through Johannes Fabian's (1983) notion of 'denial of coevalness', the point here is that, whether posited as backwards and not-there-yet or as ahead of time and 'harbingers of future history', (Comaroff and Comaroff 2012, 12), postcolonial contexts of the South are presented as belonging to a different temporal dimension than their Northern counterparts.

It is because of these limitations that, in line with the rationale underlying this volume, I would argue for a different type of positionality, one that is more multifaceted, more slippery, and emotionally more ambiguous than the South espoused by Connell and the Comaroffs, namely that of the *margins*. Such a proposal is the result of a long-standing dialogue with Christopher Stroud about "loci of enunciation" (Bhabha 1994) in the context of the establishment of the new journal *Multilingual Margins*, based at the University of the Western Cape. Marginality inherently points us towards what at a particular moment is (viewed as) non-central and non-dominant. Most importantly, marginality is not reducible to statistically measurable structural conditions (e.g., income level). Nor is it a straightforward and stable discursive position. Rather, what counts as marginal is in constant flux and is the object of continual negotiations and contestation; it is intersectionally complex and contextually relational. In this regard, Jennifer Nash (2008) highlights how an intersectional approach may be useful in revealing how 'privilege and oppression [are] . . . complex, multi-valent, and simultaneous' (12). Marginality may offer a powerful analytical tool through which to pursue an intersectional enterprise of unpacking the entanglement of privilege and oppression, not least by showing how social actors—irrespective of their socio-economic conditions—may strategically define themselves as 'marginal' in order to gain more or less momentary advantage of social visibility. Moreover, being on the fringes of the ordinary, a marginal position entails powerfully ambivalent affective components that may simultaneously encompass the feelings of pride/shame, anger/love for not being mainstream.

In arguing for margins as heuristics, I am not envisaging an all-encompassing explanatory apparatus with predictive potential. Rather, I see margins as a lens through which to interrogate some forms of political emancipation of marginal(ized) individuals and groups through *voice* and *visibility*. In order to do so, the chapter concentrates on some instances of activism on issues of sexual politics in South Africa. Through these examples, the chapter seeks to contribute to current theoretical discussions around Christopher Stroud's linguistic citizenship approach, itself grounded on Nancy Fraser's (1995) distinction between affirmation and transformation as tools of social justice. It is to such a framework that I will now turn.

The Political Semiotics of the Margins: Language, Body, Affect

In an influential article in the journal *New Left Review*, Nancy Fraser (1995) distinguishes between *affirmation* and *transformation* as strategies for the political enfranchisement of 'bivalent collectivities', that is, groups that 'may suffer both socioeconomic maldistribution and cultural misrecognition in forms where neither of these injustices is an indirect effect of the other, but where both are primary and co-original' (78). *Affirmative strategies* aim 'at correcting inequitable outcomes of social arrangements without disturbing the underlying framework that generates them' (82). In contrast, *transformative strategies* redress inequities by unsettling and dismantling the very structures that underpin social and economic divisions. Lesbian/ gay identity politics is, according to Fraser, a typical example of *affirmation* because it 'treats homosexuality as a substantive, cultural, identificatory positivity' (83) on the basis of which political recognition should be accorded. A transformative approach, instead, is advanced by queer theory, which seeks to 'deconstruct the homo-hetero dichotomy so as to destabilize all fixed sexual identities' (83). HIV/AIDS activism in the 1980s is exemplary of the latter approach, as it questioned too facile links between specific *identities* (gay, lesbian, drug addict, etc.) and illness, highlighting instead the role of sexual *practices*—irrespective of identification—in the spread of the virus.

Affirmation and transformation have not only undergirded different tactics in the politics of sexuality, but have also lain at the heart of two very different perspectives on the politics of language, namely *linguistic human rights* and *linguistic citizenship*. According to the supporters of the former (Skutnabb-Kangas 2006), state legislation should affirm linguistic minorities by according them specific rights on the basis of their speaking a particular language variety and belonging to a particular ethnic group. In contrast, Christopher Stroud (2001, 2009), who first advanced the notion of linguistic citizenship, overtly draws upon Fraser's (1995) theorizing and contests the view that languages are static and bounded entities that can be neatly mapped onto discrete identities, on grounds of which they should receive state recognition. What is proposed instead is

> an understanding of the variety of semiotic means through which speakers express agency, voice and participation in an everyday politics of language, and how non-mainstream speakers wrestle control from political institutions of the state by using their language over many modalities and giving new meaning and repurposing to reflect the social and political issues that affect them.
>
> (Williams and Stroud 2015, 408)

According to this formulation, a linguistic citizenship approach is transformative because (1) it unsettles the stability of language, acknowledging the messiness of linguistic life; (2) it highlights the fluidity of identity work; and, most importantly, (3) it captures the mundane, but no less important, forms of political agency that often happen away from government's corridors, 'outside of institutionalized contexts that one ordinarily associates with politics' (Besnier 2009, 11). Of course, the very notion of *citizenship* is not entirely unproblematic. The term is often treated in academic and lay discourse as synonymous with 'nationality', and the concomitant wielding of one or more passport(s) (see Extra, Spotti, and van Avermaet 2009). In contrast, Stroud's (2009) (see also Williams and Stroud 2015) understanding of citizenship is more complex, and can be located within a very different trajectory of thought within the social sciences and the humanities (see in particular Isin 2008; Holston 2008). According to such an intellectual tradition, citizenship is less of a *status* an individual accrues as a result of symbolic or legal affiliation to the nation-state(s) than a dynamic set of *acts* that individuals and groups perform; and, in so doing, *constitute themselves* as citizens—no matter whether they have a passport or ID-book.

The notion of linguistic citizenship sets out precisely to capture what linguistic guises these 'acts of citizenship' (Isin 2008) may take. At this point, it may be worth interrogating what falls under the very category of the *linguistic*. The empirical examples provided in linguistic citizenship scholarship consist exclusively of verbal or written interactions (see Milani and Shaikjee 2013; Stroud 2001; Stroud and Heugh 2004; Williams and Stroud 2015). In these spoken and written performances, social actors deploy a Bakhtinian plethora of accents, styles, registers, and voices in order to go against the proverbial grain and stake claims that contest and re-signify certain social arrangements. Admittedly, Peck and Stroud (2015) have recently gestured towards a broadening of the sociolinguistic so as to encompass a wider set of meaning-making resources (see also Kerfoot 2011; Milani 2015a). Writing about the burgeoning field of the study of language in public spaces, they propose that:

> one future direction in the study of linguistic landscapes might be to explore the potential of what could increasingly be viewed as a *corporeal sociolinguistics*, a merging of the concerns of contemporary sociolinguistics with corporeality and mobility with the ambit of linguistic landscape research to research place and inscription.
>
> (148)

Whilst their intervention is in the field of linguistic landscape, I'd argue that Peck and Stroud's (2015) reflections could be productively applied to linguistic citizenship as well, and thus lead us to explore the *multi-semiotic* character of acts of political claim-staking, which include the body along with other meaning-making resources. Such a turn to the body in understanding the semiotics of citizenship resonates well with Butler's (2011) observations that:

> [When] the body 'speaks' politically, it is not only in vocal or written language, . . . the performativity of the body . . . crosses language without ever quite reducing to language. In other words, it is not that bodily action and gesture have to be translated into language, but that both action and gesture signify and speak, as action and claim, and that the one is not finally extricable from the other.
>
> (4)

The examples that will be investigated below illustrate how a *die-in*—a silent, corporeal performance of death—paradoxically speaks louder than any word of dissent. They also contribute to revisiting Fraser's and Butler's theoretical points by showing how the political semiotics of the margins—whether vocal, written, or corporeal—carries a strong *affective* dimension that cannot be theorized through idealized models of rational debate (see also Deumert 2015). Put differently, it is not sufficient to take into account the propositional content of a political claim, and how it materializes semiotically; one also needs to engage with its *affective* dimensions and manifestations (see also Milani 2015a, b). In suggesting that emotions be incorporated into the analytical repertoire of linguistic citizenship scholarship, I do not wish to convey that rationality and emotion can be easily separated. Rather I want to point to 'the irreducible entanglement of thinking and feeling, knowing *that* and knowing *how*, propositional and non-propositional knowledge' (Zerilli 2015, 266, emphasis added). For in the inextricable tangle of reason and emotion lies the transformative potential of claims that do not limit themselves to redressing existing inequalities, but demand instead a radical rethinking of the current conditions of political engagement.

Enacting the Margins in Order to Unsettle Orders of (In)Visibility

It is nearly a truism for sociolinguists and linguistic anthropologists that the most insidious forms of injustice happen in cultural/symbolic domains and are rooted in unequal 'patterns of representations, interpretation, and communication' (Fraser 1995, 71). According to Fraser, cultural/symbolic injustice can take different shapes: (1) *Cultural domination*, which involves 'being subjected to patterns of interpretation and communication that are associated with another culture and are alien and/or hostile to one's own' (71); (2) *nonrecognition*, which entails 'being rendered invisible via the authoritative representation, communicative, and interpretative practices of one's culture' (71); and (3) *disrespect*, which means 'being routinely maligned or disparaged in stereotypic public cultural representations and/or in everyday life interactions' (71).

Fraser's thoughts are particularly appealing for the purpose of this book because cultural domination, nonrecognition, and disrespect together contribute to the creation of specific *orders of (in)visibility*. Such hierarchically stratified arrangements are produced by two inter-related processes: (1) The *quantitative* prevalence of the representation of certain people and not others—heterosexuals are quantitatively more frequent than their lesbian/gay counterparts in, say, print advertisements; and (2) the *qualitative* privilege accorded to certain people *at the expense* of others—the values connected to heterosexuality are typically portrayed as superior to those related to same-sex desire, which might indeed be represented but in a negative or stereotypical manner. Fraser's definitions, however, are underpinned by a rather univalent relationship between an individual and her/his culture—in the singular. But what does culture refer to here? This might prove problematic in highly diverse and multilingual contexts where what counts as one's own culture is not simply difficult to establish but ultimately analytically unhelpful. As intersectionality theorists (e.g., Crenshaw 1991; Nash 2008) remind us, domination, nonrecognition, and disrespect are not the straightforward result of one social variable, but they are determined by the simultaneous work of a multiplicity of different axes—gender, sexuality, social class, age, race, etc.,—which cannot be condensed into the concept of culture.

To take South Africa as an example, the current democratic constitution not only guarantees equality before the law but also protects against unfair discrimination *inter alia* on grounds of gender and 'sexual orientation' (Section 9, Constitution of South Africa). Legal protection notwithstanding, gender and sexual non-normativities are not only under-represented in mainstream English-language print-media, but whenever they are, they are associated with problems, violence, or are generally portrayed negatively. That being said, there is a burgeoning English-language online media industry that targets lesbian, gay, bisexual, and transgender (LGBT) constituencies. Interestingly, however, in the LGBT media, representations of non-normative sexualities are overwhelmingly coated in a racially white palette, with middle-upper class overtones. Here, black queers are portrayed as exceptional or are (re)inscribed as the new 'slave' of consumerist post-apartheid conditions (Disemelo 2014). In isiZulu newspapers, on the other hand, homosexuality is treated as something to be despised and countered because it is viewed as unAfrican (Maga 2013). These complex patterns of (mis)representation in the South African context have been interpreted by Livermon (2013) as examples of the double marginalization that non-heterosexual black individuals experience as *both* black and queer

> because cultural politics consistently mark the black queer body as the constitutive outside of blackness and the queer body is subsequently racialized as white.
>
> (314–15)

So, what to do in order to redress such multivalent cultural/symbolic injustice in order to overcome those very axes—race and sexuality—on which it rests? An important case in point is a protest enacted by the activist group *One in Nine* against Johannesburg Pride 2012, which will be presented in the next section (see Milani 2015b for a more detailed analysis).

One in Nine against Johannesburg Pride

For contextual purposes, it is important to mention that the first Johannesburg Pride march took place in the central part of the city in 1990 under the aegis of the Gay and Lesbian Organization of the Witwatersrand (GLOW). It was the first event of its kind in South Africa and in Africa, more broadly, and had an overtly political aim, being 'a call to all South Africans who are committed to a non-racist, non-sexist, non-discriminatory democratic future' (De Waal and Manion 2006, 15). Moreover, the march was the manifestation of a specific *zeitgeist*. After the release of Nelson Mandela in February 1990, a few organizations, including GLOW, started lobbying for the decriminalization of homosexuality, and advocating for sexuality-based rights to be included into the new post-apartheid dispensation.

Since the enactment of the democratic dispensation, which indeed sanctioned sexuality-based rights, Johannesburg Pride has changed its character from an openly political *march* in the city's socially mixed centre to a street *parade* in the wealthy suburb of Rosebank, followed by a profit-driven *mardi-gras* on the grass of the nearby Zoo Lake. The change of labels—from march to parade—might be itself indicative of a commercial shift towards the 'lifestylization of sexual politics' (Bell and Binnie 2000; see also Milani 2015b), which is a process that involves the collusion between the visibility of non-heterosexual identities on the one hand, and the promotion of specific consumerist practices and the lifestyles associated with them, on the other. It is also notable in this respect that, whereas black activists had been the main leaders in the original Pride marches, white middle-class entrepreneurs increasingly took over the management of the subsequent parades (Craven 2011).

It is in this context that the members of the feminist activist group One in Nine performed a so-called die-in as a form of protest against Johannesburg Pride: A group of black women carrying human-sized figures ran before the incoming parade and lay down on the street tarmac, as if dead. A few other women went to stand behind this carpet of bodies, carrying the signs *No cause for celebration* and *Dying for justice*. Their aim was to make the participants in Johannesburg Pride stop and hold a minute of silence in memory of all the black lesbians and gender non-normative individuals that had been killed in South Africa because of their non-compliance with gender and sexuality normativities.

The sudden interruption set off viciously angry responses from the jubilant walkers. As can be seen on many YouTube videos of the event, a Pride participant aggressively urged the demonstrators to 'go back to the *lokshinis* [townships]'; a parade marshal head-butted a protesting woman; Jenni Green—the Joburg Pride board member responsible for the logistics of the event—yelled from her golden Mercedes: 'This is my route'; and the chairperson of Joburg Pride Tanya Hartford ended up in a bodily confrontation with the protesters.

The clash immediately generated a chain of reactions on several media platforms. Commentators were generally unanimous in condemning the behaviour of the Pride organizers and participants. Some arguably liberal voices, though, questioned the choice of an *unannounced* die-in as the most apt political strategy of social critique because it would not have any transformative effect but would only lead to reinforce existing splits in the LGBT 'community,' and ultimately jeopardize legal advancements about sexual rights in South Africa. In light of Fraser's distinction between affirmative and transformative remedies, we might wish to ask: Is the *One in Nine's* tactic of visibility an example of *affirmation* or *transformation*? Is it a strategy through which black women can affirm their gender, race, and the specificities of their experiences vis-à-vis, say, white middle-class men? Or is it a transformative strategy through which to overcome gender, racial, and other divisions?

In order to answer these questions, it is necessary to consider how the activists of *One in Nine* strategically employed the racialized and gendered materiality of their bodies for political purposes. In an oft-cited quote, the philosopher Judith Butler (1990) argues that there is no subject behind the deed, but 'the doer is variably constructed in and through the deed' (142). According to this logic, the *One in Nine* emerges as a political subject—the agent of protest—through their die-in. Yet they are not subjects in absolute terms because the relevance of their intervention lies precisely in the nexus of womanhood and blackness vis-à-vis a South African pride parade organized by a small group of white middle-class entrepreneurs. Are these gender and racial components constructed through the deed? In the case of the *One in Nine*, it is hard to account for the meaning and potency of their action without taking into account the pre-existing gendered and racialized materiality of their bodies (see also Peck and Stroud 2015). In many ways, then, their tactic of visibility was an *affirmative* gesture, one that strategically relies on the intersectional nexus of gender and race as 'substantive' tokens, as Fraser (1995, 83) would say, for redressing that order of (in)visibility that privileges white, affluent, gay and lesbians in South Africa at the expense of working class black queer individuals. The activists affirmed themselves by positioning their gendered and racialized bodies as powerless and marginal(ized). Paradoxically, the strategic deployment of marginality allowed them to gain centre stage, and make a statement that, thanks to media coverage, became seen and heard by wider audiences.

On the other hand, though, the unannounced and emotionally jarring character of the die-in is at variance with the inclusionary nature of affirmative remedies that strive for acceptance into an existing power structure. Rather, they seem to be more in line with a transformative rejection of 'a minoritising logic of toleration or simple political interest-representation in favour of a more thorough resistance to regimes of the normal' (Warner 1993, xxvi). After the event, the organizers of Pride sought to justify their own violent and racist reactions by putting the blame on the fact that they had been taken by surprise. Accordingly, they lamented that the *One in Nine* had not communicated beforehand their intentions to perform a die-in. If they had done so, so the argument goes, a compromise could have been reached, and the One in Nine requests could have been slotted into the Pride roster. This logic, however, is based on a fundamental flaw that underpins western theories of rational public debate (see, e.g., Habermas 1989)—the assumption that everyone has equal access to discourse. As sociolinguists and linguistic anthropologists have consistently demonstrated over the last 30 years, 'not everyone is able to make statements, or to have statements taken seriously by others' (Mills 2003, 65), often because those statements have been uttered in an allegedly 'wrong', 'bad', or 'inappropriate' spoken or written language variety. So, in the unexpected character of the One in Nine protest lies a refusal to engage in a rational dialogue with Johannesburg Pride organizers, because that dialogue itself was inherently premised on unequal discursive conditions.

By the same token, the bodily and linguistic assemblage represented in Figure 9.1 is less an attempt to seek recognition from their immediate interlocutor—the incoming parade—than a powerful strategy of defiance geared to unsettle the affective structure of the parade itself. We mentioned earlier that, for Fraser (1995), a transformative approach to sexuality ultimately 'deconstructs the homo-hetero dichotomy so as to destabilize all fixed sexual identities' (83). It is not sexual identities as such that are the target of the One in Nine intervention, but the very affective glue that binds the parade together: Pride. As Sarah Ahmed (2004) notes, emotions 'work by sticking figures together (adherence), a sticking that creates the very effect of a collective (coherence)' (119). The dead bodies and the slogan *No cause for celebration* worked like a Bakhtinian 'crooked mirror' (Bakhtin 1984, 127)

Figure 9.1 Semiotic Citizenship

put in front of the parade. Pride looks at the One in Nine protest and sees itself reflected back as Shame. Since affect is always performative—it does things, it has an effect (Ahmed 2004)—it is unsurprising, albeit unjustifiable, that the production of shame set off an affective counter-response of anger from the participants in the pride parade, who experienced that as a dissolution of their collective coherence.

What Happened Next?

Two years later, the results of the *One in Nine* intervention might prove right those media commentators who saw it as a divisive initiative. The NGO that had been organizing Joburg Pride ceased operation in 2013, and two very different events arose in the vacuum that was left behind. A group of activist organizations, including One in Nine, arranged *Johannesburg People's Pride*, a march through one of the central parts of city, Hillbrow, where the first Pride march took place in 1990, and today an area that is feared by many South Africans because of its reputation for crime. In contrast, those who took part in *Johannesburg Pride* paraded through the streets of Sandton, one of South Africa's most exclusive mall districts.

Of course, one should be careful not to pour scorn too easily on commercially driven acts of sexual visibility like the Sandton parade. Even though they may in many ways reproduce dominant ideologies of, e.g., gender, sexuality, race, and class, they may nevertheless also be challenging in their own way those societal ideologies that still view same-sex desire and relations as inappropriate for public spaces. This caveat notwithstanding, my interest here is to zoom in on the people and activities that led to *Johannesburg People's Pride* 2013. For it is possible to observe how the intersectional intervention of the One in Nine was taken up and further developed. Such intersectionality is reflected in the gender, sexual, and racial diversity of the constituencies involved in the organization of *Johannesburg People's Pride*; it also emerges in their Call for Action:

> The Peoples Pride Movement would like to invite *all people* with a desire for a free and just society to join hands, feet and bodies-take to the streets of Johannesburg and demand a safe and free South Africa for all of those who live in it.
>
> We are calling on *all people in and around the margins* of what is acceptable and good. We are calling on *all people that normative society deems outlaw, all of us who are not free*. Our sexual orientation, our race, our class positions, our genders, our geographic locations, our bodies with disabilities, our refugee status and many other factors work together and are used as a basis to exploit and oppress us and place us on these margins.
>
> (http://peoplespride.blogspot.com/2013/09/call-to-action-johannesburg-peoples.html; emphasis added)

What can be seen in this extract is a tension between *universalizing* and *particularizing* discursive strategies. On the one hand, *Johannesburg People's Pride* takes a broad humanist stance calling for support from 'all people with a desire for a free and just society'. On the other hand, all-inclusivity is cut short by the more restricted hailing to 'all people in and around the margins'. Particularly relevant for the purpose of this chapter is the strategic usage of the word 'margins' as a standpoint from which to rally political activism. Interestingly, however, the deployment of a marginal position is not done in a minoritizing way that centres on the promotion of one marginalized identity excluding others. Not only does *Johannesburg People's Pride* highlight the intersections of a variety of social factors, but their appeal to 'all people in and around the margins of what is acceptable and good', also seek to mobilize a larger non-mainstream constituency of people who go against 'regimes of the normal' (M. Warner 1993).

To judge from their Call for Action, *Johannesburg People's Pride* seems to waver between two different transformative approaches for redressing social inequalities: (1) An anti-identitarian tactic that seeks to transcend identities altogether, manifested *inter alia* in the very name of the initiative—People's Pride instead of gay or lesbian pride, and the usage of the all encompassing determiner 'all'; and (2) an intersectional tactic that recognizes racial, gender, and class divisions, but with a view to achieving a broader political goal of social change that is not limited to one axis of marginalization—sexuality. These variances notwithstanding, the common denominator underlying both manoeuvres is a critique of the affirmative logic of a politics based on a single set of sexual identities (e.g., lesbian, gay, bisexual) as grounds on which rights should be granted. This is not to say that sexual rights are bad or wrong. Indeed a rights-based rhetoric was key for state recognition of sexual minorities in South Africa. But the point that both One in Nine and Johannesburg People's Pride are making is that the strategic highlighting of one axis of social identification—sexual identity—for political enfranchisement inherently obscures the social diversity within it, and, in practice, produces 'very unequal subjects with different opportunities for agency' (Stroud 2009), 198).

As an alternative to a rights-based discourse Johannesburg People's Pride proposed the notion of *erotic justice* (see also Ellison 1996). Unlike sexual rights, erotic justice 'moves away from the individualisation of sexualised subjectivities and the uncomplicated universalisation of human rights as a framework of "justice"' (Van Zyl 2015, 148). Such a perspective highlights the inherent pitfalls of a politics that strives to achieve equality through an additive recognition of sexual identity categories—the so-called alphabet soup of lesbian, gay, bisexual, transgender, asexual, queer, questioning, etc. (LGBTIAQQ+). Not only does any sexual identity category, no matter how broad and inclusive it might be, inherently exclude those who do not see themselves as fitting into it, it also fails to account for the complexity of sexual practices. For example, men who are in heterosexual relations with women but have more or less occasional sex with other men do not necessarily identify themselves as gay or bisexual, but might nonetheless be the target of stigma and violence. Taking account of the fluidity of sexuality, an erotic justice framework argues for the advancement of fairness on the basis of sexual desires and practices, including sex work.

Concluding Remarks

In contexts of social diversity, multilingualism and mobility, where a variety of social actors—including academics—struggle for social justice, it is worth reiterating Fraser's (1995) cautioning against too optimistic reliance on affirmative remedies as tools for social empowerment, as they 'work additively and are often at cross purposes with one another' (93) without challenging the underlying structures that (re)produce social inequality. Whereas the distinction between affirmation and transformation is analytically appealing, the examples from sexual activism in South Africa discussed in this chapter demonstrate that it is difficult to establish a straightforward separation between the two.

Viewed in the short-term, *One in Nine* was partly a remedy of affirmative recognition that strategically relied on and 'promote(d) group differentiation' (Fraser 1995, 84)—we black and gender-non-normative female-bodied targets of violence vs. them white, depoliticized, middle-class gay and lesbians. But the mobilization of affect also contained destabilizing elements of transformation. Through the production of shame, *One in Nine* could puncture the very idea of a South African lesbian and gay 'community', revealing its emptiness.

Similarly, the more long-term effects of such an intervention were not straightforwardly affirmative or transformative. The proliferation of different pride initiatives could be interpreted as the affirmation of specific particularities. Yet, the kind of solidarity *across* social identifications that underpins Johannesburg People's Pride is perhaps a textbook example of the effects that Fraser (1995) has in mind when arguing that transformation strategies undermine group differentiation 'so as to make room for future regroupments' (84).

So instead of dismissing a priori any strategy that might rely on a strategic essentialization of identities as necessarily affirmative, we need to develop a sensitivity to the complexities of agency for voice and visibility of socially disenfranchised individuals and groups. Cardinal points—North(ern)/South(ern)—might not offer us the most useful metaphors to capture such complex dynamics. Rather, as David Warner (2004) suggests, we should be 'developing a methodology *of the margins* that does not seek to make things intelligible in terms of the heteropatriarchy [or other structures of domination], but tries to find the words of the margins itself' (335).

Stroud's (2001, 2009) conception of linguistic citizenship gestures towards such marginality. Whereas in its original formulation this approach is presented as transformative in Fraser's terms, I'd suggest that it captures instead the *ambiguous* politics of voice and visibility from the margins in that 'it recognizes . . . the many linguistic practices through which citizenship is managed, attempting to account for the way both local and transnational solidarities are built *across* categorical identities through interpersonal negotiation in multiscaled spaces' (Stroud 2009, 209, emphasis added). That being said, the examples in this chapter illustrate how the politics of voice and visibility of the margins takes shapes that cannot be theorized with too narrow conceptions of language or rationalist models of politics. The still, pretending-to-be-dead bodies of the *One in Nine* activists were powerful, party-pooping words that sparked a chain-reaction in debates over sexuality in South Africa. It is in the multi-semiotic and affective character of the die-in that lies a key to a better understanding how the margins operate politically.

Note

1 This chapter is a substantially revised and expanded version of an article that appeared in the open access journal *Multilingual Margins* 1(1).

References

Ahmed, S. 2004. 'Affective Economies'. *Social Text* 22 (2): 117–39.

Baker P. 2008. *Sexed Texts: Language, Gender and Sexuality*. London: Equinox.

Bakhtin, M. 1984. *Problems of Dostoevsky's Poetics*. Minneapolis: University of Minnesota Press.

Bell, D., and J. Binnie. 2000. *The Sexual Citizen: Queer Politics and beyond*. London: Polity.

Besnier, N. 2009. *Gossip and the Everyday Production of Politics*. Honolulu, HI: University of Hawai'i Press.

Bhabha, H. 1994. *The Location of Culture*. London: Routledge.

Butler, J. 1990. *Gender Trouble: Feminism and the Subversion of Identity*. New York: Routledge.

———. 2011. 'Bodies in Alliance and the Politics of the Street'. *European Institute for Progressive Cultural Policies*. Retrieved from http://eipcp.net/transversal/1011/butler/en.

Comaroff, J., and J. L. Comaroff, 2012. *Theory from the South: Or, How Euro-America Is Evolving toward Africa*. Boulder, CO: Paradigm Publishers.

Connell, R. 2007. *Southern Theory: The Global Dynamics of Knowledge in Social Science*. Cambridge: Polity.

Cooper, F., and A. L. Stoler, eds. 1997. *Tensions of Empire: Colonial Cultures in a Bourgeois World*. Berkeley, CA: University of California Press.

Craven, E. 2011. *Racial Identity and Racism in the Gay and Lesbian Community in Post-Apartheid South Africa*. Unpublished Master's thesis. Johannesburg: University of the Witwatersrand.

Crenshaw, K. 1991. 'Mapping the Margins: Intersectionality, Identity Politics, and Violence against Women of Color'. *Stanford Law Review* 43: 1241–99.

Deumert, A. 2014. 'Digital Superdiversity: A Commentary'. *Discourse, Context & Media* 4–5: 116–20.

———. 2015. 'Wild Publics'. Keynote address at the conference Language in the Media 7, University of Hamburg 7–9 September 2015.

De Waal, S., and A. Manion. 2006. *Pride: Protest and Celebration*. Johannesburg, SA: Fanele.

Disemelo, K. 2014. *Black Men as Pink Consumers? A Critical Reading of Race, Sexuality and the Construction of the Pink Economy in South African Queer Consumer Media*. Unpublished Master's Dissertation. Johannesburg: University of the Witwatersrand.

Edensor, T., and M. Jayne. 2012. 'Introduction: Urban Theory beyond the West'. In *Urban Theory beyond the West: A World of Cities*, edited by T. Edensor and M. Jayne, 1–28. London: Routledge.

Ellison, M. M. 1996. *Erotic Justice: A Liberating Ethic of Sexuality*. Louisville: Westminster John Knox.

Extra, G., M. Spotti, and P. van Avermaet, eds. 2009. *Language Testing, Migration and Citizenship: A Cross-National Perspective on Integration Regimes*. London: Continuum.

Fabian, J. 1983. *Time and the Other: How Anthropology Makes Its Object*. New York: Columbia University Press.

Fraser, N. 1995. 'From Redistribution to Recognition? Dilemmas of Justice in a "Post-Socialist" Age'. *New Left Review* I/2012: 68–93.

Habermas, J. 1989. *The Social Transformation of the Public Sphere*. Boston: MIT Press.

Holston, J. 2008. *Insurgent Citizenship: Disjunctions of Democracy and Modernity in Brazil*. Princeton: Princeton University Press.

Isin, E. F. 2008. 'Theorizing Acts of Citizenship'. In *Acts of Citizenship*, edited by E. F. Isin and G. M. Nielsen, 15–43. London: Palgrave Macmillan.

Kerfoot, C. 2011. 'Making and Shaping Participatory Spaces: Resemiotization and Citizenship Agency in South Africa'. *International Multilingual Research Journal* 5 (2), 87–102.

Livermon, X. 2012. 'Queer(y)ing Freedom: Black Queer Visibilities in Postapartheid South Africa'. *GLQ* 18 (2–3): 297–323.

Maga, S. 2013. ' "But Who's the Bride?" Competing Representations of the "Traditional African Gay Wedding" '. Unpublished Honours dissertation. Johannesburg: University of the Witwatersrand.

Milani, T. M. 2015a. 'Language and Citizenship: Broadening the Agenda'. *Journal of Language and Politics* 14 (3): 319–34.

———. 2015b. 'Sexual Cityzenship: Discourses, Spaces and Bodies at Joburg Pride 2012'. *Journal of Language and Politics* 14 (3): 431–54.

Milani, T. M., and M. Shaikjee. 2013. 'Afrikaans is "Bobaas": Linguistic Citizenship on the BBC Voices Website'. In *Analysing 21st Century British English: Conceptual and Methodological Aspects of the Voices Project*, edited by C. Upton and B. L. Davies, 71–90. London: Routledge.

Mills, S. 2003. *Michel Foucault*. London: Routledge.

Mouzelis, N. 1995. *Sociological Theory: What Went Wrong? Diagnoses and Remedies*. London: Routledge.

Nash, J. C. 2008. 'Re-thinking Intersectionality'. *Feminist Review* 89: 1–15.

Nuttall, S. 2009. *Entanglement: Literary and Cultural Reflections on Post-Apartheid*. Johannesburg: Wits University Press.

Peck, A., and C. Stroud. 2015. 'Skinscapes'. *Linguistic Landscape: An International Journal* 1 (1–2): 133–51.

Skutnabb-Kangas, T. 2006. 'Language Policy and Linguistic Human Rights'. In *An Introduction to Language Policy: Theory and Method*, edited by T. Ricento, 273–91. Malden, MA: Wiley-Blackwell.

Stroud, C. 2001. 'African Mother-Tongue Programmes and the Politics of Language: Linguistic Citizenship versus Linguistic Human Rights'. *Journal of Multilingual and Multicultural Development* 22 (4): 339–55.

———. 2009. 'A Postliberal Critique of Language Rights: Toward a Politics of Language for a Linguistics of Contact'. In *International Perspectives on Bilingual Education: Policy, Practice, and Controversy*, edited by J. E. Petrovic, 191–218. Charlotte, NC: Information Age.

Stroud, C., and K. Heugh. 2004. 'Language Rights and Linguistic Citizenship'. In *Language Rights and Language Survival*, edited by J. Freeland, 191–218. Manchester: St. Jerome.

Van Zyl, M. 2015. 'Taming Monsters: Theorising Erotic Justice in Africa'. *Agenda* 29 (1): 147–54.

Vertovec, S. 2007. 'Super-Diversity and its Implications'. *Ethnic and Racial Studies* 30 (6): 1024–54.

Warner, D. N. 2004. 'Towards a Queer Research Methodology'. *Qualitative Research in Psychology* 1 (4): 321–37.

Warner, M. 1993. 'Introduction'. In *Fear of a Queer Planet*, edited by M. Warner, vii-xliv. Minneapolis, MN: University of Minnesota Press.

Williams, Q. E., and C. Stroud. 2015. 'Linguistic Citizenship: Language and Politics in Postnational Modernities'. *Journal of Language and Politics* 14 (3): 406–30.

Wodak, R. 2001. 'The Discourse-Historical Approach'. In *Methods of Critical Discourse Analysis*, edited by R. Wodak and M. Meyer, 63–94. London: Sage.

Zerilli, L. M. G. 2015. 'The Turn to Affect and the Problem of Judgment'. *New Literary History* 46 (2): 262–86.

10 Epistemic Diversity, Lazy Reason, and Ethical Translation in Postcolonial Contexts

The Case of Indigenous Educational Policy in Brazil[1]

Lynn Mario T. Menezes de Souza

'One has to persist in being white in order to be indigenous'

Much of postcolonial theory (Bhabha 1986; Gandhi 1998; Mignolo 2000, 2007; Spivak 1990) has pointed to the continuity and not the break implied in the prefix 'post-', where elements of colonial hegemony persist long after the departure and end of official colonialism.

In the case of Brazil, this is particularly apparent, given the dubious circumstances of its political independence in 1822, when power in practice remained in the hands of a white elite previously empowered by the colonial regime. This lead to the continuing subjugation of local indigenous communities, their languages, and cultures, which were subjected to the persisting colonial dilemma of either assimilating or perishing.

Indigenous Education Policy in Brazil

In its latest post-dictatorship Constitution of 1988, Brazil for the first time recognized the existence of indigenous languages and cultures within the nation, granting them rights, protection, and access to democracy. This is clearly reflected in recent public policy such as the Indigenous Education Acts (1996, 2001) which grant full autonomy to indigenous communities to define their own school curricula including indigenous knowledges and indigenous languages. However, when indigenous communities choose instead to follow the national curriculum of the 'white' mainstream, this is read as 'uninformed naive decisions' and rejected wholesale by government agencies and non-indigenous groups claiming to protect indigenous interests. These apparently pro-indigenous reactions emphatically require, ironically, that the indigenous communities conform to the federal legislation that claims to protect their interests.

This paper proposes to read this context of dissensus[2] as an example of what Santos (2002) called 'lazy reason' where dominant forms of thinking have difficulty in understanding (and 'waste') other, non-Eurocentric, and non-hegemonic forms of reason which abound within the Brazilian nation (Santos 2009). These non-hegemonic forms of reason are located within what Mignolo (2007) describes as the shadow or darker side of Modernity, referring to the inequality of knowledges that co-exist in a particular socio-historic context.[3]

I suggest that to refer to non-hegemonic knowledges as 'dark' in contrast to the dominant knowledges of the Enlightenment may result in a homogenization and simplification of the complexity of such non-hegemonic knowledges, casting them further into the shadow of the Enlightenment. Hence, in my discussion I raise the issue of how dark is dark? I do this by suggesting that three tropes from non-Eurocentric indigenous reasoning may be used to understand this situation: 'Indigenous perspectivism' (Viveiros de Castro 2002), 'the logic of predation' (Fausto 2001), and 'equivocal translation' (Viveiros de Castro 2004).

Brazil has a population of around 200 million. The official census (IBGE) of 2010 established the indigenous population of the country at 817,000, consisting therefore of 0.42 percent of the total population; this figure represents a growth of 11 percent in relation to the census of 2000. Though the percentage of the total indigenous population is small, a large part of it is concentrated in the tropical north of the country, in Amazonia, where it consists of 11 percent of the local population. In terms of ethnicity and language, the indigenous population, far from being a homogenous group, is composed of 220 different peoples who speak 180 different languages. These languages in turn belong to 30 different language families. In terms of education, the Indigenous Education Census of 2005 identified 164,000 students in indigenous schools, a rise from the previous figure of 117,000 only three years earlier. Of these, however, only 4,756 were in secondary education, located in the 72 indigenous secondary schools; this figure represents a dramatic increase from the previous figure of 18 indigenous schools three years earlier.

There is then a clear recent increase not only in the total indigenous population as a whole, but also in the interest this population has in the formal education of the official school system. This, however, has not always been the case. Until the present Constitution of Brazil was drawn up in 1988, for almost five centuries Brazil had considered itself a monolingual and monocultural country, recognizing officially only Portuguese as its national language.

As mentioned above, the Constitution of 1988, which came in the aftermath of Brazil's return to liberal democracy after 20 years of a military dictatorship, recognized officially the existence of indigenous languages and cultures within the nation and pledged to protect and preserve them. This brought to an end centuries of previous policies of assimilation and conversion to Christianity of the indigenous minorities, policies set on eradicating indigenous cultures and languages. As such, Article 210 of the Constitution explicitly states 'Regular fundamental education will be given *in Portuguese*, guaranteeing, however, to the indigenous communities, the right to use their own mother tongues and their own learning processes' (my emphasis).

It is clear in this statement that from a previous policy of assimilation and nonrecognition, the nation now recognizes the existence of the indigenous minority and establishes a differentiated, specific, bilingual, and intercultural relation with it. The bilingual and intercultural aspect of the relationship is implicit in not only guaranteeing the right to the indigenous mother tongue but also in guaranteeing the access to and use of Portuguese; the intercultural aspect is present in the recognition that indigenous cultures have their own learning processes, different from those identified with the national majority. This indirectly may also be seen as recognition of the existence of different, indigenous epistemologies and constructions of knowledge. The mediation of this intercultural, bilingual relation with the indigenous minority, is established in the Constitution as the indigenous educational system.

Radically different to what is offered to the mainstream school system, official policy permits that in the case of indigenous schools, the local indigenous community has the right to establish not only the language(s) and knowledges to be taught in the school, but also to establish who will be the teacher, and how the space and time of the school will be organized, in keeping with local cultural traditions. Thus, for example, in some communities, it is the headman or a member of his family who may be designated as teacher; in other communities it may the medicine man, a community elder, or even a young person sent to the city to be specifically trained as a teacher.

Rather than following the set school times of the mainstream school, indigenous schools may interrupt their classroom activities to accommodate student participation in traditional community activities such as hunting and planting with parents and family members. This is supported, for example, by the Law of Basic Education (LDB) of 1996, in whose Articles 78/79, the ground rules for indigenous education policy are specified in some detail. These are defined in the following terms:

(1) The recuperation of historical memory;
(2) The reaffirmation of ethnic identity;
(3) The valorization of indigenous languages; and
(4) The access to information and knowledges of mainstream society and of other indigenous societies.

It is significant for the purpose of this paper to call attention to the fact that, as we have seen, the present Constitution was the product of the recent democratization of the country, which brought with it the recognition and respect for the indigenous minority of the nation. This respect was then expressed in the later legislation that drew up specific policies of indigenous education, such as the LDB Law of 1996 mentioned above.

Within this framework, federal policy makers envisioned an indigenous school in total contrast to the previous indigenous schools based on policies which continued the colonial practices of conversion and assimilation. The new, post-1988, benevolent indigenous school, respectful of indigenous languages and knowledges would, according to the policies, be radically different from the mainstream school: The indigenous school would not only be bilingual in the indigenous language of the community concerned and in Portuguese, the national language, but would also focus on the reaffirmation of indigenous identity by emphasizing the knowledges produced by the local community and other indigenous communities; the acquisition of these two different knowledges and languages would take place simultaneously.

However, recent research (Cavalcanti 1999; Grupioni 2008) has shown that the reality of many indigenous schools is radically different. Many indigenous communities, given their constitutional and legal right to make their own decisions vis-à-vis their schools, chose mainstream knowledge and the Portuguese language as preferred content rather than indigenous languages and knowledges.

Grupioni (2008), for example, as a key participant in the formulation of policy for indigenous education, interprets this situation as a lack of understanding, on the part of indigenous communities, of the privileges and emancipatory possibilities offered to them by post-1988 educational policies. Even the Brazilian educationalist, Paulo Freire (2005) interpreted the indigenous reaction to pro-indigenous educational policies as one indicative of the 'internalization', by the socially excluded, of dominant ways of thinking which in fact exclude them and deny them access to social equity and justice.

It is my position in this paper to problematize these readings of the indigenous rejection of indigenous educational policy, and to problematize the indigenous preference for a school containing mainstream knowledges and the national language—Portuguese.

I read this situation as a complex conflict of interpretations, which demands a complex ethical and political response in order to maintain the post-1988 spirit of ethical respect for indigenous communities and to avoid repeating the pitfalls and violence of the colonial past.

Elsewhere (de Souza 2003, 2005, 2006, 2008; de Souza and Andreotti 2011), I have discussed some of the issues involved in this conflict of interpretations vis a vis indigenous educational policy in Brazil and its purported valorization of indigenous knowledges. For example, I pointed to radically different conceptions of language and writing and their relationships to knowledge on the part of indigenous communities on one hand and the mainstream, benevolent, pro-indigenous policy makers on the other. I attempted to situate these conflicts of interpretation in terms of the monolingual and monocultural bias of the policy makers, in spite of their interest in emancipatory education and the promotion of social justice for the indigenous communities. I read the interpretations of the purportedly benevolent policy makers as housed in and impeded by their own categories of culture, language, and knowledge. I tried to show how intercultural and bilingual education are not simply policy or linguistic issues, but epistemic issues.

In this paper I focus on the ethical issues of this conflict of interpretations, issues which have serious political implications for the postcolonial 'after-life' of the nation, where in the name of emancipation and social equity, social practices similar in outcome to previous colonial practices of the elimination of difference may be unwittingly pursued.

Epistemic Diversity, 'Lazy Reason', and the 'Waste of Experience'

In his ground-breaking thinking from 'other', non-dominant, non- (post-?) Western perspectives, Santos (2002, 2004, 2009) focuses on the epistemological aspect of conflicts arising from the contact between dominant and non-dominant knowledges and social practices. In these, the 'dominant' signifies a Eurocentric perspective that takes for granted and legitimates a particular conception of reason and knowledge, itself deriving from the also Eurocentric concept of science and privileging a particular form of rational, objective, and decontextualized analysis. In tracing the history of such a dominant, Eurocentric concept of valid knowledge, Santos (2002) says that the epistemological privilege of modern Science is a product of an epistemicide: It results from the historical destruction of social practices and the disqualification of social agents that operate according to other forms of knowledge. It eliminated other forms of knowledge by imposing its own single perspective, self-proclaimed as objective, rational, and scientific.

A drastic consequence of this epistemicide, according to Santos, is that contemporary social sciences, following unquestioningly this model, may have been responsible for concealing or discrediting alternative forms of knowledges, generating what he calls an enormous 'waste of social experience', whereby non-dominant knowledges not perceived as legitimate, rational or acceptable by the dominant episteme go unnoticed and un-valued.

Apart from the epistemicide that precedes it, this waste of experience is also the result of a perplexing sophism that Santos (2004) calls 'lazy or indolent reason' as referred to by Leibniz ([1710] 1985): 'if the future is necessary and what must happen happens regardless of what we do, it is preferable to do nothing, to care for nothing, and merely enjoy the pleasure of the instant.' Santos, however, expands the notion of lazy reason into four of its possible manifestations:

(1) Impotent reason—the total refraining from reasoning in the face of the perception that nothing can be done against an external necessity;
(2) Arrogant reason—the refraining from reason resulting from the perception that, because it sees itself as free, there is no necessity to reason;
(3) Metonymic reason—where a particular form of reason is perceived as the only form of rationality and therefore refrains from discovering

other forms of rationality, or if it does come across these, it appropriates them as its own;

(4) Proleptic reason—the refraining from reason in thinking the future because the future is seen as always already anticipated and, hence, known.

For Santos (2004), all of these four manifestations of 'lazy reason' have formed the basis of hegemonic Western thinking for the past centuries and mark most sociological, philosophical, and epistemological debates. The most drastic consequence of this 'lazy reason' is that in its various manifestations it presupposes a temporal concept of 'homogeneous, linear, progressive time' that 'contracts the present' and 'expands the future', and a spatial concept of 'totality'.

In terms of the temporal concept, the 'expansion of the future' (most clearly present in the manifestations of 'impotent reason' and 'proleptic reason') focuses on the future as the locus of success, development, progress, harmony, resulting in a lack of attention to the complexities, diversities, and heterogeneities of the present. It is in this sense that the present is seen as only ephemeral, merely a phase in the passage to the logically necessary and subsequent future, and is thus 'contracted' and contained. The result of this contraction of the present is the total lack of attention given to the multiple non-dominant heterogeneities and complexities of the present—invisible in relation to the promise of the supposedly 'already known' future; this in turn results in the 'waste' of alternative knowledges and practices, and produces the 'waste of experience'.

In terms of the spatial concept, Santos (2004, 2009) discusses how the dominant concept of 'totality' in rational theoretical Eurocentric thinking contributes to the 'waste of experience' by promoting a homogeneous concept of wholeness and totality which produces the invisibility of the heterogeneities and diversity that co-exist with what is perceived as the 'totality', excluding these. Once again, 'lazy reason' results in the 'waste of experience' by ignoring the alternative knowledges and practices that exist outside and together with its own privileged perception of 'totality'.

In opposition to 'lazy reason', Santos (2004, 158) calls for new, alternative epistemologies and forms of reason:

> to fight against the waste of experience, to render visible the initiatives and the alternative movements and to give them credibility, resorting to social science as we know it is of very little use. After all, social science has been responsible for concealing or discrediting alternatives. To fight against the waste of social experience there is no point in proposing another kind of social science. Rather, a different model of rationality must be proposed.

Santos calls this different model of rationality cosmopolitan reason; it is a reason based on the perception that 'the understanding of the world exceeds considerably the western understanding of the world' and its rationality tied to fixed conceptions of temporality and spatiality. This cosmopolitan reason, much unlike recent elitist and universalist concepts of cosmopolitanism, would seek to expand the present and contract the future, resignifying the concepts of time-space in order to make visible the co-extensive complexities and diversities (ecology of knowledges) existent today so that the knowledges and social practices once produced as absent and invisible—wasted—may emerge, be faced, and signified in all their complexity.

Cosmopolitan reason thus works against a 'mono' (monocultural, monological, monolingual) perspective and is based on the principle of incompleteness of all knowledges:

> The central idea [. . .] is that there is no ignorance or knowledge in general. All ignorance is ignorant of a certain knowledge and all knowledge is the overcoming of a particular ignorance [. . .] This principle of incompleteness of all knowledges is the condition of the possibility of epistemological dialogue and debate among the different knowledges.
>
> (Santos 2004, 168)

This is not a flippant form of deconstructive relativism where anything goes as knowledge. Santos affirms the necessary condition of contextual credibility of each knowledge in order to be considered legitimate and to participate in debates and dialogues with other knowledges, including scientific knowledge. This is the proposed antidote to scientific reason's hegemony grounded in its self-proclaimed legitimacy of abstract, uncontextualized, universalistic reason.

Given his critique of the exclusionary limits of concepts of totality in Western thinking, Santos is careful not to propose another general, totalizing theory that, in the name of 'including' the heterogeneities of the present, would end up like its predecessors doing exactly the opposite. In place of a totalizing theory, and as a corollary of cosmopolitan reason, Santos (2004, 168) proposes 'a theory or procedure of translation capable of creating mutual intelligibility among possible and available experiences'.

Given this importance of 'translation' as a means of establishing relations of equality among differences, without reducing any to the category of 'mono', Santos's 'cosmopolitan reason' and 'work of translation' may be seen as an ethical imperative and not a mere pluralistic theory of epistemologies. It is in this sense that Santos can contribute to an understanding of our problem of the conflicting interpretations of indigenous education in Brazil as constituting an ecology of knowledges in dire need of the work of translation so that mutual intelligibility may proliferate among co-existing varying knowledges and experiences. But first more on ethical imperatives in the midst of a perceived ecology of knowledges

Ethics and Translation: Undoing the Waste of Experience

Arguing for a non-hegemonic and non-universalistic concept of ethics in a world of complex diversity, inequalities, injustice, and social exclusion,

Caputo (1993, 4) denounces the fact that ethics is often defined in universalistic terms as an 'obligation or responsibility to an other', commonly justified as seeking to protect this other. However, Caputo reminds, us, by claiming to do this throughout history, those in hegemonic positions have often used ethics as a means of excluding a powerless other and making safe the actions of the powerful. Warning against this unethical use of ethics, Caputo (1993, 4) states: 'It [ethics] claims to lay foundations for principles and clarify concepts; it throws a safety net under the judgements we are forced to make. But obligation is not safe; ethics cannot make it safe'. Like Santos's 'waste of experience' Caputo calls for a consideration of the complexities and heterogeneities ignored by 'the powerful': 'Life is more risky and difficult' (4). Given this messy complexity of life (uncontained by lazy reason), Caputo demands that the concept of the 'other' be constantly questioned and de-essentialized; he calls for a process not unlike Santos's work of translation whereby mutual intelligibility can be established in constant dialogue. The concept of the other should be opened, he says, to include more than what the categories of the powerful permit in order to avoid the (less powerful) other being reduced to the sameness of the (powerful) self. In order for this to occur, ethics needs to be seen, according to Caputo, in local terms as culturally and historically embedded.

In a similar vein, in a move against what we have called 'lazy reason' and referring to the complex, diverse, and conflict-bound contemporary world, Butler (2004) emphasizes the urgent ethical need to listen to the other. Like Santos and his need for translation in the midst of an ecology of knowledges, Butler reminds us that though we have the ethical need to listen to the other, we have to be aware, however, of the difficulties of hearing the other. These difficulties of hearing the other are the result of the fact that one can only hear the voice of the other and give it meaning in terms of one's own experience. If one is not aware of one's location within what Sousa Santos called an ecology of knowledges, and the resulting need for translation to promote mutual intelligibility, lazy reason may set in, manifested in the strategy of metonymic reason whereby one assumes that what one understands is exactly what the other means to say. In such contacts with an 'other', proleptic reason may also manifest itself as a belief that one already knows what the other wants to say, even before he/she says it.

Aware of these traps of lazy reason in cross-cultural encounters in situations of complex diversity, Butler (2004, 17–18) like Santos and Caputo, calls for what may be also understood as translation, understood here as hearing beyond what we are able to hear: '[We need to] endeavour to recreate social and political conditions on more sustaining grounds. This means, in part hearing beyond what we are able to hear. And it means, as well, being open to narration that decentres us from our supremacy in both its right- and left-wing forms'.

This being open to the decentring of one's narratives and one's supremacy, be it on the left or on the right, politically, is a key concept in Butler's call for ethical awareness of the difficulty of mutual intelligibility whatever one's political preference may be. One needs to abandon one's 'mono'-lingual, monocultural, mono-political postures in order to appreciate the difficulty in hearing the voice of one's other, and in order to then proceed to 'translate' or seek mutual intelligibility.

Also interested in an ethical stance in unequal hegemonic relations with an other, Gramsci (1975) also calls attention to the importance of translation. For Gramsci, ethics, like every other cultural phenomenon, asks for 'translation', seen as a negotiation across differences in an effort to establish mutual intelligibility. In this sense, for Gramsci, even political and humanitarian values have to be 'translated', in order to be understood and negotiated.

Like Butler's call for the need to be aware of the impediments in hearing the other when one seeks to listen, Gramsci (1975) calls for an ethic of empathy (con-passionalità) in the translational process of seeking mutual intelligibility. This empathy or con-passionalità does not only imply a caring attitude, but more significantly, according to Gramsci, the empathy to feel the other's passions even if they are other passions, such that you would not like to share: 'not in order to share them at all costs, but to be able to talk to the other, to reach the other' Wagner (2008, 10).

Like Santos's critique of totality in lazy reasoning, Gramsci does not seek the possibility of total translation (the possibility of 'sharing at all costs'), but values the ethical stance of, once having recognized the impossibility of total translation and total mutual intelligibility, seeking nevertheless what Santos defines as 'isomorphic concerns' (2004); this term refers to the possibility of identifying corresponding similarities across differences, based on the previously mentioned concept of contextual validity. Thus, mutual intelligibility indicates the possibility of recognizing a certain equality among differences.

For Santos, the importance of isomorphic concerns and contextual validity is that they permit conjoined counter-hegemonic actions among different non-hegemonic groups, without these groups having to erase their differences. This possibility of conjoint counter-hegemonic action among otherwise disparate social groups in relation to specific mutual interests may be foreseen in Gramsci's ethical concept of empathy or con-passionalità.

Also, bringing together concerns with ethics, empathy, and translation vis a vis cross-cultural contacts between hegemonic and non-hegemonic groups in contexts of complex diversity, Spivak (2007, 276) portrays translation as an ethics of listening with empathy, and like Butler, calls attention to the problematic of listening but not hearing; like Gramsci, she speaks of ethical empathy in translation '[n]o speech is speech if it is not heard. It is this act of hearing-to-respond that may be called the imperative to translate . . . The founding translation between people is a listening with care and patience'.

This listening with care and patience, for Spivak, implies perceiving the location of one's ethical relationship with an Other within a dynamic of unequal power relations. Once again, we see in Spivak's words, the possibility signalled by Santos of mutual intelligibility across difference, the possibility of establishing isomorphic concerns.

Another important connection between Spivak's work and Santos's concept of 'lazy reason', especially in its manifestations as metonymic and proleptic reason, is perceivable in Spivak's (2004) ethical concept of 'unlearning privilege' whereby having perceived one's hegemonic superiority in relation to an other, one then perceives how this may hinder the process of mutual intelligibility and the understanding of the other, not in one's own terms, but in a process of difficult translation. One's hegemonic superiority in relation to the other (one's privilege) may impede one from hearing the other, even though one makes an effort to listen, as Butler has already pointed out above.

However, for Spivak, it is not sufficient to unlearn one's privilege; she also calls for the ethical recognition of the need of 'learning from below'. This involves 'a suspension of belief that one is indispensable, better or culturally superior; it is refraining from thinking that the Third World is in trouble and that one has the solutions; it is resisting the temptation of projecting oneself or one's world onto the Other' (2004, 6).

The Conflict of Interpretations and the Waste of Experience: The Epistemic Issue

After this excursion into theory, we now return to the problem which is the focus of this paper—the issue of the conflict of interpretations in relation to the preference of indigenous communities for apparently mainstream models of education when legislation permits them the emancipatory possibility of a bilingual indigenous school in an indigenous language with an indigenous curriculum; all this in order to undo five centuries of disrespect, exclusion, and assimilation. As we have seen, this preference of some indigenous communities for the mainstream curriculum in Portuguese is read by non-indigenous specialists as misinformed and as being the result of the introjection of dominant values by a non-dominant community, against its own interests.

However, the reason for our excursion above into the theories of ethical translation and the waste of experience was to permit, in the face of epistemic diversity and conflict, an 'other', indigenous, reading of the problem.

Is it really just another example of the internalization by the powerless of the cultural logic and ideology of the powerful? I propose that there is an urgent ethical need to seek other interpretations of this indigenous preference. In light of this, I suggest that this rather facile reading of a complex situation may be seen as the product of manifestations of lazy reason on the part of non-indigenous specialists and the proponents of indigenous education policies in Brazil. These specialists, even though they are emphatically and declaredly against the previous colonial policies of assimilation and eradication of indigenous languages and cultures, may nonetheless, and tragically, be prone to lazy reason and its preference for singular, monocultural, monolinguistic, and mono-epistemic practices and knowledge. I suggest that what needs to be considered in order to come to terms with the complexity of the situation, is, on the one hand, an epistemic issue, and on the other hand, an ethical issue.

Santos's denouncing of Western social science's complicity in lazy reason and its urgent need for a change to cosmopolitan reason is especially relevant to this situation, given that most if not all indigenous education policy in Brazil is the product of conscientious, anti-colonial social scientists: Anthropologists, sociologists and linguists. What then could possibly impede them from appreciating the full complexity of the various indigenous communities' relationship with the openness of the policies of indigenous education and the preference for what seems to be a monolingual indigenous school based on the mainstream school.

The anthropologist Roy Wagner (1981, 35) offers an answer; 'anthropologists', he says, 'study culture through culture [. . . then] whatever operations characterize our investigations must also be general properties of culture'.

The corollary of this inescapable cultural embedding of any social scientist is the impossibility of decontextualized objectivity even when applying what may be considered to be a scientific procedure grounded on tested and age-old methods and procedures. As Santos has shown and as discussed above, the very episteme of scientific knowledge is itself culturally and historically embedded and worse still, the result of epistemicidal tendencies that destroy any alternative knowledges. The irony here is that social scientists who are not critically aware of their embedding in this episteme of lazy reason may in fact not be unlike kettles calling the pot black when they accuse indigenous communities of internalizing the dominant ideologies that exclude them, apparently to their own detriment.

If these social scientist specialists are disappointed with how many indigenous communities make their varying and heterogeneous choices permitted by the openness of indigenous education legislation, they may be expecting indigenous communities in general to make the same choices—those preferred by the non-indigenous specialists (i.e., in favour of a bilingual indigenous school with indigenous knowledges in its curriculum). That is, when faced with the possibility of diverse and heterogeneous options (see Table 10.1 below for various possibilities of implementation of indigenous school) these specialists seem to expect diverse and heterogeneous indigenous communities to behave in a homogeneous, foreseeable manner, much as mainstream non-indigenous schools behave in generally standard fashion.

The mainstream non-indigenous school, however, it is important to remember, unlike the indigenous school, cannot make the innumerable choices that indigenous schools can make. It is important to remember here that all the possible choices have to be made, and are made, collectively, by the indigenous community that harbours the indigenous school; this is not at all possible for a non-indigenous school which follows curricular

Table 10.1 Various Possibilities for Configuring Implementations of Indigenous Schools in Brazil

Indigenous language as medium	Indigenous language as subject	Portuguese as medium	Portuguese as subject	Indigenous knowledge	Mainstream knowledge
X	X	X	X	X	X
X			X		X
	X	X	X	X	X
X			X		X
X	X		X		X

and methodological orientations which are homogeneous throughout the nation.

Before making the connection between these postures and expectations of non-indigenous specialists and lazy reason and its attending waste of experience, it is worthwhile recalling some of the facts we encountered at the beginning of this analysis; in spite of the reduced size of the indigenous population in Brazil, in completely un-homogeneous fashion, it consists of:

(1) 220 different peoples;
(2) They speak180 different languages; and
(3) These languages belong to 30 different language families.

Beyond this quantitative diversity and heterogeneity, one may add a qualitative dimension to this; this relates to the fact that some communities have totally lost their languages whereas others have not and yet others face the threat of the future extinction of their languages. A second dimension that adds to the complexity of the heterogeneity of indigenous communities in Brazil is that which refers to culture. Though some communities may have lost their languages, they may have maintained their culture in the form of oral traditions and knowledges. Others may have maintained their cultures together with their languages, whereas yet others may have lost both.

The bottom line here is that if it is expected that because indigenous education has its own specific legislation, then indigenous communities across the country are expected to homogeneously make the same decisions to teach and learn in a uniform manner their indigenous languages and knowledges (albeit in the name of a respect for otherness), then these communities would be benefitting very little from the openness of the legislation, and would ironically be behaving as they did under the pre-1988 standardized assimilationist policies, residually left over from colonization. Who would be the real beneficiary of this situation?

The state, whose expenses in producing materials and preparing teachers would be reduced given the possibility of implementing an economy of scale for homogenized indigenous schools? Or would the beneficiary be the community, who would apparently see its language and culture finally preserved and its knowledges occupying pride of place in the school curriculum? It is this latter possibility that seems to underlie the expectations of non-indigenous specialists.

But what of the waste of experience and the various manifestations of lazy reason on which much time and many words have been spent in this analysis. Where does this fit into the picture?

Part of the answer to this question has already been given above, where the extreme heterogeneity of indigenous communities has been alluded to, together with the fact that this seems not to have been critically absorbed by the specialists. This may now be read critically as evidence of metonymic and proleptic reasoning on the part of the specialists. The metonymic reasoning relates to the possibility that the non-indigenous specialists may be presupposing that their own logic and rationality, that of the 'cultural and linguistic preservation' should be prioritized and implemented at all costs. The proleptic reasoning here relates to the expectation that the mere implementation of indigenous educational legislation will guarantee the survival and preservation of indigenous languages and communities. Both of these (proleptic and metonymic) reasonings, in spite of the fact that they are carried out by well-meaning pro-indigenous (but non-indigenous) thinkers, activists, and policy makers, unfortunately exemplify lazy reason and bring in their wake the waste of experience.

This occurs through what Santos (2014) called the temporal and spatial concepts that accompany lazy reason: The constriction of the present and totality. First, the constriction of the present and resulting expansion of the future; these appear in the form of the non-indigenous belief that the homogeneous widespread application of an indigenous bilingual curriculum containing indigenous knowledges and teaching the indigenous language and Portuguese, will guarantee an expanded and bright future of greater self-esteem and survival and thus emancipate indigenous communities from centuries of marginalization. The attendant constriction of the present consists of the lack of awareness, on the part of the non-indigenous specialists, of alternative forms of knowledge, existent in the present, which can also boost the chances of survival of indigenous communities and emancipate them here and now from the dominance of non-indigenous epistemologies.

In second place, the spatial conception of lazy reason, which manifests itself through the notion of totality, takes the form of presupposing that policy, legislation, curriculum, and pedagogies have to be applied in totum, and in a generally homogeneous fashion. As discussed above, Santos already pointed out that the privileging of totality helps lazy reason solve the problem of what is perceived as the atomization of social reality (and hence a threat to desired and controllable homogeneity) and impose homogeneity. The social, cultural, and linguistic heterogeneity that characterizes indigenous communities in Brazil vanishes in the face of this desire for totality. Ironically, as

Santos (2002) also pointed out, this dominant desire for totality, wholeness, and homogeneity brings in its wake an impossibility of social transformation; this impossibility arises from the idea of self-sufficient organization and 'self-explanatoriness' that a totality proffers, there being no space for difference or alternatives from which change and transformation may surge.

The real waste of experience in this consideration of the epistemic issues involves the concepts of 'language and cultural preservation' that permeates much of the official policies of indigenous education. Here the waste of experience, in the sense of ignoring alternative non-dominant knowledges, lies in the conflict of interpretations around the notion of preservation and its profound cultural embeddedness.

To begin with, the concept of cultural and language preservation presumes that both culture (in the form of knowledge) and language are substances which have some kind of material existence which can and should be preserved. This concept of substantivity then grounds the desire for a general homogeneity in the application of policies of indigenous education as discussed above.

Non-indigenous specialists, as we have seen, also strive for a bilingual indigenous school that would teach and hence preserve the indigenous language and culture of the community concerned. The beneficiary of such a desired (on the part of the non-indigenous specialists) outcome is seen to be each indigenous community that successfully implements and sustains the corresponding policy.

We have also seen, however, that the reality of the situation is very different. The ideal indigenous school as envisaged by policy foresees a school similar to that described in the first row of Table 10.1 above, and such a school is difficult to find. It is my contention that what is at stake is a conflict of interpretations of not only the concepts of preservation, culture as knowledge, language, but also of the very concept of education and school. Once again, the waste of experience lies in the difficulty in perceiving the differences in these concepts between the dominant Eurocentric culture and the indigenous cultures. This becomes a serious issue as a manifestation of the waste of experience when one remembers that the specialists involved in this conflict are social scientists themselves and therefore presumably critical thinkers aware of the embeddedness of these sociocultural concepts.

In order to clarify this situation further, one needs to pursue another excursion, this time into Amazonian indigenous philosophies in order to reverse the process of wasted experience.

Translating Amidst an Ecology of Knowledges: The Case for Equivocal Translation and the Ethical Issue

As is well known among social scientists, and more specifically, among anthropologists in Brazil, a large part of the indigenous cultures of the

Amazon region (where the indigenous population is concentrated) construct their epistemologies on the cultural precept of what Viveiros de Castro (2014) has called 'indigenous perspectivism'. This in turn is the product of an ontology that sees all living beings (human, animal, mineral, vegetal, and spiritual) as interconnected manifestations of the same life force that permeates, in an undifferentiated manner, all forms of life. What all living beings are seen to share is culture (and not nature, as in Eurocentric humanism). This concept of culture refers to the cognitive capacity to think, make meaning, and produce knowledge. Thus, what distinguishes one species from another is a difference in knowledge where each form of knowledge is seen as that species' specific response to its needs for survival. Thus, similar to Santos's concept the indigenous philosophy of perspectivism sees the world as being constituted by an ecology of heterogeneous knowledges.

As all living beings are seen as interconnected, relationships between them are seen to be essential for survival. However, this interconnectedness or phenomenological unity is purely pronominal and not substantive. This means that any species of subject perceives itself and its world in the same way that we perceive our world and ourselves. Given the diversity of such perceptions, the issue involved in relating across species is not of discovering the common referent to differing representations, but on the contrary, of making explicit the equivocation in believing that the differences may relate to the same (Viveiros de Castro 2009).

Once again, in a similar fashion to that proposed by Santos, who postulated the 'work of translation' as an important means for relating within an ecology of knowledges, Viveiros de Castro identifies in indigenous philosophy the process of equivocal translation.

The objective of equivocal translation, as a tool for cross-species relationships, is not to find a synonym (a co-referential translation) for the representations of others, as if to speak of the 'same thing'; the aim, Viveiros de Castro (2009, 62) says, is not to lose sight of the difference concealed within equivocal, apparently 'synonymous' representations, between our language and the language of the other species, 'since we and they are never talking about the same things'. Thus, even though a jaguar and a human may each see itself as consuming 'beer', the beer of the jaguar (the blood of its prey, for example) is not the same as the beer of the human.

This process of equivocal translation more than a means of simple epistemic translation, consists of an ethical dimension in the relationship with an other, much like that suggested by Caputo, Spivak, Gramsci, and Butler above. Thus, despite sharing an equal ignorance about the Other, with the subject one is relating to, it is important to be aware that the Other of the Other is never exactly the same as the Other of the Same, i.e., there is no point of convergence, no external referent, no way of saying whose perspective is the true perspective.

The necessary contact with Otherness in a world perceived as inescapably interconnected requires a perception of the ethical need for translation as inescapable equivocation (Viveiros de Castro 2009):

> *a good translation is one which allows the alien concept to deform and subvert the translator's conceptual toolbox, so that the intention of the source language can be expressed within the new one.*

Thus, the referent is not fixed and external (as in Eurocentric universalism)—it is the referent that changes. This may be exemplified by the traditional perspectivist indigenous saying:

> The jaguar sees itself as human and sees the human as a jaguar; I don't.

The perspectivism emphasizes the fact that in a human-jaguar confrontation, both the jaguar and I know that we see ourselves as human and the other as jaguar, but we have no way of ascertaining whose perspective is the real perspective.

This is not a case of traditional Eurocentric relativism, since what I know can only be the product of my species' capacity to produce knowledge; the only way that I can know what the jaguar knows is by becoming the jaguar.

This, however, would mean acceding to the perspective and thus the knowledge of the jaguar and would result in my ceasing to exist as myself, and becoming the jaguar.

The ethical relationship suggested by this indigenous perspectivism is that one should be aware of the equality in difference between one's own knowledge and that of the other at the same time as one is fully aware that one is not the other, and is therefore different. This is not unlike Santos's concept of translation as a means of acceding to mutual intelligibility, through isomorphic concerns, attentive always to the fact that total intelligibility is impossible.

This concept of equivocal translation then establishes the eminently ethical relationship necessary in relating to epistemic difference, even when total mutual illegibility is not possible. This is also not unlike Butler's, Spivak's, and Gramsci's metaphors of the ethical need to listen to the other at the same time as perceiving the difficulty in hearing or understanding the other given the insuperable differences between oneself and the other. Nonetheless, translation, empathic or equivocal, as the need for engagement and mutual intelligibility among non-hegemonic practices and knowledges, facilitates aggregation for counter-hegemonic action.

Changing the course of this excursion into indigenous philosophy back to the issue of the conflicts of interpretation vis-à-vis the preference of many indigenous communities for a non-indigenous school within the domain of indigenous educational policies, one may now risk more empathic translations of this preference, away from the accusations of uninformed actions or the internalization of dominant ideologies. To begin with, it is essential to remember that these preferences and practices of indigenous communities occur within their cultural epistemologies and ontologies of indigenous perspectivism and its ensuing ethic of equivocal translation. As such, given their cultural awareness of the 'isomorphic' sameness in difference of knowledges between their own indigenous knowledges and those of the mainstream school, the much-maligned preference for a mainstream curriculum in Portuguese occurs, one must remember, in their own indigenous community school and not on the territory of an other.

Being a community school, the teacher together with the students, belongs to the very same community. Moreover, as permitted by indigenous educational legislation, it is the community that controls the time and space of the community school. Thus, in spite of the fact that it is a mainstream curriculum teaching mainstream and not indigenous knowledge in Portuguese that is preferred in the community school, the process of construction of knowledge within the school (call it schooling) coexists with indigenous knowledges in the local indigenous language outside the school; hence, students continue to interact with traditional practices and knowledges—such as planting and hunting with their parents (call it education)—while at the same time learning the dominant knowledge and the dominant language. Seen from the philosophical stance of indigenous perspectivism, this schooling-education practice may be understood as the need to relate to different others (and their knowledges) with whom one is interconnected (in this case the dominant non-indigenous, national community); it may also be seen as the ethical and epistemological need, intrinsic to indigenous philosophy, to have access to the perspective and knowledge of the dominant other whilst at the same time being aware of (and hence avoiding) the danger of becoming the other. All this within the same indigenous philosophical framework that considers that knowledge is produced in response to each species need for survival.

The Human Talent for Antagonism

In conclusion, far from a facile and apparently dark (as opposed to the enlightened reasoning of modernity) abandoning of one's own language, culture, and knowledge supposedly in favour of equally darkly adopting the hegemonic language, culture, and knowledge of the nation, and far from a mechanical uncritical dark internalization of the dominant ideology, the apparently simple practice of preferring a mainstream curriculum in the mainstream language reveals itself as a complex philosophical process of equivocal translation, cultural survival, and cosmopolitan reason, attesting to the strength, resilience, and complexity of indigenous epistemologies in the face of epistemic diversity, bringing to the fore that what may have been simply perceived as dark and non-hegemonic, implies in fact, in its complexity what may be perceived as various shades of darkness where indigenous epistemologies are imbricated and interacting with non-indigenous episte-mologies in a current political, linguistic, and cultural context.

The same sophistication and resilience unfortunately cannot be perceived in the posture of some mainstream social scientists who claim to be pro-indigenous, and in favour of the preservation of indigenous languages and epistemologies. These specialists often seem to be trapped within the bounds of their own Enlightenment epistemologies, apparently with great difficulty for engendering translation and the search for mutual intelligibility in the midst of epistemic diversity and dissensus.

When they claim to listen to the indigenous other, they apparently only hear their own voices and values, seemingly overtaken with difficulty for escaping from the bounds of lazy thinking, and thus liable to waste the wealth of experience of the ecology of knowledges that surrounds them but remains invisible to their eyes. The lingering inheritance of coloniality and its unequal distribution of knowledges, bodies, and languages seems to persist. This may be something that Applied Linguistics, in its focus on education, needs to be aware of in order to avoid, albeit unwittingly, continuing the legacy of colo-niality. And here I end with a timely warning expressed by Todd (2009, 9):

> The idea that education can ameliorate certain global conditions under the sign of humanity is a worrying proposition . . . it fails to recognise that the very injustices and antagonisms which are the targets of such education are created and sustained precisely through our human talent for producing them.

Notes

1 Reprinted with permission from *Interfaces Brasil/Canada 2014*, 14 (2), 36–60.
2 Rancière (2010) defines dissensus as a 'difference within the same', or 'a sameness of the opposite', referring to the diversity that constitutes and not separates com-munities. For Rancière, dissensus in this sense is the 'actual reality of politics'.
3 Grosfoguel (2008) and Quijano (1997), among others, refer also to the fact that within coloniality, besides knowledges, bodies (races and genders) and languages are also distributed unequally within unequal power relations. For the purposes of brevity, our discussion in this paper will not focus on this aspect.

References

Bhabha, H.K. 1986. 'Remembering Fanon: Self, Psyche and the Colonial Condi-tion'. Foreword to Fanon. F. *Black Skin, White Masks*. London: Pluto Press.

Butler, J. 2004. *Precarious Life: The Powers of Mourning and Violence*. London/New York: Verso.

Caputo, J. 1993. *Against Ethics: Contributions to a Poetics of Obligation with Con-stant Reference to Deconstruction*. Bloomington: Indiana.

Cavalcanti, R. 1999. *Presente De Branco, Presente De Grego? Escola e Escrita em Comunidades Indígenas do Brasil Central* [*White Man's present or Trojan Horse? School and Writing in Indigenous Communities in Central Brazil*]. Unpublished MA thesis, Federal University of Rio de Janeiro.

de Souza, L. M. 2003. 'Voices on Paper: Multimodal Texts and Indigenous Literacy in Brazil'. *Social Semiotics* 13 (1): 29–42.

———. 2005. 'The Ecology of Writing among the Kashinawa: Indigenous Multimodality in Brazil'. In *Reclaiming the Local in Language Policy and Practice*, edited by S. Canagarajah, 73–95. Mahwah: Lawrence Erlbaum.

———. 2006. 'Entering a Culture Quietly: Writing and Cultural Survival in Indigenous Education in Brazil'. In *Disinventing and Reconstituting Languages*, edited by S. Makoni and A. Pennycook, 135–69. Clevedon: Multilingual Matters.

———. 2008. 'Going beyond "Here's a Culture, Here's a Literacy": Vision in Amerindian Literacies'. In *Literacies, Global and Local*, edited by M. Prinsloo and M. Baynham, 193–213. Amsterdam: John Benjamins.

de Souza, L. M., and V. Andreotti, eds. 2011. *Postcolonial Perspectives on Global Citizenship Education*. London: Routledge.

Fausto, C. 2001. *Inimigos Fiéis: História, Guerra e Xamanismo na Amazônia*. São Paulo: EdUSP.

Freire, P. 2005. *Pedagogia da Tolerancia [A Pedagaogy of Tolerance]*. São Paulo: UNESP.

Gandhi, L. 1998. *Postcolonial Theory*. New York: Columbia University Press.

Gramsci, A. 1975. *Prison Notebooks*. New York: Columbia University Press.

Grosfoguel, R. 2008. 'Transmodernity, Border Thinking, and Global Coloniality: Decolonizing Political Economy and Postcolonialstudies'. *Revista Critica de Ciencias Sociais* 80. Retrieved from http://www.eurozine.com/articles/2008-07-04-grosfoguel-en.html. (Accessed 3 March 2014).

Grupioni, L. 2008. *Olhar Longe, Porque O Futuro É Longe: Cultura, Escola E Professores Indígenas No Brasil [Looking Afar, because the Future Lies Far Ahead: Culture, School and Inidgenous Teachers in Brazil]*. Unpublished Ph.D. thesis, University of São Paulo.

Leibniz, G. W. [1710] 1985. *Theodicy: Essays on the Goodness of God, the Freedom of Man, and the Origin of Evil*. La Salle, IL: Open Court.

Mignolo, W. 2000. *Local Histories/Global Designs: Coloniality, Subaltern Knowledges, and Border Thinking*. Princeton, NJ: Princeton University Press.

———. 2007. 'Delinking'. *Cultural Studies* 21 (2): 449–512.

Quijano, A. 1997. 'Colonialidad del Poder, Cultura y Conocimiento en América Latina' ['The Coloniality of Power, Culture and Knowledge in Latin America']. *Anuario Mariateguiano* 9: 117–31.

Rancière, J. 2010. *Dissensus: On Politics and Aesthetics*. Translated by Steven Corcoran. London/New York: Bloomsbury Academic.

Santos, B. de S. 2002. *A Critica da Razão Indolente: contra o Desperdício da Experiência [A Critique of Lazy Reason: Against the Waste of Experience]*. São Paulo: Cortês.

———. 2004. 'A Critique of Lazy Reason: Against the Waste of Experience'. In *The Modern World-System in the Longue Durée*, edited by I. Wallerstein, 157–97. London: Paradigm.

———. 2009. 'Um Ocidente Não-Ocidentalista? A Filosofia à Venda, a Douta Ignorância e a Aposta de Pascal ['A Non-Occidental West? Philosophy for Sale, Learned Ignorance and Pascal's Wager']. In *Epistemologias do Sul [Epistemologies of the South]*, edited by B. de S. Santos and M. P. Meneses, 445–87. Coimbra: Editora Almedina.

———. 2014. *Epistemologies of the South: Justice Against Epistemicide*. Boulder, CO: Paradigm Publishers.

Spivak, G. C. 1990. *The Postcolonial Critic: Interviews, Strategies, Dialogues*. Routledge: London.

———. 2004. Righting Wrongs. *The South Atlantic Quarterly*, 103 (2–3): 523–581.

———. 2007. 'Translation as Culture'. In *Translation: Reflections, Refractions, Transformations*, edited by P. St. Pierre and P. C. Kar, 263–76. Amsterdam and Philadelphia: John Benjamins.

Todd, S. 2009. *Toward an Imperfect Education*. London: Paradigm.

Viveiros de Castro, E. 'O nativo relativo'. *Mana* 8 (1): 113–48.

———. 2004. 'Perspectival Anthropology and the Method of Controlled Equivocation'. *Tipiti* 2 (1): 3–22.

———. 2009. *Métaphysiques cannibales*. Paris: Presses Universitaires de France.

———. 2014. *Cannibal Metaphysics*. Minneapolis: Univocal.

Wagner, B. 2008. 'Cultural Translation: A Value or a Tool? Let's Start with Gramsci!' *Forum Postkoloniale Arbeiten / Postcolonial Studies*. Retrieved from http://www.goethezeitportal.de/fileadmin/PDF/kk/df/postkoloniale_studien/wagner_cultural-translation-gramsci.pdf. (Accessed 23 October 2010).

Wagner, R. 1981. *The Invention of Culture*. Chicago: University of Chicago Press.

11 Re-Placing and Re-Centring Southern Multilingualisms

A De-Colonial Project

Kathleen Heugh

Things fall apart; the centre cannot hold.
—(William Butler Yeats 1919, 'The Second Coming')

Introduction

The first decade and a half of the twenty-first century have been accompanied by socio-political and economic changes, environmental catastrophes, conflict-induced ruptures (Heugh 2014a) and turbulence (Stroud 2015) on a global scale. These far-reaching changes have reverberated within the northern 'academy'. We now live in a world in which centre(s) of global political and economic power are shifting from North Atlantic countries to countries or blocs of countries located in Asia, Africa, and South America. Such changes are bringing to the surface systems of knowledge and belief that have been overlooked by many scholars. Christianity appears to be on the retreat, although it was powerful in European cosmology and epistemology through the Renaissance (fourteenth to sixteenth centuries) and Reformation (sixteenth to seventeenth centuies), and although it was introduced and consolidated in the 'New World' through colonial expansionism. One reason may be the demise of the European nation-state empires after World War II. The influence of the U.S. as the major global power in the second half of the twentieth century, after only six decades of ascendancy, also appears to be in decline. The Global Economic Crisis of 2008 and the loss of momentum in the U.S., the largest economy of the world, coupled with the military failures of northern allied countries in Central Asia and the Middle East, indicate decline on several fronts. Economic, political, and military strengths that coalesced in Europe and the US during the twentieth century now appear to be changing places—from north back to south and east according to scholars such as Cooper and Morrell (2014); Durant ([1935] 1954); Maddison (2007); and McGann (2015); and influential global economic advisers, AT Kearney Inc. (2015).

In this chapter, my main focus is on an emerging southern challenge to the academy, a revisiting of northern-held historical narratives that have manufactured an 'abyssal line' (Santos 2012) between north and south, an uncovering of ongoing entanglements and co-dependencies that criss-cross the line, and a replacing of southern knowledges and expertise within the academy. I attempt to illustrate these changes through the lens of world views that recognize heterogeneity or diversities, particularly linguistic diversities. These views dispel the mirage of homogeneity which was fashioned through the scientific rationalism of the seventeenth and eighteenth centuries and carried on into nineteenth- and twentieth-century ideologies of the nation-state. World views recognizing heterogeneity and diversities anticipate and signal fundamental revision and recalibrations within the academy. Such recalibrations do not establish a mirror image or reverse of the abyssal line. Instead, they offer restoration and re-establishment of order through a 're-placement' of southern multilingualisms and through them diversities of knowledge, belief, and ways of being.

We can trace the southern challenge in Africa to twentieth-century writers who echo Yeats's prescient observations regarding the fraying nature of the centre. Chinua Achebe's novel, *Things fall apart* (1958), addresses the colonial impact on African societies ironically coinciding with the unravelling of European colonialism. Ngugi wa Thiong'o wrote of *Moving the Centre* (Ngugi 1993) after the completion of independence and early signs of US decline. These authors signalled assertions (and critiques) of endogenous or Indigenous knowledge systems (IKS). Their critiques were to be followed by contributions from scholars in Australia, New Zealand, and Africa (e.g., Cooper and Morrell 2014; Hountondji 2013; Odora Hoppers 2002; Smith 1999; Warren, Slikkerveer, and Titilola, 1989) that questioned northern hegemony and claims regarding ownership of knowledge production. In Argentina, Rodolfo Kusch explored *Indigenous and Popular Thinking in América* (Kusch [1970] 2010).[1] These strands of thought now interlace with debates identified as southern across the global south, articulated in 'southern theory' (Connell 2007) and 'southern epistemologies' (e.g., Santos 2012), and they resonate with the reclaiming of histories and wisdoms among southern communities (cf. Chakravarty 2011) at a time when the proximities of south and north draw closer. The challenge is not simply to a northern political economy. Southern authors from South Asia, Africa, the Americas, and Australasia draw attention to the hubris of an 'academy' that erases southern and eastern systems of knowledge, being, and world view in time and space. Such re-emergences are relevant for those with an interest in contexts of heterogeneity, including linguistic heterogeneity.

Although diversity in the first decade of the twenty-first century brought renewed attention to multilingualism as a global phenomenon (as noted by Agnihotri 2007; Cenoz, Gorter, and Heugh 2011; Edwards 2012; Lo Bianco 2014; Martin-Jones and Gardner 2012; May 2013; Singleton et al. 2013; Stroud and Heugh 2011 and Wiley, Lee, and Rumberger 2009), its immediacy has now become pressing. It is all the more pressing as significant differences are beginning to appear in terms of how multilingualism is understood. Some recent discussions of multilingualism that have gained traction in the northern academy appear suspended in time, harking back to colonial and postcolonial ideologies (or insensitivities) that continue to take little note of southern experiences and expertise. They do not appear to be attuned to the ways in which contemporary conflict and human mobility bring southern peripheries towards northern centres of fading power. In this chapter, I thus attempt to illustrate southern experiences of diversity and multilingualism in the light of contemporary global shifts and in relation to perceptions of epistemological supremacy that linger in the northern academy. At first sight the discussion may be mistaken for essentialism or drawing an impermeable 'abyssal line' between discussions of diversity (multilingualism in particular) and between north and south during a time of global change and uncertainty. It is neither. In order to find a way through uncertainties and the growing sense of unease that is accompanying the scale of mobility and change (Ippolito and Trevisanut 2016) witnessed in Europe, I argue that it is necessary to prise apart epistemological and other entanglements of south and north that have become distorted over time. In the process of prising apart it may become easier to see where and how northern perceptions have eclipsed southern experiences and expertise. It may be easier to see where southern expertise might now bring opportunities to approach human diversity with greater clarity and ethical practice.

My use of the term 'south' in this chapter is not simply as a metaphor of resistance but as one that points to an opportunity for recentring and rebalancing perceptions of human diversity. It is an opportunity for a 're-placement' of context in discussions of linguistic diversity and other diversities. It is an opportunity to overcome the constraints of academic hubris so that we might learn to listen, to unlearn, and to relearn from one another (e.g., de Souza and Andreotti 2009), and this is as important in the discipline of sociolinguistics as in other areas of the humanities. It is a 'de-colonial' (Mignolo 2011) project that is as relevant in northern contexts as it is in southern ones, as centre and periphery draw closer once more.

Challenges Before Us

My argument begins with the challenge to northern-held assumptions about history, about the locus of knowledge, and about epistemic hegemony that have become bedded down with nation-state ideologies of homogeneity. I argue that a trajectory towards the universality of scientific thought, along with nation-state interests in homogeneity, is theoretically incompatible with diversity. In the current age of 'de-coloniality' (Mignolo 2010, 2011) it is anachronistic and hegemonic. In northern contexts, representations of diversity are filtered through the twin lenses of universality and nation-state homogeneity. However, there are differing representations of diversity among and within southern communities. Diversity does not reduce to one-ness (or universality). Diversity in one physical or temporal setting is not the same as diversity in another. Diversity is not static; it is dynamic and multidimensional. Similarly, there is no oneness or sameness in Indigeneity (Chakravarty 2011), Aboriginality (Watson 2009, 2014), or 'multilingual-ity' (Agnihotri 2014; Heugh 2014b). Experiences of multilingualism in one northern setting are not those of a second northern setting and they are cer-tainly not those of any southern setting (Heugh 2013, 2014a, b). This means that attempts to articulate a universally applicable theory of diversity, for example, of linguistic diversity or multilingualism, are likely to be flawed.

We also need to untangle some of the history of south-north exchanges of knowledge and expertise as these connect with the epistemologies, ontolo-gies, and cosmologies that southern communities hold and experience. We need to examine the way that historical documents are written in a handful of languages and unpeel the many layers and dimensions of multilingualism(s) that present and convey knowledge. For southern communities, experience, belief, and knowledge are held in balance with humanity. Place and time are dimensions that neither disappear nor lose significance (see also Cooper and Morrell 2014). As the late twentieth century, the northern centre has taken on southern characteristics, diversity in all its dimensions has enveloped us wherever we are. The contemporary nature of diversity urges a re-exami-nation of how the academy reflects knowledge, experience, and expertise from the very diverse communities and contexts of the world. Thus far, it has often (mis)represented this knowledge, experience, and expertise. It also urges individual members of the academy, whether they are located in northern or southern settings, to reflect on complicity with what may turn out to be fragile theories and pedagogies rooted not in plurality, but in sin-gularity, homogeneity, and universality.

The first purpose of this chapter then is to pose a challenge. If diversity does not reduce to singularity, and if the default position of dominant dis-courses of the academy is universality (and singularity), then contemporary diversities and pluri-versalities of southern experiences and thinking bring the most serious challenge to the academy in recent times. The second pur-pose of this chapter is to move the debates beyond what Santos (2012) char-acterizes as an 'abyssal line' between southern and northern thinking, and to begin to explore what it is that southern perspectives might contribute to global understandings of diversities, and with them, multilingualisms. For many of us in the academy this means trying to understand, recognize, and interpret both northern and southern perspectives simultaneously. Kusch (2010), writing from Argentina in the 1970s, offers a useful perspective here. He refers to 'mestizo consciousness', arguing that this does not refer to people of mixed ancestry (Mignolo 2010) but rather to a consciousness arrived at through a lived understanding of both Indigenous and European (northern) world views. Mestizo consciousness may contribute to reflex-ivity and a reorientation of the academy in ways that admit pluri-versal perspectives of knowledge and diversity (including multilingualism). The third purpose of my chapter is to draw attention to an ethics of reflexive research practice that draws on learning to slice through cacophonies of hubris to listen to and see wisdom in silences.

Recontextualizing Entangled Exchanges of Knowledge

In this part of the discussion, I suggest that it is necessary to untangle southern and northern histories, many of which are captured in European texts and represent world views that emerged during the ascendancy of European expertise and knowledge. Although most Western histories dwell on the contributions of the ancient Greek and Roman empires to modernity and scholarship, there is a growing body of scholarly work that challenges these historical accounts. Some 80 years ago, Will Durant ([1935] 1954), asserted that Western representations of ancient civilizations had missed or glossed over the significance of historical records from ancient Egypt, the East, and the Americas.

> At this historic moment—when the ascendancy of Europe is so rapidly coming to an end, when Asia is swelling with resurrected life . . . the provincialism of our traditional histories, which began with Greece and summed up Asia in a line, has become no merely academic error, but a possibly fatal failure of perspective and intelligence.
>
> (Durant [1935] 1954, viii–xi)

Durant also refers us to the knowledge and expertise carried by merchants along the Silk Road from China to Africa, the Mediterranean and Italy, and back, the significance of which has been lost in conventional histories. Yet, the dominance of nineteenth-century views such as those of Hegel, who never visited Africa, has lingered. Hegel declared in his *Lectures on the Philosophy of History* (1822–1830), that:

> What we properly understand by Africa, is the Unhistorical, Undeveloped Spirit, still involved in the conditions of mere nature, and which had to be presented here only as on the threshold of the World's History.
>
> (Hegel 2001, 117)

Such views endured well into the twentieth century as evident in the work of British historian Hugh Trevor-Roper:

> Perhaps, in the future, there will be some African history to teach. But at present there is none, or very little: there is only the history of the Europeans in Africa. The rest is largely darkness, like the history of pre-European, pre-Columbian America. And darkness is not a subject for history.
>
> (Trevor-Roper 1965, 9)

Durant's concerns had been with ancient civilizations but he skirted documentary evidence of African histories south of Egypt, although there must already have been traces of this in the scholarly documents and archives pertaining to the Silk Road leading to and from China. At least one of the routes of the Silk Road ventured into East Africa and the activities of Abyssinian (Ethiopian) merchants and scholars have been well-documented in medieval Europe. There is earlier documentary evidence in Greece and Rome of Nubian ascendancy in East Africa dating back to 5,000 BC. There are also maps that indicate the presence of pyramids in Kush and Nubia (present-day Sudan), which show these to be more numerous than in Egypt (e.g., Nordström 2014; Welsby and Davies 2002). Kush was located at the point at which the two major tributaries of the Nile, the Blue Nile from Ethiopia and White Nile from Uganda come together. It was strategically located for the passage of highly prized goods from Eastern sub-Saharan Africa towards the Mediterranean.

We know that despite Hegel's nineteenth-century statements regarding Africa's apparent lack of scholarship and Trevor-Roper's claim about its intellectual darkness, Africa was nevertheless home to at least 80, possibly 95 scripts, and accompanying literacies (Mumin 2014, 40). Many of these evolved from or alongside hieroglyphics that had spread south along the length of the Nile and Great Rift Valley into East and Central Africa. Sometime later, from the seventh to the fourteenth centuries, Arab traders carried Ajami script across the Maghreb in North Africa, to the south and into the Sahel, where it was adopted and used with as many as 79 languages of West Africa (e.g., Mumin 2014, 45). A long-held Western view that nineteenth-century European scholarship is responsible for revealing some of the secrets of ancient Egypt has been challenged by Okasha El Daly (2005), who argues that there existed a continuum of Coptic and Islamic scholarship of Egyptology, and Islamic study of hieroglyphics, that can be traced a thousand years earlier, to the ninth century. Recent archaeological findings in Diepkloof Cave in Howieson's Poort in South Africa of systematic etchings on ostrich egg fragments that date back 60,000 years suggest that the early precursors to writing systems can be traced in Southern Africa more than 30,000 years earlier than elsewhere (Texier et al. 2013). Together, these and other challenges to Western representations of pre-colonial Africa, and indeed of Central and South America, or of Australia, have not yet been fully understood with regard to their significance in the past or what they may signify for the present, or the extent to which some of the foundations of modern, Western thought, are thus dislodged.

The claim that Africa or South America had no history or scholarship may be ascribed to the frailties of scholars such as Hegel or Trevor-Roper, or others who have repeated such claims. These claims illustrate that knowledge and historical documents may be distorted, that southern expertise has been overlooked, elided, or erased, and that such erasure endures over the passage of time. However, we also see new evidence that disrupts old narratives.

We also need to take account of the role of language as a conduit for the dissemination of knowledge and as a lens through which we glimpse other worlds, ways of seeing, hearing, and being (e.g., de Souza and Andreotti 2009). Although only four percent of the world's languages (286 languages, according to Lewis et al. 2016) originate in Europe, not all of these have been included across a full range of purposes for documenting and disseminating knowledge over the last two centuries (see also Franceschini 2013; Heugh 2014a, 2014b). Kusch (2010) names six 'imperial' languages,[2] English, French, German, Italian, Portuguese and Spanish, in addition to ancient Greek and Latin, as the languages in which scholarship has been imagined in northern contexts beginning with the Reformation (of the Catholic Church in Europe) from the late sixteenth century onwards. These languages have not been used to convey the richness of either minority European languages or southern knowledges and expertise to the academy, rather they have been used to invisibilize (Skutnabb-Kangas 2000) or obscure southern and minority experience and expertise (Chakravarty 2011; Kusch 2010; Medina 2014; Mignolo 2010). Thus, global knowledges and histories held in over 7,000 languages and practices of multilinguality (Agnihotri 2007) come to be inaccurately filtered through a mere handful of languages. Furthermore, Kusch (2010) and Mignolo (2010) argue that these languages are employed to preserve a semblance of northern ownership of and entitlement to rank the value of, or exclude, southern knowledge/s. This raises a dilemma for critical and postcolonial theorists.

Recent attempts to articulate universal theories of multilingualism that draw from northern experiences but that appear to elide southern knowledge, the human agency of southern expertise, and spatial and temporal context, are therefore problematic. From a southern perspective, such elision appears possible only through a process in which the subject is objectified and/or ethical practice is disrupted with dishonesty and predation (Odora Hoppers 2002; Smith 1999; Watson 2014). This is a matter of concern for linguists, especially if we espouse postcolonial and critical stances. If we assume that scholarly knowledge of value is adequately captured in a handful of languages that have gained ascendancy in Europe and North America, and if we pursue a universal view of multilingualism, we are at risk. We are at risk of eliding knowledge, belief, and ways of being conveyed through the 7,000 or more spoken and signed languages and practices of multilinguality that do not make their way into published texts of the academy. Theory that overlooks contexts of place and time, and that overlooks the agency of communities beyond a few mainstream northern contexts, is not theory (cf. Kitching 2008). It invites or approaches dogma.

Nevertheless, if southern systems are often eclipsed, they have not been eliminated, as is evident in the cracks through which diversity reappears. As 'pluri-versality' (Kusch 2010; Mignolo 2010) re-emerges it becomes less feasible to hold exclusionary views of world knowledge, even within the academy. Pluri-versality is obvious to most people in Africa, Asia, Central and South America, and the Pacific, as it is also obvious to Indigenous and politically weakened linguistic communities that have been minoritized elsewhere (e.g., Extra and Gorter 2001; McCarty 1997; Skutnabb-Kangas 2000; Wiley et al. 2014). A pluri-versal view of multilingualism is multidimensional and dynamic, and partly captured in the explanation, 'multilingualism is the African lingua franca' (Fardon and Furniss 1994, 4), where multilingualism is not a collection of separate parts but rather a systematic and fluid horizontal whole. Multilingualisms in Africa and India, for example, occur in both horizontal layers that permit equitable and functional practices of communication, and also vertical hierarchical layers of inequality, marginality, exclusion, privilege, and access. Access to full participation in civil society for speakers of a Tribal language in Orissa state in India may mean, for example, proficiency in the Tribal language, Saora; the state language, Oriya; Hindi and English (Mohanty 2012). The more marginalized one's community, the greater the likelihood it is that one requires knowledge of at least four languages, plus fluency in multilingual repertoires that bridge these. Similarly, (self-reported) communicative repertoires of people who live in the Limpopo Province of South Africa often include expertise and resources in as many as nine languages (Pan South African Language Board 2000). These resources are needed for instrumental purposes in a linguistically diverse northern region of the country that experiences a significant degree of cross-border mobility and informal trade. Access to higher education, formal employment, and government services or employment is dependent upon written proficiency in at least one language, preferably two (see also Benson and Kosonen 2013; Shoba and Chimbutane 2013). In other words, in those parts of the world where communities have long-established systems of multilingualism, there are at least two dimensions of multilingualism, the vertical and the horizontal (Heugh 2015). But there is far more to multilingualisms in these settings.

Languages, in southern communities, are knitted into the interlacing of epistemology, ontology, and cosmology (e.g., Chakravarty 2011; Eden 2007; Lewis-Williams 1996; Watson 2014). The languages of living and ancestral beings (living and metaphysical, human and non-human) are understood and practised in multidimensional ways that differ from mainstream northern understandings of language. (Trans)languaging practices flow through song, dance, and trance, facilitating communication among the living, ancestors, eland, and shamans for the San of Southern Africa (Lewis-Williams 1996). There is no abyssal line that divides multilingual knowledge of the languages of animals and insects inscribed across a desert canvas in the Kalahari, and the inscriptions and paintings that leave historical records of events for the San of Southern Africa, Aboriginal communities in Australia, and Tribal communities in India. Nor is there an abyssal line between the knots of the quipus in South America and spoken texts. There is also no abyssal line between the physical and metaphysical networks of communication of many communities of the world. Multilingualisms occur in different dimensions, layers, and scales. For some communities they are *de facto* necessities, for example, in communities where kinship laws require exogenous marriage in some Aboriginal communities, and yet one also needs to retain one's own language:

> You have to know your language because you'll never be able to learn your Dreaming and if you don't know your Dreaming you can't identify where you belong. If you don't identify where you belong you may as well say you're dead.
> (Bowden and Bunbury 1990, 32–3, cited in Walsh 2005, 12)

For the Mari people who observe paganism in Russia, knowledge of Mari language is essential in order to convey the dying in their transition from life to the immaterial world. The process cannot be accomplished satisfactorily through Russian or any other language.[3] Belief, knowledge, and language practices are intimately intertwined for some communities in ways that are entirely different for others. The practices of people who inhabit peripheries, 'borderlands' that are both literal and figurative, such as the Mexican-US borderlands invoked by Anzaldúa (1987, in her literary employment of a broad repertoire of Spanish, English, and moments between), and later by Mignolo (1996) prefigure contemporary discussions of (trans)languaging.

Anzaldúa (1987), however, goes much further. She offers multidirectional and multi-scaled understandings of and expertise in the richness of linguistic fluidity, repertoire, and multilingualisms in which the language broker exercises agency and resistance, and where necessary, also complicity. Anzaldúa recognizes the power of the vertical form of American English to grant or deny access to citizenship, and she recognizes her own agency to transgress and to conform in written and spoken texts.

Anzaldúa's perspectives, chiming with southern voices elsewhere, differ from those in recent discussions of multilingualism and multilingual education in which an abyssal line is drawn between the conformist or vertical and the transgressive or horizontal dimensions of multilinguality. A strand of European and North American literature, recently turned towards multilingualism, runs the risk of dichotomizing understandings of language/s. This is where an understanding of language as bounded or fixed (as in ideologies of standard, minority, national languages) is rejected in favour of an understanding of the fluidity of language (e.g., Makoni and Pennycook 2007). The dichotomous, either-or, view is carried in discussions of bi-/multilingualism and bi-/multilingual education (e.g., translanguaging) (see Blackledge and Creese 2010; García and Li Wei 2014; Heller 2007). Even if this dichotomy were to hold fast in northern contexts, this would not necessarily mean that it would do so in southern contexts.

The first reason for this is that owing to the scale of linguistic diversity in postcolonial or southern societies (96 percent of the languages of the world, their coexistence [Lewis, Simons, and Fennig 2016], and continua [Djité 2008]), it is obvious that multilingualism involves fluidity in everyday practices of the majority of people in civil society. The second reason is that it is equally obvious in southern contexts that multilingualism simultaneously involves hierarchical layers of languages that intersect with institutionalized gate-keeping mechanisms, including vertical fixities of 'form'. Even if sociolinguists agree that the standardization of languages involves artifice, the artifice has taken on a materiality, and this materiality is recognized by those who hold power and those who do not. Successful access to the 'standardized' national or official language represents aspirational and symbolic capital. For example, the aspiration towards the 'form' or 'variety' of English that will open doors has become both palpable (cf. Coleman 2011) and out of reach for most, and this only serves to increase its vertical materiality. Thus, whereas in Europe, multilingualism may be associated with minority communities on the periphery (Pietikäinen and Kelly-Holmes 2013), the scales weigh differently in Africa and many parts of Asia. These are places in which layers of pre-colonial, colonial and postcolonial multilingualisms peripheralize majority populations on the vertical plane while they also facilitate horizontal mobilities.

Such differences have relevance for bi-/multilingual education. Seldom in the northern literature is multilingual education discussed or understood within a context of the plurality of multilingualisms as multidirectional, multi-scaled, and multi-purposeful. Seldom are multilingualisms represented as fluid in the sense that, depending on context, they may transverse human, animal, spiritual, and ancestral worlds. As human mobility continues and as the peripheries move towards the centre, our gaze needs to widen and to bring into focus a more nuanced and robust view of multilingualisms that includes the experiences of the majority of the world's linguistic communities that have thus far remained largely invisible.

Re-Placing: Multilingualisms, History, and Knowledge

In this section of the chapter, I retrace my steps in order to take a closer look at how perceptions of multilingualism have diverged, from northern and southern perspectives. As suggested earlier, the reach of written evidence of multilingualism is long, from the clay tablets of the Sumerians 4,600 years ago (Franceschini 2013) and the early Egyptians (Durant 1954). Ninety-six percent of the world's languages (Lewis, Simons, and Fennig 2016) have been used in various ways by communities in Africa, the Americas, Asia, and the Pacific for many purposes, including education and scholarship, governance, economics, science and technology, and trade and mobility (Chakravarty 2011). In particular, multilingualism has a long history in education linked to faith, systems of belief and law in East, North, and West Africa (e.g., Heugh 2011, 2013), India (e.g., Agnihotri 2014; Dua 2008), and Australia (e.g., Walsh 2005; Watson 2014).

The multilingual education practices in African and Asian settings pre-date colonialism. With the advent of colonial and postcolonial education systems, covert practices of multilingualism and multilingual education emerged from beneath the layers of colonial and postcolonial educational administrations. More recently, different forms of multilingual education have come into being as part of large-scale, system-wide language policy implementation in several countries after 'independence' (e.g., South Africa, Guinea Conakry, and Ethiopia). These forms of multilingual education have sometimes been introduced as a function of multi-stakeholder language planning (e.g., Chiatoh 2014, in Cameroon; Sentumbwe and Heugh 2014, in North West Uganda) and sometimes as a result of top-down system-wide education.

In contrast, the re-discovery of multilingualism in northern contexts has been a relatively recent phenomenon. The nineteenth century and early twentieth century focus on the teaching of classical and foreign languages in Europe and North America was followed, from the mid-twentieth century onward, by a focus on second language teaching and learning (with reference to groups of immigrant origin) and on bilingual education (with reference to regional minority groups and groups of immigrant origin). In a growing literature, from this period onward, we see North American and European exploration of different forms of bilingual education, immersion programs, and partial and dual immersion. As pointed out by Blackledge and Creese (2010); García (2009); and Heller (1999, 2007), such bilingual programs have been designed using direct method or other pedagogies that are typically restricted to teaching languages in parallel and separately. Yet approaches to bilingual education introduced in some minority contexts do not involve such 'language separation'. Take, for example, the case of some schools and classrooms in Wales where there is explicit use of two languages (Welsh and English) together, including two-way translation and purposive code-switching, rather than strict separation of languages in parallel silos (Gorter and Cenoz, forthcoming 2016; Lewis, Jones and Baker 2012).

Although northern ideas of separating languages across curricula or school timetables have influenced educational policies in southern settings, these have seldom been implemented in practice. Where the majority of students and teachers speak or use languages other than a target language that has limited use or traction in the community, the default language practices of the classroom involve various forms of multilingualism. There have also been various different approaches to bilingual education which involve systematic use of two-directional translation-translanguaging over the last 100 years (Malherbe 1946). Yet, in a good deal of recent literature on bi-/multilingual education there is an assumption of oneness, a single model/pedagogy orientation, i.e., universality. This makes little sense to people who live and use multilingualism in southern contexts (drawing daily on the multiple linguistic resources in their repertoire and on their multilingual capabilities) (e.g., Agnihotri 2007). It makes little sense to people who have long histories of non-formal and formal education that foster multilingual-ity (Agnihotri 2014; Heugh 2015), including those invented, monitored, and controlled by children (Wolff 2000). If multilingual education were understood as merely an extension of northern models of bilingual educa-tion (e.g., immersion programs), southern experiences of multilingualism in (non-formal and informal education) and southern knowledge of, ways of being, and belief are then erased.

It is also important to note that the scholarship of eminent linguists from Africa (e.g., Ayo Bamgbose 2000; Beban Chumbow 2009; Blasius Chiatoh 2014; Paulin Djité 2008) and from India (e.g., Ajit Mohanty 2012; Hans Dua 2008; Rama Agnihotri 2007) is seldom given more than a passing nod, along with that of many others from the south. Their contributions to the literature on multilingualism are often overlooked even when written in English. Their contributions to language policy and planning (from below) and insights on the nature of languages in diversity somehow escapes the mainstream literature, although it is reflected in various UNESCO, UNI-CEF, and UNDP Reports and Policy statements (e.g., Alidou et al. 2006; Ouane and Glanz 2011).

The extent to which this is simply a blind spot due to centuries of ori-enting to northern scholarship or due to global publishing practices is not clear. We do know that in South Africa, subsequent to political change in the 1990s, numerous linguists visited South Africa. What was particularly attractive to visiting scholars were constitutional changes in 1994 that extended a century long 'official bilingual' policy (with several bilingual school models) to make provision for multilingual policy. Close proxim-ity to key language policy stakeholders, language policy development, and language legislation of two NGOs, the National Language Project and the Project for the Study of Alternative Education in South Africa, was of partic-ular interest to northern scholars. Whereas many researchers subsequently observed ethical research protocols, others elided, under-represented, and sometimes misrepresented their sources, including proposals for multilin-gual education arrived at through multilingual interventions in schools that pre-empted later discussions of 'flexible bi-/multilingualism' and 'functional multilingualism' (see Agnihotri 1995; de Klerk 1995; Heugh, Siegrühn, and Plüddemann 1995; Versfeld 1995). A rich vein of research on the use of multilingual resources in meaning-making in the classroom has been devel-oped over the last two decades in South Africa. It includes carefully nuanced ethnographic studies of multilingual classroom practices that have revealed the purposeful nature of code-switching and translanguaging (e.g., Kerfoot and Bello-Nonjengele 2014; Makalela 2015; Makoe and McKinney 2009; Probyn 2015). The significance of this work is that it concerns majority rather than minority populations of students and it involves pluri-versal multilingualisms.

The shift of focus in Europe and North America from bilingual educa-tion and bilingualism to multilingual education or multilingualism, along with pedagogies and terminology similar to those found in South Africa in the 1990s, is unlikely to be coincidental or unrelated to the multilingual debates and or associated discussions in sub-Saharan Africa and South Asia at this time.

Yet, for the most part the connections have gone. What we find in many contemporary publications of multilingualism are models, pedagogies, and ancillary programs trialled among minority communities, mostly in northern settings. Seldom do we find rich understanding of how multilingual education is practised purposefully, either as a covert system beneath the surface in Africa and South Asia or in its system-wide implementation (e.g., South Africa, Ethiopia). It is these experiences that are familiar to communities who now live in northern cities. It is southern experience and expertise in system-wide interventions that are needed to address socio-economic, linguistic, and faith-based diversities now evident in northern settings. Yet, with some disbelief, southern scholars and practitioners watch muddled attempts to reinvent the wheel in the face of increasing diversity.

The processes involved in the invisibilization of southern agency and expertise that I have referred to above also feature in the critiques put forward by Chakravarty (2011); Kitching (2008); Mignolo (2010); and Smith (1999). These scholars expose the fragility of a critical and postcolonial theory that is restricted to a mainstream northern gaze that loses sight of the longue durée of history. Since influential scholars in the academy look north and draw theory from restricted contexts (in time and place), many southern scholars have also felt the need to follow suit. Postcolonial habitus includes complicity with a belief that contemporary northern theory is in advance of southern scholarship. Southern scholars need to reflect on ways in which we sacrifice southern scholarship in order to buy back ill-fitting northern scripts that re-lay colonial hegemonies.

Scholars, whether southern or northern, need to find a way to de-link Southern knowledges of multilingualisms and diversities from northern frameworks in which they have become entangled, and to replace them. This is because we retain memory of communal responsibilities, custodianship, and pluri-versalities which we need if we are to contribute together towards solutions for the present.

Cleavage, De-Linking, and Mestizo Consciousness

Kusch (2010), the Argentinian scholar, is regarded by Mignolo (2010) as the source of de-colonial thinking. He offers us a methodological and conceptual path for de-linking and untangling. Kusch and other scholars (e.g., Anzaldúa 1987; Mignolo 2010; Santos 2012) who critique northern hegemony in the Americas are not alone. Parallel but contextually different critiques have been put forward in Africa (e.g., Cooper and Morrell 2014; Hountondji 2013; Odora Hoppers 2002), Australia (e.g., Connell 2007; Watson 2014), India (e.g., Chakravarty 2011) and New Zealand (e.g., Smith

1999). Together they take southern (but not identical) perspectives directed towards the epistemological cleavage between theory that emerges from southern and northern thinking. One of these, 'de-coloniality' (Mignolo 2007), involves a de-linking from colonialism and its progeny, post-colonialism. Mignolo (2010, 2011) argues that de-coloniality poses a far greater challenge to northern hegemony than does postcolonial and critical theory of Fanon or Foucault, which he and Chakravarty (2011) position as northern not southern thought.

However, although it may be possible to de-link, it is impossible to untangle historical threads of interconnectedness. Yet, Kusch offers us something more: He offers us the lens of 'mestizo consciousness'. For Kusch, this means experiencing displacement (from the northern centre), being of migrant background, recognizing not-belonging; yet living and working in and recognizing the complexities of community relationships with (well-) being, knowledge, and the cosmos. It also means understanding that which brings about Northern theory. Mestizo consciousness is neither Indigenous nor European (Northern), but it is Southern.[4] If we toil towards or reach mestizo consciousness, it may offer those of us who have been schooled in theory framed mostly in northern contexts and yet who live and work in southern contexts, a lens. It is a lens through which we can tease apart dissonances between (decontextualized or universalized) theory, and knowledge, experience, and contextual pluralities. Although southern scholars have the potential for mestizo consciousness, I understand this brings us to a difficult choice. We may choose to acquiesce to authors who are oriented towards seeking universal relevance and a central space within the Northern academy. We may do this for reasons of pragmatism if we are caught within the web of pressures to conform within contemporary academia. Most of us are. So, we are therefore drawn towards (southern) epistemic suicide as we decline mestizo consciousness. The alternative is 'epistemic disobedience' (Mignolo 2009) which may lead to academic or career suicide in front of 'the academy'—particularly if we reclaim the relevance of place and time together with pluri-versality. Epistemic disobedience extends to those of us who from a mestizo consciousness argue that epistemology, ontology, and cosmology are interconnected for communities in the south (e.g., Eden 2007; Bolaane 2014; Watson 2009, 2014) and often for northern minority communities. We exercise epistemic disobedience when we argue that diversities and interconnectedness cannot be decontextualized. Attempts to decontextualize diversities result in eliding human agency and expertise, and this is a form of knowledge predation (Smith 1999). If we were able to recognize interconnectedness and co-dependence, however, this may allow us to navigate through current disarray towards re-balance and re-order (see also Deumert 2015; Stroud 2015).

In the current climate in which academics everywhere are under pressure to publish in 'international' journals or volumes, we recognize that compliance with recently published work of eminent (Northern) scholars in our field (see also Medina 2014) results in publication. The dilemma of mestizo consciousness and epistemic disobedience includes reflexivity regarding research ethics and recognizing for whom the consequence of disobedience matters. Do we, scholars who are well-schooled in Northern theory, take our cue from self-interest and individualism, an apparent attribute in many northern contexts? Or, do we take our cue from the social milieux from which we come, in which we are immersed and in which we recognize non-linear (historical) relationships among community, place, knowledge, being, and belief that are pluri-versal and dynamic—including in their south-north entanglements? This is an important dilemma, because as south moves north the architecture of northern systems will undergo revision and renovation. The turn offers a choice: either we choose to exchange northern with southern hegemony, or we choose to replace hegemony and predation with reciprocity. Chance or fate brings scholars, whether southern, eastern, or northern—a pause, an interruption—at a moment of considerable disruption caused by large-scale human conflict, environmental disaster, and displacement of people within the global south and from south to north. It comes at a time in which the political and economic power blocs are moving south and east (AT Kearney Inc 2015; Durant [1935] 1954; Maddison 2007; McGann 2015). At this time of global turbulence and disruption we have an opportunity to reconsider the history of our interconnectedness, entanglements, and complicities. Mestizo consciousness permits us to de-link from colonial and postcolonial habitus in which universality and homogeneity are embedded. It permits us to understand both northern and southern contexts, to bridge the abyss, and to replace universal with pluri-versal views of multilingualisms. As southern communities understand their obligations that include custodianship of place, the past, and the future, so too have we, as (socio) linguists, custodial responsibilities for the health of our discipline.

Acknowledgements

I should like to thank anonymous reviewers and also the generous advice of Caroline Kerfoot, Kenneth Hyltenstam, Marilyn Martin-Jones, Christopher Stroud, and Irene Watson on earlier drafts of this paper. Frailties in the argument are mine.

Notes

1 Hereafter, Kusch (2010).
2 Both Durk Gorter and Marilyn Martin-Jones point out that Kusch has omitted Dutch in his list of imperial languages.
3 Personal Communication with Erik Juzykain, Ministry of Culture and Inter-Ethnic Affairs, Yoshkar Ola, Mari-el Republic, Russian Federation 6 June 2001.
4 My understanding of mestizo consciousness draws from Mignolo (2010); however, if I have misrepresented either Kusch or Mignolo, this is my error. Mignolo

distinguishes mestizo consciousness from Anzaldúa's (1987) consciousness of 'la mestiza' in her borderlands theory, where la mestiza refers to people who identify as mestiza/o by reason of ancestry. I understand Anzaldúa to mean people who live, experience, and perform mestiza-nesses, in literal and figurative peripheries or borderlands.

References

Achebe, C. 1958. *Things Fall Apart*. London: William Heinemann.

Agnihotri, R. K. 1995. 'Multilingualism as a Classroom Resource'. In *Multilingual Education for South Africa*, edited by K. Heugh, A. Siegrühn, and P. Plüddemann, 3–14. Johannesburg, SA: Heinemann.

———. 2007. 'Towards a Pedagogical Paradigm Rooted in Multilinguality'. *International Multilingual Research Journal* 1 (2): 79–88.

———. 2014. 'Multilinguality, Education and Harmony'. *International Journal of Multilingualism* 11 (3): 364–79.

Alidou, H., A. Boly, B. Brock-Utne, Y. S. Diallo, K. Heugh, and H. E.Wolff. 2006. *Optimizing Learning and Education in Africa: The Language Factor: A Stock-Taking Research on Mother Tongue and Bilingual Education in Sub-Saharan Africa*. Paris: UNESCO and Association for the Development of Education in Africa (ADEA).

Anzaldúa, G. 1987. *Borderlands/La Frontera*. San Francisco: Aunt Lute.

AT Kearney Inc. 2015. *Global Economic Outlook: Beyond the New Mediocre?* AT Kearney Global Business Policy Council, AT Kearney Inc. Retrieved from https://www.atkearney.com.au/documents/10192/5498252/Global+Economic+Out look+2015–2020—Beyond+the+New+Mediocre.pdf/5c5c8945–00cc-4a4f-a04f-adef094e90b8. (Accessed 14 October 2015).

Bamgbose, A. 2000. *Language and Exclusion: The Consequences of Language Policies in Africa*. Münster, Germany: Lit Verlag.

Benson, C., and K. Kosonen, eds. 2013. *Language Issues in Comparative Education: Inclusive Teaching and Learning in Non-Dominant Languages and Cultures. Comparative and International Education: A Diversity of Voices, vol. 1*. Rotterdam: Sense.

Blackledge, A., and A. Creese. 2010. *Multilingualism: A Critical Perspective*. London: Bloomsbury.

Bolaane, M. 2014. 'San Cross-Border Cultural Heritage and Identity in Botswana, Namibia and South Africa'. *African Study Monographs* 35 (1): 41–64.

Bowden, R. and Bunbury, B., eds. 1990. *Being Aboriginal: Comments, Observations, Stories from Aboriginal Australians*. Sydney: ABC Books.

Cenoz, J., D. Gorter, and K. Heugh. 2011. 'Linguistic Diversity'. In *Diversity Research and Policy: A Multidisciplinary Exploration*, edited by S. Knotter, R. De Loebel, L. Tsipouri, and V. Stenius, 83–98. Amsterdam: University of Amsterdam and Pallas.

Chakravarty, K. K. 2011. 'Introduction'. In *Voice and Memory: Indigenous Imagination and Expression*, edited by G. N. Devy, G. V. Davis, and K. K. Chakravarty, xiii-xxv. Hyderabad: Orient BlackSwan.

Chiatoh, B. A. 2014. 'Community Language Promotion in Remote Contexts: Case Study on Cameroon'. *International Journal of Multilingualism* 11 (3), 320–33.

Chumbow, B. S. 2009. 'Linguistic Diversity, Pluralism and National Development in Africa'. *Africa Development* 34 (2): 21–45.

Coleman, H., ed. 2011. *Dreams and Realities: Developing Countries and the English Language*. London: British Council.

Connell, R. 2007. *Southern Theory: The Global Dynamics of Knowledge in Social Science*. Cambridge: Polity.

Cooper, B., and R. Morrell, eds. 2014. *Africa-Centred Knowledges: Crossing Fields and Worlds*. Woodbridge, Suffolk: James Currey and Rochester, NY: Boydell & Brewer.

de Klerk, G. 1995. 'Three Languages in One School: A Multilingual Exploration in a Primary School'. In *Multilingual Education for South Africa*, edited by K. Heugh, A. Siegrühn, and P. Plüddemann, 28–33. Johannesburg: Heinemann.

de Souza, L. M. T. M., and V. Andreotti. 2009. 'Culturalism, Difference and Pedagogy: Lessons from Indigenous Education in Brazil'. In *Cross-Cultural Perspectives on Policy and Practice: Decolonizing Community Contexts*, edited by J. Lave and M. Moore, 72–86. London: Routledge.

Deumert, A. 2015. 'Beyond Southern Data and towards Southern Theory'. Paper presented at the Sociolinguistics of Globalization Conference. (De)centring and (De)standardising, Hong Kong, 3–6 June.

Djité, P. G. 2008. *The Sociolinguistics of Development in Africa, Vol. 139*. Bristol, UK: Multilingual Matters.

Dua, H. 2008. *Ecology of Multilingualism, Language, Culture and Society*. Mysore: Yashoda.

Durant, W. [1954] 1935. (26th printing). *The Story of Civilization: Part One: Our Oriental Heritage*. New York: Simon and Schuster.

Eden, C. 2007. 'How Can I Bring Ubuntu as a Living Standard of Judgement into the Academy? Moving beyond Decolonisation through Societal Reidentification and Guiltless Recognition', 38–73. Ph.D. University of Bath. Retrieved from http://www.actionresearch.net/living/edenphd.shtml. (Accessed 10 August 2015).

Edwards, J. 2012. *Multilingualism: Understanding Linguistic Diversity*. India: Continuum.

El Daly, O. 2005. *Egyptology: The Missing Millennium: Ancient Egypt in Medieval Arabic Writings*. London: University College London (UCL) Press.

Extra, G., and D. Gorter, eds. 2001. *The Other Languages of Europe: Demographic, Sociolinguistic, and Educational Perspectives*, 118. Bristol, UK: Multilingual Matters.

Fardon, R., and G. Furniss. 1994. *Frontiers and Boundaries: African Languages as Political Environment*. London: Routledge.

Franceschini, R. 2013. 'History of Multilingualism'. In *The Encyclopedia of Applied Linguistics*, edited by C. Chapelle. New York: Blackwell. doi:10.1002/9781405198431.Wbeal0511.

García, O. 2009. *Bilingual Education in the 21st Century: A Global Perspective*. Chichester, UK: Wiley-Blackwell.

García, O., and Li Wei. 2014. *Translanguaging: Language, Bilingualism and Education*. Basingstoke, Hampshire: Palgrave Pivot.

Gorter, D., and J. Cenoz. Forthcoming. 'Language Education Policy and Multilingual Assessment'. Special Issue, *Language and Education*.

Hegel, G. W. F. 2001. *The Philosophy of History: Georg Wilhelm Friedrich Hegel*. Prefaces by C. Hegel and the Translated by J. Sibree (M.A Hegel's Lectures on The Philosophy of History 1822–1830). Kitchener, ON: Batoche Books.

Heller, M. 1999. *Linguistic Minorities and Modernity: A Sociolinguistic Ethnography*. London: Longman.

————. 2007. *Bilingualism: A Social Approach*. Basingstoke: Palgrave Macmillan.

Heugh, K. 2011. 'Discourses from without, Discourses from within: Women, Feminism and Voice in Africa'. *Current Issues in Language Planning* 12 (1): 89–104.

————. 2013. 'Multilingual Education in Africa'. In *The Encyclopedia of Applied Linguistics*, edited by C. Chapelle. Published Online: 5 November 2012. doi: 10.1002/9781405198431.Wbeal0782.

————. 2014a: 'Turbulence and Dilemma: Implications of Diversity and Multilingualism in Australian Education'. *International Journal of Multilingualism* 11 (3): 347–63.

————. 2014b. 'Multilingualism, "The African Lingua Franca" and "The New Linguistic Dispensation"'. In *Language Rich Africa: Policy Dialogue: The Cape Town Language and Development Conference: Looking beyond 2015*, edited by H. McIlwraith, 80–7. London: British Council.

————. 2015. 'Epistemologies in Multilingual Education: Translanguaging and Genre: Companions in Conversation with Policy and Practice'. Special Issue. *Language and Education* 29 (3): 280–5.

Heugh, K., A. Siegrühn, and P. Plüddemann, eds. 1995. *Multilingual Education for South Africa*. Johannesburg, SA: Heinemann Pearson.

Hountondji, P. J. 2013. *Sur La Philosophie Africaine: Critique de L'Ethnophilosophie*. Cameroon: Langaa RPCIG, African Books Collective.

Ippolito, F., and S. Trevisanut, eds. 2016. *Migration in the Mediterranean: Mechanisms of International Cooperation*. Cambridge: Cambridge University Press.

Kerfoot, C., and B. O. Bello-Nonjengele. 2014. 'Game Changers? Multilingual Learners in a Cape Town Primary School'. *Applied Linguistics* 37 (4): 451–73. doi: 10.1093/applin/Amu044.

Kitching, G. N. 2008. *The Trouble with Theory: The Educational Costs of Postmodernism*. Philadelphia, PA: Penn State University Press.

Kusch, R. [1970] 2010. *Indigenous and Popular Thinking in América*. Durham, NC: Duke University Press.

Lewis, G., B. Jones, and C. Baker. 2012. 'Translanguaging: Origins and Development from School to Street and Beyond'. *Educational Research and Evaluation: An International Journal on Theory and Practice* 18 (7): 641–54.

Lewis, M., G. F. Simons, and C.D. Fennig, eds. 2016. *Ethnologue: Languages of the World*, Nineteenth Edition. Dallas, TX: SIL International. Retrieved from http://www.ethnologue.com.

Lewis-Williams, J. D. 1996. "'A Visit to the Lion's House": The Structure, Metaphors and Sociopolitical Significance of a Nineteenth-Century Bushman Myth'. In *Voices from the Past:/Xam Bushmen and the Bleek and Lloyd Collection*, edited by J. Deacon and T. A. Dowson, 122–41. Johannesburg, SA: Witwatersrand University Press.

Lo Bianco, J. 2014. 'A Cerebration of Language Diversity, Language Policy, and Politics in Education'. *Review of Research in Education* 38 (1): 312–31.

Maddison, A. 2007. *Contours of the World Economy 1–2030 AD: Essays in Macro-Economic History*. Oxford: Oxford University Press.

Makalela, L. 2015. 'Moving out of Linguistic Boxes: The Effects of Translanguaging Strategies for Multilingual Classrooms'. *Language and Education* 29 (3): 200–17.

Makoe, P., and C. McKinney. 2009. 'Hybrid Discursive Practices in a South African Multilingual Primary Classroom: A Case Study'. *English Teaching* 8 (2): 80–95.

Makoni, S., and A. Pennycook, eds. 2007. *Disinventing and Reconstituting Languages: Vol. 62*. Bristol, UK: Multilingual Matters.

Malherbe, E. G. 1946. *The Bilingual School: A Study of Bilingualism in South Africa*. London: Longman.

Martin-Jones, M., and S. Gardner. 2012. 'Introduction'. In *Multilingualism, Discourse and Ethnography*, edited by S. Gardner and M. Martin-Jones, 1–15. New York: Routledge.

May, S. 2013. *The Multilingual Turn: Implications for SLA, TESOL, and Bilingual Education*. New York: Routledge.

McCarty, T. L. 1997. 'American Indian, Alaska Native, and Native Hawaiian Bilingual Education'. In *Bilingual Education Vol. 5, Encyclopedia of Language and Education*, edited by J. Cummins and D. Corson, 45–56. Dordrecht: Kluwer.

McGann, J. 2015. *2014 Global Go to Think Tank Index Report*. Think Tanks and Civil Societies Program, International Relations Program, University of Pennsylvania. Retrieved from Http://Repository.Upenn.Edu/Cgi/Viewcontent. Cgi?Article=1008&Context=Think_Tanks. (Accessed 14 October 2015).

Medina, L. R. 2014. *Centres and Peripheries in Knowledge Production*. New York and Abingdon, OX: Routledge.

Mignolo, W. 1996. 'Linguistic Maps, Literary Geographies, and Cultural Landscapes: Languages, Languaging, and (Trans)Nationalism'. *Modern Language Quarterly* 57 (2): 181–97.

———. 2007. 'Delinking'. *Cultural Studies* 21 (2–3): 449–514.

———. 2009. 'Epistemic Disobedience, Independent Thought and De-Colonial Freedom'. *Theory, Culture & Society* 26 (7–8): 159–81.

———. 2010. 'Introduction: Immigrant Consciousness'. In *Indigenous and Popular Thinking in América*, edited by R. Kusch, translated by M. Lugones and J. M. Price, xiii–lxxiv. Durham, NC: Duke University Press.

———. 2011. *The Darker Side of Western Modernity: Global Futures, Decolonial Options*. Durham, NC: Duke University Press.

Mohanty, A. K. 2012. 'MLE and the double divide in multilingual societies: Comparing policy and practice in India and Ethiopia'. In *Multilingual Education and Sustainable Diversity Work: From Periphery to Centre*, edited by T. Skutnabb-Kangas and K. Heugh, 138–50. New York: Routledge.

Mumin, M. 2014. 'The Arabic Script in Africa: Understudied Literacy'. In *The Arabic Script in Africa: Studies on the Use of a Writing System*, edited by M. Mumin and K. Versteegh, 41–76. Leiden and Boston: BRILL.

Ngugi, Wa Thiong'o. 1993. *Moving the Centre: The Struggle for Cultural Freedoms*. London: Heinemann.

Nordström, H.-Å. 2014. *The West Bank Survey from Faras to Gemai 1: Sites of Early Nubian, Middle Nubian and Pharaonic Age*. London: The Sudan Archaeological Research Society.

Odora Hoppers, C. ed. 2002. *Indigenous Knowledge and the Integration of Knowledge Systems: Towards a Philosophy of Articulation*. Claremont: New Africa Books.

Ouane, A., and C. Glanz, eds. 2011. *Optimising Learning, Education and Publishing in Africa: The Language Factor*. Hamburg, Germany: UNESCO Institute for Lifelong Learning.

Pan South African Language Board. 2000. *Language Use and Language Interaction in South Africa: A National Sociolinguistic Survey*. Pretoria: Pan South African Language Board.

Pietikainen, S., and H. Kelly-Holmes. 2013. *Multilingualism and the Periphery*. New York: Oxford University Press.

Probyn, M. 2015. 'Pedagogical Translanguaging: Bridging Discourses in South African Science Classrooms'. *Language and Education* 29 (3): 218–34.

Santos, B. de S. 2012. 'Public Sphere and Epistemologies of the South'. *Africa Development* 37 (1): 43–67.

Sentumbwe, G., and K. Heugh. 2014. 'Local Languages and Primary Education in Northern Uganda: Post-Conflict Community and Local Partnerships'. In *Language Rich Africa: Policy Dialogue: The Cape Town Language and Development Conference: Looking beyond 2015*, edited by H. McIlwraith, 132–5. London: British Council.

Shoba, J., and F. Chimbutane, eds. 2013. *Bilingual Education and Language Policy in the Global South*. London: Routledge.

Singleton, D., J. Fishman, L. Aronin, and M. O'Laoire, eds. 2013. *Current Multilingualism: A New Linguistic Dispensation: Contributions to the Sociology of Language 102*. Berlin: Mouton De Gruyter.

Skutnabb-Kangas, T. 2000. *Linguistic Genocide in Education: Or Worldwide Diversity and Human Rights?* London and New York: Routledge.

Smith, L. T. 1999. *Decolonizing Methodologies: Research and Indigenous Peoples*. London: Zed Books.

Stroud, C. 2015. 'Afterword: Turbulent Deflections'. In *Language, Literacy and Diversity: Moving Words*, edited by C. Stroud and M. Prinsloo, 206–16. London: Routledge.

Stroud, C., and K. Heugh. 2011. 'Language Education'. In *Cambridge Handbook of Sociolinguistics*, edited by R. Mesthrie, 413–29. Cambridge: Cambridge University Press.

Texier, P.-J., G. Porraz, J. Parkington, J.-P. Rigaud, C. Poggenpoel, and C.Tribolo. 2013. 'The Context, Form and Significance of the MSA Engraved Ostrich Eggshell Collection from Diepkloof Rock Shelter, Western Cape, South Africa'. *Journal of Archaeological Science* 40 (9): 3412–31.

Trevor-Roper, H. 1965. *The Rise of Christian Europe*. New York: Harcourt Brace.

Versfeld, R. 1995. 'Language is Lekker: A Language Activity Classroom'. In *Multilingual Education for South Africa*, edited by K. Heugh, A. Siegrühn, and P. Plüddemann, 23–7. Johannesburg: Heinemann.

Walsh, M. 2005. 'Languages and Their Status in Aboriginal Australia'. In *Language and Culture in Aboriginal Australia*, edited by M. Walsh and C. Yallop, 1–13. Canberra: Aboriginal Studies Press.

Warren, D. M., L. J. Slikkerveer, and S. O. Titilola. eds. 1989. 'Indigenous Knowledge Systems; Implications for Agriculture and International Development'. In *Studies in Technology and Social Change No. 11: Ames, Iowa: Technology and Social Change Program*. Ames, IA: Iowa State University.

Watson, I. 2009. 'Sovereign Spaces, Caring for Country, and the Homeless Position of Aboriginal Peoples'. *South Atlantic Quarterly* 108 (1): 27–51.

———. 2014. 'Re-Centring First Nations Knowledge and Places in a Terra Nullius Space'. *Alternative* 10 (4): 508–20.

Welsby, D. A., and W. V. Davies, eds. 2002. *Uncovering Ancient Sudan: A Decade of Discovery by the Sudan Archaeological Research Society*. London: The Sudan Archaeological Research Society.

Wiley, T. G., J. S. Lee, and R.W. Rumberger, eds. 2009. *The Education of Language Minority Immigrants in the United States: Vol. 74*. Bristol, UK: Multilingual Matters.

Wiley, T. G., J. K. Peyton, D. Christian, S. C. K. Moore, and N. Liu, eds. 2014. *Handbook of Heritage, Community, and Native American Languages in the United States: Research, Policy, and Educational Practice*. New York: Routledge.

Wolff, E. 2000. *Pre-School Child Multilingualism and Its Educational Implications in the African Context*. Cape Town: PRAESA.

Yeats, W. B. 1919. 'The Second Coming'. In Yeats, W.B. 1921. *Michael Robartes and the Dancer*. Whitefish, Montana: Kessinger Publishing, LLC.

A Postscript on the Postracial[1]

Christopher Stroud

It's Saturday at the Old Biscuit Mill, and this Saturday—like every Saturday—it is packed to breaking point, standing room only. The Old Biscuit Mill is an old red factory, revamped and gentrified, that promotes itself as 'a vibrant, warm-hearted little village in the heart of Woodstock where talented people come together to share, collaborate and well, . . . show off their heart-felt passion' (Homepage, 25 November 2015). It is best known for its weekly Saturday market, and has recently been remapped as part of the Cape Town must-see destinations (TripAdvisor). It is a 'transnational village' in the sense of Cabral and Martin-Jones (this volume).

Amiena, Mooniq, David, and myself watch as two gay guys in their mid-twenties,—clearly Hipsters—make their way to the Pizza store at the back of the mill, threading themselves through the clamour of families and singles, tourists, and locals, standing chatting and drinking at the different food stands. Nobody pays them any attention—all are intent on managing their meats and cheeses, pizza slices, and pâté, washed down with glasses of champagne, beer, or wine. This is what the Biscuit Mill is about: eating, drinking, chatting, and laughing in a drama of sound and conspicuous consumption; it is about sharing food and feeling good in the company of others.

However, scratch under the surface, and the eating and drinking at the OBM reveals itself to be about more than mere banal, carnal enjoyment. Or rather, and more correctly, banal carnal enjoyment is about more than just eating and sharing food. The OBM, together with the malls and food courts of the South, like Benjamin's arcades, are factories for the production of contemporary modernity. The OBM in particular is a preeminent site for the inscription of a 'global/racial hierarchy, itself entangled with other hierarchies' (Kerfoot and Hyltenstam, 5) in the form of a coloniality of structural whiteness or the new postracial. The postracial, says Goldberg (2015), is the contemporary articulation of racism. It is the belief that racist actions and utterances—when they occur (which they do with alarming frequency)—are individual and occasional rather than systemic and systematic. Postracism is the *illusion* of non-racism.

What the papers in this collection offer me in particular is a rich array of tools and refined conceptual frameworks precisely for understanding the production of the postracial. Each contribution focuses in one way or another on the ubiquitous and pervasive dynamic of the contemporary transnational social order, one configured around the production and circulation of 'absence'—a fundamental building block of the postracial. Invisibilities and absences—of people and their identities, places and their histories, and circuits of mobility—are what is constitutive of modern, global postracial society. And although written from a variety of positions and dealing with a range of topics, each paper provides valuable insights into the important *capillary* nature of the global, postracial social order.

How are the subject positions of 'absent postracial other' actually manufactured at the OBM? In what ways does the simple practice of conspicuous carnality, trivial as it may seem, reaffirm the centrality of a social order where privileged bodies partake of the benefits of structural whiteness and absent others are discarded? What is the role of the framing of consumption in talk about and around food'? How does the way commodities and activities are packaged by the semiotic landscape of the mill impact on orders of visibility?

Juffermans and Tavares remark on how mobility is relational and embedded in power. The OBM privileges particular types of mobilities and mobile bodies, and actively excludes others. As part of a transnationally linked geography and spatial imaginary of distinction, the OBM is an institutional incarnation of 'colonially imposed geopolitical divisions' and 'contemporary political economies that render some bodies and some languages [and material and spiritual objects] more able to travel' (Kerfoot and Hyltenstam, 4) than others. It is predominantly northern tourists with white bodies and northern tongues who visit the OBM, as one stop on their circuit of Cape Point, the penguins of Boulder Beach, Table Mountain, and the Stellenbosch vineyards. This is apparent to us as we walk through the mill. What is also apparent is the almost complete absence of local foodstuffs. Amiena remarks on the paucity of local Halal stalls among the offerings of Italian, Spanish, Korean, and other national delicacies. Complementing the rich variety of foods is the rich variety of languages audible around the stalls and eating spaces, although the majority of them are cut to the same typological cloth.

The cheeses, olives, and fine meats, ciders and boutique beers, champagnes and wines have travelled long distances to the counters of the OBM—the further they travel, the greater their potential distinction. The speed, trajectory, and mode of transport through which the goods and tourists are transported, as well as the space of leisure (the OBM) in which they are consumed, are reflected in the price (measured in cost per kg). The value of exotic sweetmeats is compounded by processes of semiotic refinement, where the material realities of speed, distance, origin, and mode of transport are semiotically framed in indexicalities of distinction, such as chalked slate boards, chef/clad bodies, handwritten labels, fine plates and embroidered boxes, and other props of the semiotic landscape.

Most significant is the purity of the language of signs, something that resonates with Wee's point in this volume that disentanglement is manifested linguistically as 'fixed multilingualism'. The smoothing of entanglements into ordered juxtapositions reflects 'the universal logic of monolingualism bound up with essentializing ethnic and linguistic hierarchies' (Kerfoot and Hyltenstam, 4, and Wee; cf. also Lindberg and Sandwall on institutional discourses).

The counterpoint to the ordered juxtaposition of distinction and the mobility of its northern patrons is the hybridity and mix of spaces of waste and margin, the converse, of course, of places of distinction. It is in these spaces that we find those 'excluded from [global] flows, [. . .] those who do not travel well but remain invisible in global ethnoscapes' (Juffermans and Tavares, 99–100). At the entrance to the mill, on the other side of the barbed wire fencing, the coconut cleavers, the local bands, gumboot dancers, 'coloured' car guards, or the little black boys from the townships that ask tourists for money or food, ply their trades. In the streets behind the mall, we find the *very* absent others (often from other parts of the African continent) who live on the litter and remains of food that spill across the carefully guarded back doors. These are the black bodies that travel in other circuits, but that sometimes attempt to also exploit and reverse the well-trodden North-South trajectories as refugees or job seekers. They travel slowly and with many interruptions. Wrapped in the torn packaging of leaking boats, they carry with them assortments of odds and ends that nobody wants—except their credit cards and mobile phones. They are kept apart from the visitors to distinction by discreet gatekeepers at the doors and open spaces whose job it is to prevent 'leakage' from the polluted and transgressive spaces beyond.

Bock's paper asks 'to what extent do participants reproduce or transform inherited racial discourses' (59): Although the OBM surely hosts stories of racial transformation, other narratives that reproduce racial status quos appear more in line with the modus operandi of the OBM. The contemporary postracial of the OBM shares the systematic production of invisibilities and absences with older, more recognizably racial stories of disengagement and non-interaction. This illustrates what Alcoff (2015) calls 'the incoherence of white supremacy' that in certain sites and historical moments is realized through organizations such as the Ku Klux Klan and in others through gentrification and eviction of black residents in the name of urban development.[2]

David and I, having secured benches at the Pizza stand, get caught up in a sticky conspiratorial conviviality woven around things that are not said (not even 'sayable') but that are massively present in their absence. We are talking with two elderly sisters, South African by birth but of Portuguese heritage. After 20 years of uninterrupted 'exile' in the U.S., they are in Cape Town to visit their son. Today, they complain, Cape Town is so much more crowded than they remember it from their youth, and the roads are *chock-a-block* with 'bad drivers'. They go on to recount how the weekend before, while driving to visit an old childhood friend some kilometres north of Cape Town, they take a wrong turn off the N2 highway and find themselves unexpectedly on the outskirts of . . . —uncertain of the name, they hesitate and the son of one of them hurries to fill it in: 'Langa'.[3] Sick with apprehension, and alert to the unwanted possibility of moments of unpredictable entanglement with locals, they quickly change places with a black passenger they are travelling with, and allow themselves to be driven back to the safety of the N2 highway prostrate on the backseat of the car. Later in the story, as an afterthought, when the sisters assure us that 'they are not against anybody but wish they would stop talking *their* languages and worshipping *their* ancestors', and 'allow *themselves* to be civilized', the increasingly embarrassed son asks:

Son: Mother, what do you mean by 'they'?
Mother: Well, you know, the ethnics.[4]

The significance of this narrative lies in how it is structured around what is *not said*. In order for it to work, it relies on both the speaker and the audience sharing conventions on how to interpret propositional vagueness and referential ambiguity. There is a *complicity* of the audience in establishing the presuppositions and implicatures of the story, as well as in the co-construction of the story-lines. In many respects, this story-line is similar to the private, lived experiences of the *thread* in the online discussion sites studied by Hanell and Salö. But here it is the very *lack of* entextualization—an entextual vacuum—that serves to re-centre the unfolding of the discourse. We are left to our own devices to source the implicit references and the unspoken, insinuated, consequences of a wrong left turn off the N2.

This narrative then is one of a set of tactics and modalities of disengagement. One of its foremost characteristics is that the tellers are building their story around 'spectatorship', where there is an overlayering of an interpretative frame on events (the unsaid and unsayables) that point to non-involvement in the lives of those recounted, and an experienced alienation to these others' everyday lives (Muni Toke). The story is saturated with a stance of ignorance of the people 'talked about'. The register is one that presupposes an overhearer; it is a *censorial authorship*, the way privilege talks in the presence of the servants standing around the dinner table. It carries the distinction of an authorial voice that speaks from a position of authority ('we need to teach them English'), and of otherness ('I wish they would stop worshipping the ancestors'). The purpose of the narrative is less to recount a chain of events, and more to bring across, co-construct, and share, a stance or attitude to the *experience* of the teller. There are more than a few parallels to the French overseas colonials (e.g., Muni Toke's medical consultation), who reproduce a *colonial gaze* in the telling of personal experiences with exotic (and ultimately non-fathomable) Others.

The frailty of the two elderly sisters conceals the power of this narrative to slight without apparent effort, and to co-construct an *absent presence* (cf. Kerfoot and Tatah). The narrative 'unsaid' of invisibility reflects the way invisibility is materially articulated as an absence located beyond the perimeters of the OBM. It shares the modality of engagement with others—spectatorship—with the modality of being at the OBM, one of looking, watching (as well as eating and drinking).

It is not only the materiality of the OBM that (re)traces colonial circuits or erases trajectories and the visibility of their travellers. Narratives figure here also.

David recorded and transcribed the following event at the wine shop in the far corner of the mill. It is an endearing story of the slave origins of connoisseur wines from vineyards in Stellenbosch, the premier wine-growing region in the Western Cape.

Vendor: (In the 1680s) they built a slave house which you can still go
        and see today.
        It is next to our natural museum.
        It became a slave house.
        So she grew up there.
        And her owners (inaudible) behind the castle, they built a
        garden, where they grew their vegetables.
        And those vegetables were given to ships as they came in.
        And she was there.
        And she met the soldier.
        And the soldier fell in love with the slave.
        And then a lot of things started.
        That is the story behind this.
        So our red wine is named after her.
        So it's a true story.
Customer 1:   That's awesome.
Customer 2:   That's a beautiful story.
Vendor: ((proceeds to present other wines))

This is a contemporary story of optimism and belief in the human potential to live together non-racially in close communion (cf. Bock). In its telling, however, the narrative mimics semiotically what the mall accomplishes through its material dynamics, namely, the production of absence and invisibility. The story joins sites and bodies and emotions across time and place creating complex (post)colonial entanglements: the emotions and experiences of arrogant seventeenth-century colonialists are tied to those of contemporary transnational travellers (tourists) in a fairy-tale romance of a Dutch soldier falling in love and marrying a freed slave girl. It also links the tourist as audience to different spaces of enunciation—this very same story is told at the vineyard itself, at other points of sale besides the OBM boutique, on the website of the winery (and will surely be told at the dining tables of the tourists on hosting dinners and wine tastings when back home). In the telling, the story highlights the contemporary actuality of old colonial trade circuits (such as the Stellenbosch vineyard, the ship, the Dutch lowlands)—routes now travelled by the tourists—at the same time as it celebrates the importance of these circuits and sites for the happy trajectory of the slave girl. More than 400 years later, the mobility of the slave girl out of bondage is the mobility sought by the East Timorese migrants of Cabral and Martin-Jones or the Lusophone African migrants stuck in the waiting rooms of visa offices (cf. Juffermans and Tavares).

This narrative is a powerful resemiotization/entextualization of the material workings of the OBM as a dynamo of absence. The force of the narrative resides in being framed by privilege; who tells, who listens, and the stance towards the telling informed by the quality of the wine tasted. Although we rejoice in the good fortunes of the slave girl (whom we can assume is some shade of black), we concede the agency for her salvation to the soldier (who we may assume is white). We recognize in this story the forgiveness in the slave girl of a magnificence worthy of Nelson Mandela—no privilege lost, but much gained. The narrative is to all intents and purposes an instantiation of the very South African desire for a 'rainbow nation'. The authorial voice of the story, the setting of its telling, the distinction of the participants in its co-construction and its *sens moral* are enactments of a particular order of visibility. It is a fairy tale, and the *sens moral* of fairy tales cannot be contested. Nevertheless, what is left untold, of course, is that interracial marriages remain all but non-existent in South Africa; that 80 percent of the arable land remains in the hands of a small percentage of white settlers, and that all is not well in the postracial nation.

Perhaps more importantly, though, is that although the name of the slave girl labels the wine, her voice remains invisibilized or absent in the telling. She is acknowledged in the soldier's interpellation of her as the object of his desire for marriage. Her pain and indignity, the extent of which we can only guess, serve merely as titillating precursors to real happiness. Colonial slavery is thus relegated to a background text for the celebration of the fortitude and humanity of the soldier (or his desires), and as a romantic setting for a love story. In some sense, this legitimizes *post hoc* her predicament which is presented as a historical parenthesis. In other words, the narrative, although engaging the best emotions of an empathetic audience, nevertheless contributes to the firming of a racio-linguistic hierarchy (Kerfoot and Hyltenstam, 3) where the perspective and stance is that of structural whiteness (Muni Toke, and Kerfoot and Tatah). Whereas Bock's participants saw social engagement and interaction across racial boundaries as key to a nonracial future, this story suggests that it is rather the echoes of the postracial present we are hearing.

This story is in all essentials a production of North-South co-construction of whiteness that is simultaneously a mutual constitution of the colony and metropole here, and a reinforcing of a decidedly contemporary white perspective on southern realities. The OBM is where privilege can massage and assuage the guilt of privilege. This is not 'the inextricable tangle of reason and emotion' within which Milani claims 'lies [. . .] transformative potential' (178). Rather, sentiment and reason here affirm the status quo, and contribute to a form of white (re)mooring (Cabral and Martin-Jones), no less powerful because of its function as a sales pitch for an exclusive wine.

Complication

The gay couple has reached the Pizza bar at the far end of the biscuit mill. With every step, the physical fact of their blackness had been incrementally and symbolically bleached. Their blackness has never been that of the absent presence of those on the perimeters of the biscuit mill. Nor has it been that of those who live on the waste of the OBM in the back streets, or reside off the N2 in the locations around Cape Town. Rather, it is the blackness of polite society—perhaps of the same mettle as the slave girl. It is not the absent presence, but a blackness invisibilized more than erased, made absent. It is the way blackness becomes when inserted into the circuits of distinction. This is the blackness that led the infamous Penny Sparrow, when interviewed by a black DJ on a breakfast show, to exclaim with true astonishment 'That's surprising, are you black? You speak very well, were you educated?' And this is where the key dynamic of the OBM resides—not so much in the maintenance of whiteness, but in the reduction of the meaning of blackness once more to the structural *terms* of whiteness. More than the maintenance of whiteness alone, the OBM is just as much about refiguring 'blackness' in an ongoing history of white fragmentation of the black subject, and the undermining of other, more agentive, forms of black representations of blackness (cf. Kerfoot and Tatah).

Resolution: Unmooring/Disentangling

Lionel Wee asks how it comes to be that 'things that might otherwise be intertwined are kept within distinct boundaries' (137)? He suggests that disentangling intertwined things (complex social formations) is one way of 'sustaining perceptions of order or control' (138) and that orders of visibility serve such purposes. The OBM is a hub of entanglements, of identities, spaces, and histories. It serves as an affordance for the reproduction of a particular order of visibility—a hierarchy of 'objects, social relations, ways of knowing, being, and saying embedded in the common sense and taken for granted [...] practices' (Kerfoot and Hyltenstam, 7) at the mill that privilege structural whiteness and the contemporary postracial. The OBM is about reaffirming the privilege and power of whiteness and the relative invisibility of blacks. It is a space for the *carnal* production, processing, and semiotic packaging of dreams and evasions of the postracial. The small stories, the wine tasting, the consumption of luxury in moments of leisure, are all about the production, circulation, and fit of bodies to Alcoff's incoherent whiteness as a 'fluid amalgam of sometimes contesting interpretations and practices' (2015, 15). As Kerfoot and Hyltenstam point out in the introduction, these are co-constructed of the 'north' and 'south'—'not as separate or literal places of belonging but as a relation'—that opens a 'window onto a world of flows and connections" (1) (cf. Cabral and Martin-Jones) and, one could add, of blockages (Juffermans and Tavares). Heugh's paper argues persuasively for a need for the development of epistemologies, ontologies, and moralities grounded in the perspective of the *mestizo*, one who straddles both North and South. This is even more important as these co-conscripted flows and connections are what produce the epistemological absences and the silenced agents noted by Santos (2014, 154). The OBM smoothes over, unties, and re-knots difficult encounters into the more palatable package of the postracial. It is a complex machinery for a multimodal and multivocal complex of discourses that together redefine the significance of whiteness and blackness—ways of knowing bodies through the underlying dynamic of distinction mediated through viscerality, affect, and censorial authorship. Above all, it is about the construction of the 'absent presence'.

Notes

1 This tangle of reflections emanate—as is usually the case for me—out of the enjoyment of many entangled conversations with students and colleagues in both the North and South. In this particular textual order of visibility—the afterword—some of these entanglements are more visible (Amiena Peck, David Karlander, Mooniq Shaikjee, and the authors in this book) and some less visible (Quentin Williams, Sibonile Mpendukana, Ana Deumert). However, all are equally entangled. A special note of thanks to Kenneth Hyltenstam, Don Kulick, Kathleen Heugh, and Caroline Kerfoot, with whom I have been hanging for 115 years collectively, and counting.
2 On the 27 of August 2016, in an unprecedented development, the black and coloured families facing eviction on Bromwell Street demonstrated at the Old Biscuit Mill in Cape Town against the Woodstuck Hub, appealing for the City to stop the eviction. http://www.groundup.org.za/article/woodstock-residents-occupy-old-biscuit-mill/
3 A township on the outskirts of Cape Town, historically occupied by black workers.
4 An expression which is never used in South African parlance for the purpose of referring to blacks or coloureds.

References

Alcoff, L. M. 2015. *The Future of Whiteness*. Cambridge, UK: Polity.
Goldberg, D. 2015. *Are We All Postracial Yet?* Cambridge, UK: Polity.
Santos, B. de S. 2014. *Epistemologies of the South: Justice against Epistemicide*. Boulder, CO: Paradigm.

Contributors

Zannie Bock is a Senior Lecturer in the Department of Linguistics at the University of the Western Cape. Her current research interests include discourse and narrative analysis, digital media, and the role of language in the construction of youth identities, particularly racial identities. Recent publications include work on racializing discourses among university students, emerging styles in youth instant messaging chats, and the ways in which affect and stance are encoded in texts. Earlier publications include discourse analyses of testimonies given before South Africa's Truth and Reconciliation Commission.

Estêvão Cabral (PhD in Political Science from Lancaster University, UK). He has done research on the political history of Timor-Leste, on literacy during the years of Resistance to the Indonesian invasion and occupation of East Timor and on language policy in East Timor. His current research focus is on the transnational migration of East Timorese. He is an affiliated member of Babylon, Centre for the Study of Superdiversity, Tilburg University, The Netherlands.

Lynn Mario Trindade Menezes de Souza is Professor of Language Education at the University of São Paulo, Brazil. His expertise is in the area of Language Education with research interests in language policy and politics, literacy, literary criticism, and postcolonial literature.

Linnea Hanell is a sociolinguist with a particular interest in the intersections of discourse and action. The paper included in this volume is a part of her PhD project at Stockholm University, which is broadly concerned with discourse, health, knowledge, and the initiation into parenthood in the welfare state of Sweden. Her publishing record also includes an article in *Language & Communication* concerned with multiliteracies and academic knowledge production.

Kathleen Heugh is based in the Research Centre for Languages and Cultures, University of South Australia. She focuses on research in multilingual education, policies, and practices in sub-Saharan Africa. She has undertaken several system-wide and multi-country studies for governments and development agencies. With Christopher Stroud she initiated the Southern Multilingualisms and Diversities Consortium to draw attention to the knowledge and linguistic expertise of marginalized people located in the global South.

Kenneth Hyltenstam is Professor Emeritus at the Centre for Research on Bilingualism, Stockholm University. He has been Professor of Bilingualism since 1992 and prior to that Associate Professor of Bilingualism since 1981. His main research area is second language acquisition, but his research also covers several other topics (bilingualism and dementia, language maintenance, language policy, and language and education). He has published six volumes internationally and several books in Swedish. Recent research appears in *Applied Linguistics, Bilingualism: Language and Cognition, Language and Speech, Language Learning, Sociolinguistica*, and *Studies in Second Language Acquisition.*

Kasper Juffermans works at the University of Luxembourg where he is a postdoctoral researcher and principal investigator in the STAR project, the multi-sited project funded by the Luxembourg National Research Fund described here. He has 12 years of fieldwork experience in West Africa (Gambia and Guinea-Bissau), tries to speak two West African languages (Mandinka and Guinean Creole), and recently published *Local Languaging, Literacy and Multilingualism in a West African Society* (Multilingual Matters, 2015).

Caroline Kerfoot is Associate Professor at the Centre for Research on Bilingualism, Stockholm University. She was previously Head of Language Education, University of the Western Cape, South Africa. Her current research focuses on multilingualism, identities, and epistemic access in educational sites characterized by high levels of diversity and flux. Recent publications appear in *Applied Linguistics, Linguistics & Education, International Multilingual Research Journal*, and *Language & Education.*

Inger Lindberg is Professor of Bilingualism with special focus on second language learning at Stockholm University. Her research focuses on sociopolitical and sociocultural aspects of second language learning and teaching as well as literacy development in multilingual school contexts.

Marilyn Martin-Jones is an Emeritus Professor at the MOSAIC Centre for Research on Multilingualism, University of Birmingham, UK. Her main research focus has been on multilingual discourse practices and literacies, in classroom and community contexts, and on the ways in which such discourse practices and literacies are bound up with local and global relations of power. She currently edits (with Joan Pujolar) the Routledge book series: *Critical Studies in Multilingualism.*

Tommaso M. Milani is Associate Professor of Linguistics at the University of the Witwatersrand, Johannesburg. His areas of research encompass language politics, media discourse, multimodality, and language, gender, and sexuality. His publications include the edited books *Language Ideologies and Media Discourse* (co-edited with Sally Johnson, Continuum 2010) and *Language and Masculinities: Performances, Intersections, Dislocations* (Routledge, 2015). He is co-editor of the journal *Gender and Language* and sole editor of the book series *Advances in Sociolinguistics* (Bloomsbury Publishing).

Valelia Muni Toke, PhD, is a permanent research fellow in Social Sciences at IRD—Institut de Recherche pour le Développement—and a member of the joint research unit SeDyL (CNRS—INALCO—IRD). Her research examines the use of political ideologies in language sciences, the applicability of scientific knowledge to language policy, and the management of linguistic diversity in institutional settings. Her current fieldwork is based in French overseas territories (Wallis, South Pacific; Mayotte, Indian Ocean) and focuses on linguistic issues regarding equality in access to health care.

Linus Salö holds a PhD in Bilingualism from Stockholm University. He conducts research in the fields of sociolinguistics, qualitative sociology, and linguistic anthropology. His research interests encompass language politics, academic publishing, and mother tongue education, with an eye towards exploring entextualization, language ideology, regimentation, and habitus. His works are published in several key journals of his fields. He also has a forthcoming book on the sociolinguistics of academic publishing (Palgrave, 2017).

Karin Sandwall, PhD, is the director of the National Centre for Swedish as a Second Language at Stockholm University, Sweden. Karin is also an experienced teacher in sfi, the Swedish basic language program for adult immigrants. In her research, Karin explores and problematizes sfi students' opportunities for interaction and language learning at work placements and the relation between informal and formal learning. Also, pedagogical implications concerning the integration of (in-)formal learning within and between the contexts are in focus.

Christopher Stroud is a Senior Professor of Linguistics at the University of the Western Cape and Director of the Centre for Multilingualism and Diversities Research. He is an affiliated Professor of Transnational Multilingualism at Stockholm University. His research foci in recent years encompass the sociolinguistics of multilingualism in southern Africa.

Gwendoline Jih Kouotou Tatah is a Writing Fellow in the Department of Language Education at the University of the Western Cape. She holds a PhD in Language and Literacy from the University of the Western Cape and her research focuses on multilingualism and identities in schools. She was previously a teacher of English and literature in her native Cameroon.

Bernardino Tavares is a doctoral researcher in the STAR project at the University of Luxembourg. He obtained a BA in Modern Languages (French and English) and an MA in Anglo-American Studies with a focus on creole linguistics from the University of Coimbra. As a West African migrant in Europe himself, he is interested in sociolinguistic aspects of migration between Africa and Europe, language ideologies of Creole societies, and multilingualism.

Lionel Wee is a Professor in the Department of English Language & Literature at the National University of Singapore. A linguist by training, he has strong interests in language policy, new Englishes, and social theory. He is currently working on a book about *The Singlish Controversy* (Cambridge University Press).

Appendix A
Transcription Key

Turns:	1,2,3
Clause:	i, ii, iii
O:	opening move
D:	developing move
P:	prolonging move
R:	reacting move
Res:	response, supporting
Rej:	rejoinder, confronting
()	seconds
text	French
text	Cameroonian Pidgin English
TEXT	Duala
(*text*)	translation
[text]	stage notes
TEXT	louder volume
↑	rising pitch in the following segment
↓↑	pitch falls and rises within the next word
¨	very high stress
::	lengthened speech
=	latched speech
[[	beginning of overlap of speech or nonverbal actions
(.)	a pause of less than a second
(0.0)	approximate time of pause

Index

Printed in Great Britain
by Amazon